# OPERATION
# IDRIS

INSIDE THE BRITISH ADMINISTRATION
OF CYRENAICA AND LIBYA, 1942–52

**RICHARD SYNGE**

SILPHIUM
PRESS

# OPERATION IDRIS

## INSIDE THE BRITISH ADMINISTRATION OF CYRENAICA AND LIBYA, 1942–52

### RICHARD SYNGE

Produced by Silphium Press, an imprint of
The Society for Libyan Studies
c/o British Academy
10–11 Carlton House Terrace
London SW1Y 5AH
www.societyforlibyanstudies.org

ISBN 978-1-900971-25-6

Cover and interior design by Chris Bell
Edited by JMS Books LLP
Index by Alex Bell

Printed by Marston Book Services Ltd, Oxfordshire

# contents

# acknowledgements

WITHOUT THE ENTHUSIASM and support of others at every stage, this book would have been unlikely ever to see the light of day. As it emerged from a transcription exercise of my father's diaries and memoirs to become a more coherent account of the British Military Administration of Cyrenaica, I was especially fortunate to meet Jason Pack in 2012. Jason's intensive research into Libya's past had already given him a remarkably clear focus on the period covered here. He has been generous in sharing his understanding and insight, in providing crucial guidance to the available archival material and the wider scholarship, and in reading and commenting on the text as it evolved, for all of which I am extremely grateful.

John Wright gave my efforts a warm vote of confidence at key moments in the process, while Barnaby Rogerson, Russell McGuirk, George Joffé and Saul Kelly provided advice that helped the story take on substance and I thank them all warmly. For crucial assistance as I compiled the closing chapters, my thanks go to Richard and Alan Cassels for permission to draw on the memoir of their father, Gervase P. ('Jeff') Cassels. With the text continuing to expand even as publication loomed, I was extremely lucky to be able to count on the constructive support and encouragement of Victoria Leitch of the Society for Libyan Studies.

Two good friends deserve special mention. Elissa Jobson urged me to persist with the transcription effort when it seemed to be a rather thankless task, while Jane Bryce applied a literary perspective to my father's cultural milieu of the time and made useful comments on his ways of seeing, behaving and writing. This launched me on a fascinating and ultimately very useful diversion into understanding the world of Alexandria in the early and middle years of the 20th century (not least the works of Constantine Cavafy, E. M. Forster and Lawrence Durrell).

None of this would have happened of course without my father's own dogged determination, in diary and memoir, to spell out what he saw and did, as well as where he stood (often regardless of whether others agreed with him). Additionally, his subsequent peripatetic career provided me with the early experiences that did so much to form my own life's journey and world view. When my late brother, Patrick Synge, passed me the memoir shortly before he died in 2006, he provided the initial urge to attempt something along these lines. From these origins, this project has developed a life of its own and has produced numerous wholly unexpected discoveries.

I am especially grateful for the consistent support of my wife, Casey Synge, and especially for her many incisive comments that helped give final shape to this work.

*Richard Synge, December 2014*

# foreword

HE GOAL OF THE memoir editor should be identical to that of the biographer: to shed light on the past by putting the reader inside the mind of a remarkable or representative individual from a bygone era.

Even though the British Military Administration (BMA) of Libya (1942–51) ended roughly 65 years ago, the logic and psychology of its protagonists is already largely buried by the sands of time. Western attitudes towards the Orient, imperialism, 'natural leaders', 'native states' and 'pure Arabs' have changed so rapidly that it requires a great feat of empathy to inhabit the minds of British imperial administrators during and after the Second World War. In the specific case of the BMA in Cyrenaica (eastern Libya), the feat of imagination is further complicated by the dearth of explanatory secondary literature on the subject. In fact, Professor Anna Baldinetti, one of the few authorities on this period of Libyan history, has noted that 'a complete study concerning the British administration [of Cyrenaica and Tripolitania] still needs to be written'.[1]

The publication of Peter Synge's diaries and memoirs, along with the insightful commentary and historical background provided by his son Richard, an Africa specialist and prolific author, represents a significant first glimpse into the 'official mind' of Libya's British rulers.[2] Peter's narrative of day-to-day events – as edited, scrutinised and contextualised by Richard – is a unique and valuable document on at least three counts: its composition, its voice and its organisation.

---

[1] A. Baldinetti, *The Origins of the Libyan Nation: Colonial legacy, exile and the emergence of a new nation-state*, Abingdon, 2010, footnote 18, Chapter 6, p183.

[2] For an explanation of how cliques within the British policymaking bureaucracy were prone to form an 'official mind', see the seminal texts of R. Robinson, J. Gallagher, A. Denny, *Africa and the Victorians: The Official Mind of Imperialism*, London, 1961, and T. G. Otte, T*he Foreign Office Mind: The Making of British Foreign Policy, 1865–1914*, Cambridge, 2011.

Other major players of the BMA (e.g. Duncan Cumming, Lord Rennell of Rodd, Eric De Candole, Edward Evan Evans-Pritchard, Norman Anderson) have not left unfiltered personal reminiscences. They may have written memoirs, like De Candole, official histories, like Rennell of Rodd, or left extensive private papers, like Anderson, but for different reasons these all deliberately present sanitised accounts, aiming to burnish the author's legacy, glorify their favourites, justify their actions and portray the BMA as a benign monolith, while ignoring the psychological drama that unfolded among its main protagonists. Conversely, Peter Synge was able to leave an unfiltered account because he was not a professional diplomat, administrator, Orientalist or scholar. In fact, as a factory manager in Egypt's interwar cotton industry, who found himself transformed into a mid-level player in the administration of Cyrenaica by the exigencies of wartime, he seems not to have envisioned that future generations would be sufficiently interested in his diaries or memoir to study the BMA or his role within it. Written, therefore, primarily for himself and his family, Peter's compositions are refreshingly honest and straightforward.

Not only were his diaries written as the events described took place, but Peter was not one to toe the party line. Within the BMA, he was an outsider by professional formation and personal conviction – he also had an axe to grind. Yes, Peter was a middle-class Briton with a public school education, extensive experience in the Middle East and the ability to speak conversational Arabic – all similar to his superiors – but he was not a trained Arabist administrator with an Oxbridge pedigree.[3] The BMA's upper echelons were dominated by former Sudan Political Service men who harboured romantic ideas about the Sanussiyya, indirect rule, 'pure' desert Arabs, and the natural kinship between Briton and Bedouin.[4] Among these ideologues, Mohammed al-Mahdi Idris al-Sanussi presented himself as the archetypical 'natural leader'. Lacking

---

[3] Peter Synge was one of six sons from a once prominent Anglo–Irish family with an ecclesiastical tradition. Peter and all his brothers attended King's School Bruton in Somerset, yet Peter was the only one not to proceed afterwards to Oxbridge. Poor performance in school exams led the family to conclude he might benefit from a 'fresh start' in the colonies. His black sheep status relative to both his school and familial environments might have led him to feeling underappreciated, resentful towards authority and an 'outsider' – all psychological traits which came out in his interactions and reflections in Cyrenaica.
4 To quote Lord James Rennell of Rodd, who personally played a key role in creating the diplomatic framework for the Anglo–Sanussi relationship as British Ambassador to Italy during WWI and whose son was a key administrator and official historian of the BMA, 'the blood of his [Ahmed Hassanein's] Beduin forefathers made intimacy [with his peers at Oxford] easier since the Briton and the Beduin not infrequently find in one another a certain kinship of instinct which compels mutual regard.' Rennell Rodd, Introduction, A. M. Hassanein Bey, *The Lost Oases*, London, 1925, p14.

the requisite professional formation and outlook, Peter did not fully share this matrix of ideas, but was in a position to witness them from up close. He was therefore the best kind of eyewitness: an insider's outsider. Moreover, Peter bore many personal grievances against his superiors and out of professional frustration deliberately critiqued the underlying assumptions of the BMA. This ensemble of factors lends a uniqueness to Peter 's voice which is, perforce, entirely absent in the official correspondence of the BMA.

Due to his feelings of exclusion and under-appreciation, Peter was deeply disaffected and confrontational in his dealings with his superiors. His marginalisation speaks volumes about how the imperial ethos constructed a monolithic narrative and necessitated personal conformity from its functionaries. Therefore, although not the voice of a colonised Libya struggling with the complexity of her colonised identity, Peter Synge's 'voice' is nonetheless an authentically subaltern one.

To best showcase that voice, Richard Synge has organised this volume in an original fashion, interlacing sections of commentary and historical background with the blow-by-blow accounts from Peter Synge's diaries and memoir. This approach makes the volume accessible to the scholar and lay reader alike. For the lay reader, Richard's succinct yet careful presentation of the history surrounding the BMA transforms the diary entries into a gripping story that provides insights into the larger political and social phenomena of the BMA. For the scholar, this 'light-touch' approach to editing, allows the reader to reconstruct the inner workings of the BMA without any over-editing, theorising, or cherry-picking by the author inhibiting the reader's direct engagement with the primary material.

***

From my vantage point as someone who has pored over tens of thousands of BMA documents at the British National Archives at Kew and guided Richard through the relevant War Office and Foreign Office files, Peter's diary and memoir provide a novel form of confirmation concerning the centrality of the Anglo–Sanussi relationship as the focal point for British attempts to govern Cyrenaica.[5] Peter's accounts also

---

[5] The Anglo–Sanussi relationship was a diplomatic and political reality, with deep economic, administrative, personal and ideological roots predating the British conquest of Cyrenaica by over half a century. My forthcoming book, provisional title *Britain's Informal Empire in Libya? The Anglo–Sanussi Relationship, 1882–1969*, Hurst & Co, 2017, will explore in depth the origins, evolution and impact of the Anglo–Sanussi relationship on British policy towards Cyrenaica.

stress how the relationship was constructed out of a web of disparate personal connections and yet operated as an integral whole with its own psychology, aspirations, romance, initiation rituals and shibboleths. This volume shows how the senior figures of the BMA were truly obsessed with cultivating Sayyid Mohammed Idris as the figurehead for their project of indirect rule in Cyrenaica.

While Idris remained in exile in Egypt, the British governed with his blessing, and when opposition arose, they needed him to return to Cyrenaica so that he could first mediate with its inhabitants on behalf of the British government, and later rule Cyrenaica directly, in a way that was legitimate to the populace and would also protect Western interests. To believe wholeheartedly that a combination of Idris and the notables of the *sa'ada* tribes[6] was the only way that Cyrenaica should be governed, an upper-level BMA official needed to be enamoured with Idris and the Sanussiyya, and to have an Orientalist's vision of Cyrencaica's 'pure Arab tribes'.[7] The political irrelevance of the urban population, along with the Sanussiyya's default pre-eminence in Cyrenaica and their loyalty to the British imperial cause, formed 'articles of faith' for the 'official mind' of the BMA; questioning them, as Peter Synge did, was tantamount to heresy.

To acquire this 'proper' belief system, a British official needed to be predisposed to it by the 'correct' professional formation. This theme is excellently demonstrated by Richard Synge in Chapters 8, 9 and 10, where he discusses the Sanussi Settlement Scheme, an impracticable

---

[6] The *sa'ada* are tribes not in a client status to any other tribe and claim to be able to trace their genealogy back to the 11th-century Ibn Hillal invasions of Arabian nomads. The Sanussiyya, as outsiders to the Cyrenaican tribal system, tended to draw their upper-level functionaries from the *sa'ada* tribes. The BMA also preferred to reinforce rather than challenge pre-existing tribal hierarchies. For more on the origins of the *sa'ada* tribes and their unique positions in Cyrenaica society and the BMA consult Emrys L. Peters's *The Bedouin of Cyrenaica: Studies in Corporate Power*, Cambridge, 1990.

[7] In his *Cyrenaica Handbooks Part VIII: The Tribes and Their Divisions* (an internal War Office publication of 1943 available at the National Archives in FO 371/46112), Edward Evan Evans-Pritchard draws on texts concerning the Ibn Hillal invasions of the 11 th century to concur with eminent French Orientalist, Louis Massignon, that the Arabs of Cyrenaica are of four-fifths purity of Arab blood – a higher proportion than he postulates for those of Palestine, Iraq or Syria. 'Culturally they are Arab. Indeed, they are as completely Arabised as any people in the world, Tamim and Quraish not excepted.' p1. This conception is repeated later frequently in internal BMA documents and may explain why prevailing notions about peninsular Arabs are applied to Cyrenaicans but not to Tripolitanians who were viewed as Arabo–Berbers. These racial notions made Cyrenaica fit for the implementation of an Arab princely state akin to Jordan, Kuwait and the Trucial States, which also were viewed in British Arabist circles as possessing a high proportion of 'pure' Arab blood. For more on this theme, see Jason Pack, 'British State-Building in Cyrenaica during the War Years (1941–45)', MSt dissertation, Oxford University, 2011.

plan to transplant the exiled Sanussiyya back into Cyrenaica as a form of landed nobility. That the Sanussiyya, a family of itinerant Sufi scholars, were manifestly ill-suited for such an endeavour and would form a poor basis for creating a modern state structure in Cyrenaica should have been quite clear to any neutral observer. Yet, the ideas behind the Sanussi Settlement Scheme were perfectly in keeping with the prevailing Orientalism and 'Ornamentalism'[8] that characterised the 'official mind' of the experienced Arabist administrators of the BMA. Peter Synge saw through the BMA's blind spots: for speaking truth to power, he was eventually dismissed.

Peter's experience reveals that British administrators who lacked an Arabist and Sudan Political Service background were unable to 'naturally understand' the psychological and emotional rationale of the Anglo–Sanussi relationship, and nor were they able to grasp why Britain should make so many compromises to govern Cyrenaica indirectly through the Sanussiyya. A further demonstration of this psychological drama within the BMA is the reception given to Brigadier J. W. N. Haugh, a career soldier without any Arabic skills. Appointed at the war's end as Cyrenaica's Chief Administrator, he was quickly reviled by both his staff and his Cyrenaican interlocutors. His sin was to disregard the very fundamentals of the Anglo–Sanussi relationship.

In viewing Richard Synge's historical glosses through the lens of the Anglo–Sanussi relationship, the two-sidedness of this personal and political connection emerges: key protagonists in the BMA rarely faulted Idris personally for his demands for money, threats to withdraw from political life, or even direct attacks on the British administration. Instead, they directed any criticisms at members of Idris's entourage, like Omar Sheneib. Conversely, Idris frequently used his pro-British credentials and shrewd negotiating tactics to secure his goals, similar to Nuri Al-Said's behaviour as Prime Minister in Iraq in the 1940s and 1950s. Idris knew that the nascent administrative machinery in Cyrenaica required his approval or even his physical presence to function properly and hence he drove an increasingly hard bargain with the British to achieve his personal and national objectives. The necessity of Idris's collaboration is manifest in Richard's acute observation that

---

[8] See D. Cannadine, *Ornamentalism: How the British Saw their Empire*, London, 2001, for a definition and discussion of the neologism 'Ornamentalism', which roughly equates to the particularly Victorian, Edwardian and Georgian proclivity of the British upper and upper-middle class to envision non-European societies as containing versions of feudal, hierarchical and aristocratic features, as English society was increasingly losing those features.

from the end of the war until Idris's permanent return to Cyrenaica in late 1947, the position of the British declined precipitously. This volume shows that the British administrators were hamstrung by the international high politics surrounding the fate of Italy's former colonies, which prevented pro-Sanussi BMA administrators from simply creating the client state they envisioned until after the United Nations decisions of 1949. Unfortunately for modern-day scholars, Peter Synge was summarily transferred to Eritrea in 1947 and we cannot benefit from his insights into the crucial years of 1949–51, when the United Kingdom of Libya was cobbled together by UN Commissioner Adrian Pelt and the British around Sayyid Mohammed Idris.

\*\*\*

For those fascinated by more than just high politics, the diary excerpts (more so than the memoir) allow the reconstruction of Libyan social mores prior to the country's rapid urbanisation and conservative turn following the discovery of oil in 1959. The diaries are replete with choice anecdotes: British administrators having to close an 'Oriental café' because too many Libyans were drinking and causing social disturbances; drunk American troops cavorting with and molesting Libyan women; Libyan women who danced publicly in front of mixed audiences while veiled; the rare occurrence of a Libyan prostitute who specialised in catering to the tastes of the occupying forces becoming embroiled in a web of jealousy and blackmail –juxtaposed against the existence of a successful girl's school in Benghazi at a time when overall literacy rates in Cyrenaica were less than 10 per cent.

These various insights into Libyan society are perhaps inevitably outnumbered by the diaries' extensive coverage of life in the British Officers' Mess. The BMA's insularity was truly paradigmatic and the sense of British racial and cultural supremacy was as yet unharmed by the setbacks Britain had suffered on the international stage. For Peter, games of bridge and tots of whisky appear not so much as diversions from the gruelling duties of administration, but as reaffirmations of his identity in a strange and foreign land. The social dysfunctionality and trauma of many of the main British participants, such as Peter Synge and Bill Bailey, expose quite clearly the myth of the innate British talent for governance of 'native peoples'. Although the diaries are written in dry and unsentimental prose, the psychological complexity of both Libyan society and the British Officers' Mess simply leaps off the pages.

Reading Peter Synge's reminiscences in the memoirs with the benefit of hindsight, we see that the 1940s represented a time of great flux for Libya, not only politically and economically, but in terms of social mores, regional identities and attitudes towards Europeans. Following the narrative account presented in the diaries and memoirs, we see that in the span of a few years the British were transformed from liberators to occupiers in the eyes of much of the populace. We also discover that the history of the British Military Administration of Cyrenaica, like most episodes of human history, was not simply an arena for the interplay of impersonal military or ideological forces, but rather a forum for a psychological drama among various protagonists – struggling to understand other cultures, to cope with slights to their honour and to fulfil their duties to conscience and country.

*Jason Pack, Cambridge, 2014*

# glossary

| | |
|---|---|
| 'ammiyya | vernacular Arabic |
| fushaa | literary Arabic |
| ghaffir | watchman |
| gharri | horse-drawn cart |
| ghibli | a sandstorm caused by wind from the Sahara (a similar phenomenon in Egypt is known as a *khamsin*) |
| mamour | police magistrate (as deployed in Sudan) |
| mudir | district administrator |
| mukhtar | local administrative official |
| mustashar | government-appointed adviser to tribal sheikhs |
| naja | camp |
| omda | chief |
| qadi | judge administering Islamic law |
| qaimaqam | district governor (an Ottoman title) |
| sofraggi | house servant |
| zawia (zawiyya) | Sufi lodge or meeting place |

# abbreviations

| | |
|---|---|
| **ACAO** | Assistant Civil Affairs Officer |
| **APO** | Assistant Political Officer |
| **BG** | British Government |
| **BMA** | British Military Administration |
| **CAO** | Civil Affairs Officer |
| **CCAO** | Chief Civil Affairs Officer |
| **CDF** | Cyrenaica Defence Force |
| CinC | Commander in Chief |
| **CO** | Commanding Officer |
| **CPO** | Chief Political Officer |
| **CSM** | Company Sergeant Major |
| **DC** | District Commander |
| **DCCAO** | Deputy Chief Civil Affairs Officer |
| **DCPO** | Deputy Chief Political Officer |
| **ENSA** | Entertainments National Service Association |

| | |
|---|---|
| **GHQ** | General Headquarters |
| **GMC** | General Military Court |
| **HMG** | His Majesty's Government |
| **LAF** | Libyan Arab Force |
| **MP** | Military Police |
| **MOI** | Ministry of Information |
| **Naafi** | Navy, Army and Air Force Institute (providing catering in regular British military establishments) |
| **NCAL** | National Constituent Assembly of Libya (1950–52) |
| **NO** | Naval Officer |
| **PIO** | Principal Information Officer |
| **PMO** | Principal Medical Officer |
| **PT** | Egyptian piastre, 1,000th of an Egyptian pound |
| **RASC** | Royal Army Service Corps |
| **REME** | Royal Electrical and Mechanical Engineers |
| **S&T** | Supplies and Transit Department |
| **SCAO** | Senior Civil Affairs Officer |
| **SDF** | Sudan Defence Force |
| **SHO** | Senior Health Officer |
| **SNO** | Senior Naval Officer |
| **wef** | with effect from (relating to promotions in rank) |

# note on the text

The main text of this book follows current prevailing conventions in the English spelling of people and places, with the exception of quotations and the extended extracts from the primary and secondary sources being reproduced or cited, where the transcription is as close as possible to the original. Thus the name Sanussi appears in various renderings, e.g. Sanusi, Senusi and Senussi, according to their use in these different sources, and in the diaries many of the place names reflect the way they had previously been spelt in Italian.

# LESSONS FROM LETHE'S GROTTO

O N THE OUTER fringes of the city of Benghazi, amid otherwise largely barren surroundings of bare limestone, lies the underground cavern of Lethe, known in ancient times as the source of waters which, when consumed, resulted in forgetfulness, oblivion or death.

The water flowing in the grotto seems to be part of a larger subterranean lake and, locally, people assume that it flows towards the sea, emerging near a seaside bathing spot known as the Blue Lagoon. The same water probably also feeds a series of hollows in the surrounding area that are marked by vegetation flourishing in this otherwise rocky terrain. But even now, in the 21st century, no one really knows where the Lethe river actually rises or where it flows to.

Getting down into the cavern itself is no easy matter because the path is often slippery from the droppings of rock doves that nest in the cliff ledges above its narrow entrance. Those who have stood on the cramped, muddy ledge in this gloomy spot say that the water is from a stream that flows away through two tunnels that disappear into complete darkness.[1] The uninspiring appearance of the cavern and the difficult access could well have given rise to the idea that the waters here are not for the living but more for the dead, or strictly speaking, for the ghosts of those who have only just departed. The classical myth of Lethe, one of five rivers of the underworld, declares that before they can be reincarnated, the ghosts of the dead have to come here to drink its waters, so as to forget their previous life and become ready to enter a new body.

---

[1] Vivid descriptions of Lethe are given by Gwyn Williams in *Green Mountain: An informal guide to Cyrenaica and its Jebel Akhdar*, London, 1963, pp26–7, and by Anthony Thwaite in *The Deserts of Hesperides: An Experience of Libya*, London, 1969, p62. A recent glossy brochure portraying Benghazi as the 'Venice of North Africa' highlights the waters of Lethe as one of 'a string of pearls' for visitors interested in the city's history and archaeology.

That a place so closely resembling the surviving descriptions of Lethe's Grotto can be found in Libya is a reminder that the ancient Greek world once extended across the Mediterranean and fully incorporated most of this land once known by the Greeks as Pentapolis (after its five cities) and by the Romans as Cyrenaica (after Cyrene), and then later as Barqa (after the city of Barca) by Arab settlers. During the Greek era, the region developed its own unique personality and reputation. Cyrene's school of philosophy was famous for encouraging people to strive towards happiness and good cheer. And in both Greek and Roman times a local herb called *Silphium* was greatly sought after as a valuable cure for aches and pains of all kinds, a powerful seasoning and, some claimed, an aphrodisiac.[2]

For over 1,000 years, the empires of Greece, Persia, Egypt and Rome all had dealings with and made their impact in this country, but it lost its importance after a succession of earthquakes damaged many of the earliest buildings and its magic herb *Silphium* became extinct through over-harvesting. Even before the Arab invasion of the 7th century AD, the ancient cities were easy targets for marauding nomads driven up from the Sahara as the desert encroached towards the coastline. But Cyrenaica's historic marvels and mysteries have continued to exert a strong appeal for those who have passed this way ever since.

In the rocky mountain range now known as the Jebel Akhdar (the Green Mountain), the ruins of Cyrene stand on a plateau at 488 m and command a stunning view over a steep escarpment towards the little port of Apollonia (also know as Susa) and the vast blue Mediterranean beyond. The ancient city's unique Sanctuary and Temple of Apollo, its amphitheatres and its huge and fully colonnaded Roman forum have all managed to survive the ravages of time, earthquakes and the weather, as well as the relentless assaults of treasure hunters. According to UNESCO, this is 'one of the most impressive complexes of ruins in the entire world'. Although a new wave of theft and vandalism since the upheavals of 2011 has done untold damage, its special status is sure to continue for many years yet.

Looking back at events in the 20th century, it might seem that ruination and destruction had returned to symbolise the fate not just of Cyrene but of most of Cyrenaica too. Certainly, over two hellish years in 1941 and 1942, some spectacular infrastructure – only recently installed by the Italians in the late 1930s – was in its turn reduced to rubble.

---

[2] A good account of the history of ancient Cyrenaica can be found in John Wright's *A History of Libya*, London, 2010.

A succession of heavily armed campaigns and airborne attacks by the British on the Italians, the Germans on the British and finally the British on the Germans devastated the two port cities of Tobruk and Benghazi, destroyed roads and bridges and littered the whole country with the wreckage of war, tanks, trucks, unexploded mines, shells and bombs.

After its centuries of neglect, Cyrenaica had turned out to be extremely strategic, mainly because of its proximity to Egypt and the Suez Canal, which in 1942 Adolf Hitler was still supremely confident that Rommel could invade and control. Italy's colonial presence had turned this territory into the key zone of conflict between Axis and Allied territory in North Africa. And at the war's end, its strategic value continued to be appreciated.

The era represented in this book may be largely forgotten now, but unlike the ghosts of Lethe, some people succeed in defying oblivion by recording their memories for future generations. Those set out here are a combination of on-the-spot diary entries covering 1943 and 1944, kept by Peter Synge, an officer with the British Military Administration (BMA) in Cyrenaica, and a summary, written later, of his experiences up to the time of his departure in October 1947. I have supplemented these with my much more recent research in the official archives relating to that era and the key events he recorded.

The story of the British period in Cyrenaica is not widely known and has only recently come to be studied closely by academic historians.[3] It was a period of transition, an interregnum, between the pre-war Italian colonisation and the United Nations-sponsored independence for the whole of Libya, but it was also an intense effort to steer events in the British interest at a time of profound upheaval throughout the Middle East.

Describing the crisis that overwhelmed the British Empire in the Middle East in the late 1940s, the American historian William Roger Louis makes the astute observation that in Cyrenaica the British were presiding over 'the birth of a state, though this was not obvious to many contemporary observers and sometimes not even to those directly involved'.[4] This is an uncannily appropriate characterisation of the proceedings recorded by Peter. His account serves to confirm that, from the outset, few of the BMA's officers were fully aware of the ultimate outcome that they or their successors were working towards. Of the

---

[3] One example of the revived interest in the period is the account given by Anna Baldinetti in *The Origins of the Libyan Nation: Colonial legacy, exile and the emergence of a new nation-state*, Abingdon, 2010, pp113–5.

[4] W. R. Louis, *The British Empire in the Middle East, 1945–1951*, Oxford, 1984, p268.

many different characters in the story, only a handful had a grasp of the bigger picture.

The diary that Peter Synge painstakingly kept remained unread by anyone but him until I decided to examine it closely in 2011, mainly because I was intrigued to see if there were mentions of the same places that were at the time appearing daily on the news, as the uprising against Muammar Qadhafi ripped through Libya in the course of that year. I discovered that my father had served two long spells of duty in Benghazi (where the rebellion first erupted in February 2011 and where the first NATO action was taken to prevent the city's recapture by Qadhafi on 18 March 2011). Peter had also been administrator in Agedabia (Ajdabiyya, the town where young fighters resisted Qadhafi's forces early in the rebellion, and which in 2013 and 2014 went on to become the centre of a tussle for control of eastern Libya's oil revenues) and he had held postings at Beda (al-Bayda, close to the ancient ruined city of Cyrene) and Tobruk, with the result that he came to know the country extremely well in the four and a half years he spent there.

I had always been aware that at some time during the war my father came into close personal contact with the future king, Mohammed al-Mahdi Idris al-Sanussi, but I knew none of the details with any certainty. As my father told it, the story was a humorous one, involving the loan of his underwear when Idris complained of feeling cold. Now, on checking through the memoir, I discovered his rather more significant claim that this action had helped save Idris's first historic visit to Cyrenaica in 1944 from turning into an embarrassing setback for the emerging British game plan for the country. Once the wider context becomes clearer, this story now seems to be an almost perfect metaphor for the sensitivities surrounding the complex negotiations with Idris over a prolonged period. It was, in fact, a crucial early moment in the process I have dubbed 'Operation Idris'. But this did not immediately become apparent when I first read my father's detailed reports of his day-to-day work. There was plenty of drama in the sequence of events he recounted, but it was only after extensive further research that I began to see the bigger picture.

For corroboration and perspective, I made a close comparison of the on-the-spot diary entries and the overall sequence of events in Cyrenaica, as recorded in the files of the War Office and the Foreign Office at the British National Archives. It was soon obvious that this personal story fills a clear gap in the available accounts of the period and provides a fresh angle on some of its dramas. It gives full and vivid substance to the brief – and absurdly over-simplified – summary given by the man who followed my father as Chief Secretary, E. A. V. De Candole, of 'friendly young Englishmen in khaki shirts and shorts … dashing about the countryside in dilapidated fifteen-hundredweight trucks, [who] distributed food supplies and helped the tribal and urban leaders to re-establish their affairs on Arab lines.'[5]

Peter Synge's most original contribution to this story comes during the first nine months of 1943, when the candour of his language reflects the fact that he was still finding his feet and dealing with a wholly unfamiliar set of circumstances. Despite being kept almost excessively busy with a wide range of duties, he had a sharp interest in the action around him and was not afraid to criticise several of his British colleagues. Similarly in 1944, his day-to-day entries show exactly how the temporary administration operated and help establish a more complete account of the first visit of Sayyid Mohammed Idris (as he was then known) to his homeland after 22 years of exile – a key moment for him and for Britain – than others I have found.

Starting out at middle management level, Peter was promoted to a more senior role in Cyrenaica at the end of the war, just as the British presence was entering a highly uncertain phase. The authorities were keeping their options open over the timing and tactics for establishing a new nation and also as to whether the focus should be on Cyrenaica or the whole of Libya. Although his memoir neatly describes the uncertainties that followed the war up to the time he left Cyrenaica in October 1947, only the archives fill out the background and take the story forward by a crucial matter of weeks. These were tense and difficult months in which the BMA faced rising local political opposition, but, very much behind the scenes, the way was being prepared for the permanent return of Sayyid Mohammed Idris.

Idris took up residence in a house near Lethe's Grotto in November 1947, whereupon he went on to take the political lead in Cyrenaica, initially as amir (the equivalent of 'prince'), then as king – first of Cyrenaica in 1949 and then of newly independent Libya in December 1951. The cultivation of this largely artificial kingdom – at the time seen as a good guarantee of solid Anglo–Libyan relations for the foreseeable future – raised inevitable difficulties and prompted some controversial decisions along the way. The very issues that contributed to my father's departure from Cyrenaica – he was one of a number who were removed to make way for a new group of administrators in 1947 – turn out to be a revealing part of the larger history.

---

[5] E. A. V. De Candole, *The Life and Times of King Idris of Libya*, published privately 1990, p73.

Amid rapidly changing dynamics across the Middle East in 1946 and 1947, significant elements of British strategy in the region were being kept highly secret and the relevant documents that clarify the decision-making processes at the time only came into the public domain decades later. And of those who were closest to these processes, there was an inevitable constraint on speaking openly about their work, as the remarkable evidence of my father's immediate successor as Political Secretary, Gervase P. ('Jeff') Cassels, presented in Chapter 13, makes abundantly clear. He was on the spot for the first phase of Cyrenaican independence in 1949 and for the emergence of the whole of Libya as an independent kingdom in 1951–52. His refreshingly honest account of the conduct of the post-independence elections more than confirms the importance Britain placed on seeing Libya become a friendly client kingdom.

If the initial restoration of order after the chaos of war was efficient and returned a measure of stability to Libya, the overall British intentions for the country in the 1940s turn out to have been not only highly complex, reflecting new realities across the region, but also somewhat contradictory at a time of imminent imperial withdrawal from both Palestine and India. Choosing to set the clock back rather than forward, Britain relied on its familiar tactic in the Middle East of finding and bolstering a client monarch who would agree to satisfy its strategic interests and act as a brake on threatening pressures from extremist elements.[6] In the process, considerable intellectual and organisational effort was expended on justifying the Sanussi cause of Idris and installing him in office on the model of the amirate-cum-kingdom in Transjordan (present-day Jordan). In Libya, it was an extraordinary gamble that happened to pay off for the next two decades.

My father was both a witness to, and a key participant in, the crucial first phase of this intensive British involvement. Although he rarely talked about this period of his life, no doubt out of habitual reticence and because of an inevitable preoccupation with day-to-day matters, his memoir captures many moments of significance. And in clear defiance of those shadows of forgetfulness, oblivion and death inherent in the Lethe legend, he made a special effort to preserve his Libyan diaries, knowing that his daily observations might prove enlightening to others at some time in the future. More than anything, it was these on-the-spot insights that convinced me that his was a story worth deciphering and telling for the first time.

---

[6] As William Roger Louis succinctly put it, 'the case of Libya reveals the classic themes of British imperialism recast in a post-war world.' *The British Empire in the Middle East, 1945–1951*, Oxford, 1984, p265.

# chapter 1

# REBUILDING FROM THE RUINS
## CYRENAICA, 1942–43

WHEN BRITAIN'S fortunes of war changed in November 1942, with General Bernard Montgomery's decisive victory over Germany's desert army at al-Alamein, the Eighth Army was quick to consolidate its advantages. Britain's rapid reoccupation of eastern Libya facilitated the onward allied push across North Africa. Key priorities were the strategic ports and airfields at Tobruk and Benghazi, both of which had already been under British control in the course of 1941 until stopped by the first incursion of Field Marshal Erwin Rommel's Afrika Korps and then again by Rommel's even more successful advance in 1942. In the struggle for supremacy in the Mediterranean arena, the territory here had been continuously fought over for two full years.

On 13 November 1942, the Eighth Army entered the devastated port of Tobruk and a week later managed to secure the principal city of Benghazi, from where it soon launched a long and rain-soaked trek along the coast towards Tripoli in mid-December. With Tripoli taken on 23 January 1943, the North African war entered its final phase. German and Italian forces held out for a further three months in Tunisia until being finally dislodged on 13 May by the combined operations of American and British forces. With these victories, Britain found itself responsible for running both Cyrenaica and Tripolitania, which together had made up the greater part of the Italian colony of Libya, while Free French forces controlled the southern desert zone of Fezzan.

After two previous short-lived attempts to run Cyrenaica, which had changed hands no fewer than three times in two years and had suffered massive destruction of its towns, roads and other infrastructure, this time Britain was determined to settle in and take charge more effectively, and it was keen to gain the cooperation of the war-weary local

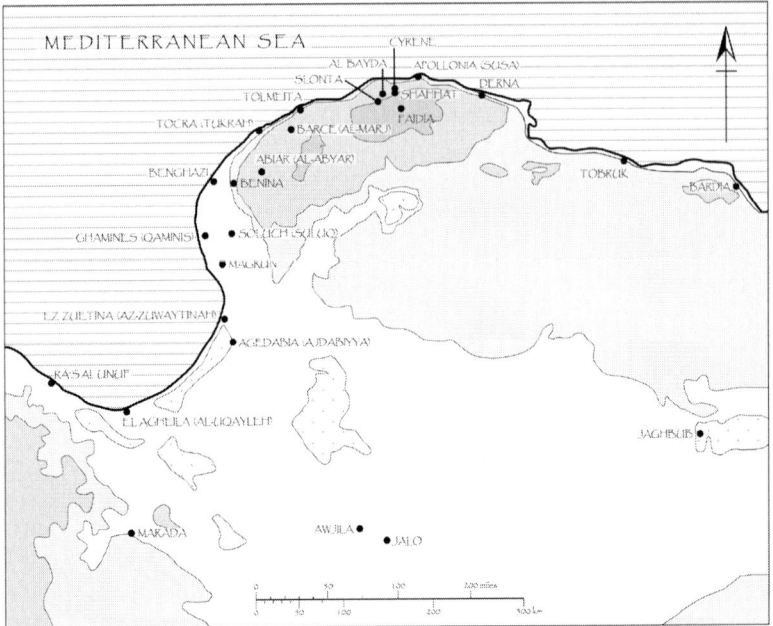

Figure 1. *Map of the places mentioned in the text.* Created by Maxine Anastasi.

population. In legal terms, along with other Italian colonies, Cyrenaica was regarded simply as 'occupied enemy territory', with its future to be determined by a peace treaty at the end of the war, but this eastern region of Libya, known in Arabic as Barqa, had special significance to the Middle East Command based in Cairo. And so Montgomery delivered a 'message to the people of Barqa' on 11 November 1942, in which he repeated an earlier official promise made by Britain's Foreign Secretary, Anthony Eden, to the territory's well-known spiritual leader, Sayyid Mohammed al-Mahdi Idris al-Sanussi, that his followers would 'not again be subject to Italian rule'.[1] Without making a specific promise of independence for Cyrenaica or Libya – as Idris and his supporters wanted – Montgomery reassured them of the importance of their special relationship with Britain, emphasising that 'while the British Army

---

[1] The diplomatic thinking behind Eden's declaration is discussed in Saul Kelly, *War and Politics in the Desert: Britain and Libya during the Second World War*, London, 2010, pp111–121. The status of Idris was anomalous in that although the Italians, before the arrival in power of Benito Mussolini, had acknowledged him as amir (prince), the British in the 1940s were initially reluctant to bestow such a title, preferring the formulation of sayyid – a term of respect accorded to certain recognised descendants of the Prophet Muhammad.

rules the country, it wishes to establish friendly and cordial relations with the people.'[2]

As soon as the Eighth Army knew it could secure Cyrenaica, the go-ahead was given for the recruitment of a small band of administrators to provide a form of temporary government. Britain could present itself as its primary liberator from the hated Italians, against whom the Sanussis had fought a bitter guerrilla war in the 1920s, and there was every chance that the relationship might develop further to the satisfaction of both sides.[3] The main strategic concern for Britain was to preserve long-term access to the valuable naval and air facilities along Cyrenaica's coastline, which British strategic papers would later refer to as 'the western bastion of the Middle East'.[4]

## THE WORK OF THE BRITISH MILITARY ADMINISTRATION (BMA)

By mid-December 1942, an initial group of 27 British men had been hastily recruited as potential administrators for Cyrenaica, although their boss, Brigadier Duncan Cumming, was clearly worried that few of them were of the calibre he hoped for. He complained that 'only a fifth of the officers of the military government will know sufficient Arabic to do this work with reasonable facility in that language' and was therefore concerned about his ability to maintain 'the accepted standard of administration'.[5]

Peter Synge was one of the 27 men handpicked in December 1942 to go into Cyrenaica as soon as it could be arranged. Although he spoke conversational and commercial Arabic (acquired in his previous job as a cotton ginnery manager in Egypt), Peter had no experience of civil administration and so he could well have been one of the new recruits about whom Cumming had doubts. The story that emerges from his account is that he and his colleagues were thrown in at the deep end of a very uncertain situation and given a wide range of challenging duties. Few in number, they had to shoulder huge responsibilities for which

---

[2] Rennell of Rodd, *British Military Administration of Occupied Territories in Africa during the years 1941–1947*, London, 1948, p251, and S. Kelly, *War and Politics in the Desert: Britain and Libya during the Second World War*, London, 2010, p160.

[3] All remaining Italian settlers had been evacuated before the final British advance of November 1942. In an effort to understand the tribal affiliations of the local rural population, the new military administration was at first guided by information gained during the first two occupations, as noted by Jason Pack in 'British State-Building in Cyrenaica during the War Years (1941–1945)', MSt dissertation, Oxford University, 2011, pp21–4.

[4] S. L. Bills, *The Libyan Arena: The United States, Britain and the Council of Foreign Ministers 1945–1948*, Ohio, 1995, p22, from Brig. R. D. H. Arundell, 'Future Policy in Cyrenaica' 13 November 1945, FO 371/50790.

[5] D. C. Cumming in Barce, to GHQ Cairo, 18 December 1942, WO 230/151.

they clearly had had little serious preparation, but this was a time of war, when extraordinary things so often become par for the course.

As members of a military administration, the men posted to each of the six main districts in Cyrenaica were expected, first and foremost, to support the ongoing war effort in whatever way might be needed and, secondly, to act as benign administrators – or effectively as civilians who just happened to be in uniform. The exact rules and procedures of the BMA seem never to have been comprehensively defined because the situation demanded that these should evolve in pragmatic fashion in response to whatever challenges might arise. According to the official historian of this period, 'it was necessary to create an administrative authority, however rudimentary, at once', adding 'the art of government is not in the making of laws but in knowing what laws can be made. To make laws, orders or rules, which are disregarded and cannot be enforced, is to discredit the authority of government.'[6]

As is vividly confirmed by Peter Synge's diary and memoir, the evidence of the official files indicates that he and his BMA colleagues were on duty seven days a week and were expected to turn their hand to any number of tasks. Some of the key elements of their work can be identified as: (i) organising adequate food supplies for the population, as well as purchasing local crops and livestock; (ii) collecting any useful war equipment left lying around the country to send to the frontline, first in North Africa and later in Italy; (iii) maintaining order with the help of the Cyrenaica Defence Force, a kind of gendarmerie staffed by former members of the Libyan Arab Force, which had been recruited with the help of Idris and had fought alongside the British army; (iv) cultivating good relations with the mainly Bedouin tribal chiefs (or sheikhs) in rural areas, as well as with members of the political and business elite in the main cities; (v) resolving any disputes that could arise between the mostly nomadic tribes (for example, over access to water wells); (vi) acting as magistrates to enforce a system of basic justice; (vii) facilitating the running of the key farms and agricultural estates in the country, before handing them over to new owners; (viii) initiating the collection of local taxes or rates; (ix) keeping financial accounts; (x) facilitating repair of the worst of the devastating war damage to schools, hospitals, buildings, harbours and roads that Cyrenaica had suffered; (xi) in particular, acknowledging and

---

[6] Lord Rennell of Rodd, *British Military Administration of Occupied Territories in Africa during the years 1941–1947*, London, 1948, p29. The implication of this was that the wholesale departure of the Italian administration in Cyrenaica meant it was more difficult to apply the rules of war – as spelt out by the Hague Convention of 1907 – in this part of Libya than was the case in Tripolitania.

Figure 2. *Fighter aircraft of the US Air Force fly into the Marble Arch landing ground west of El Agheila, December 1942. The arch, erected on Mussolini's orders in 1937 to symbolise Italy's conquest of Cyrenaica and Tripolitania, straddled the Via Balbia coastal road linking both territories.* By permission of The Imperial War Museum ME RAF 7245.

fostering the special status of Idris and his entourage during any visits or tours that he or they made in Cyrenaica.

At first, those recruited were to be called Political Officers, but early in 1943 this was changed to Civil Affairs Officers (CAO) to underline their broadly administrative functions.[7] But because this was formally a military government, answerable to the War Office, each officer had to be known by an army rank, and this often led to a mismatch between the responsibilities they took on and their military status, as Peter was keenly aware throughout his service. Having been commissioned as a

---

[7] The renaming was part of a process in which the temporary administrations in all the former Italian colonies came to resemble colonial governments, while being 'military only in form'. Rennell of Rodd, *British Military Administration of Occupied Territories in Africa during the years 1941–1947*, p456.

31

first lieutenant, after gruelling training at a boot camp in the Egyptian desert, he had to lobby hard to be made a captain as he had originally been promised once he assumed his civil affairs responsibilities but, after that, he was overlooked for further promotion for nearly three years. Seeing other younger or (in his opinion) less worthy colleagues being promoted above him sometimes made him seethe with indignation.

The man in charge of the BMA in Cyrenaica, Brigadier Duncan Cumming, was himself from a civilian background, having been a senior administrator in Sudan before the war. Appointed as Deputy Chief Political Officer (DCPO) for Cyrenaica in May 1942, even as Rommel was still pushing the battlefront deep into Egypt, Cumming had prepared himself well, and was determined above all to make a good impression on the people of the territory once he got his chance. The first fitful efforts at administering Cyrenaica had been made after the Italians had been first driven out in early 1941, but these had been cut short twice after Rommel's Afrika Korps intervened prior to its final grab for Egypt. But after al-Alamein, with the German army finally forced into a categorical retreat, there was an opportunity to take charge definitively, and perhaps to live up to the promises made to Idris, whose established loyalty to the British had enabled the recruitment of the symbolically useful Libyan Arab Force to help fight the Axis forces over the previous two years.[8]

Cumming set out the aims of the BMA succinctly in a semi-official letter dated 11 November 1942, in which he pointed out:

> The military government ... is temporary and is only required until the future of the country is settled in the Peace Treaties. Consequently it enjoys a number of privileges denied to other governments, particularly in a colonial territory. For instance, there is no question about its right to rule; it can legislate with maximum ease and it can avoid becoming involved in politics even though it must be keenly alive to the political atmosphere. It is, however, this easy exercise of absolutism that provides the greatest danger to good government. We shall not aim at good government in any theoretical sense but as the best practical solution to the rather complicated problem than Cyrenaica presents.[9]

---

[8] 'Consisting of five battalions, the Libyan Arab Force wore the Sanussi emblem, a white crescent and star on a black field, as a badge.' R.B. St. John. *Libya: From Colony to Independence*, Oxford, 2008, p85.

[9] Rennell of Rodd, *British Military Administration of Occupied Territories in Africa during the years 1941–1947*, p249. Duncan Cumming's outline of the BMA's intentions implied adapting Britain's obligations under the rules of war agreed by the Hague Conventions of 1899 and 1907.

Cumming kept a tight rein on the men under his command, who were an odd mix of people, many of them drawn from civilian life and unused to the kind of military discipline that their status now implied. As Peter Synge's diary shows, the *esprit de corps* was sometimes close to breaking point. To avoid the personal clashes that arose among members of his team, the brigadier resorted to a constant shifting of responsibilities. Because there were no opportunities for entertainment in the early days, the men seemed to find what consolation they could in the limited quantities of alcohol that were available and in obsessive games of bridge in the evening. As time went on, their rather austere existence was relieved by sports and by occasional visits from the Entertainments National Service Association (ENSA).

## KEY PERSONNEL

The British presence in the Libya of the 1940s was unusual in several respects. It was enacted by a small body of administrators supported by the very limited resources available in wartime, essentially mimicking colonial methods in use in Sudan and Palestine. In Cyrenaica, the eastern half of the country adjoining Egypt, policy was guided by a belief in the importance of a British alliance with the Sanussiyya – an Islamic religious movement that had influence in the Sahara and across the remoter parts of north-eastern Africa. Although there is still much discussion among historians over the actual political credentials of the Sanussi order, the alliance originated in early British colonial dealings in the surrounding region.[10] Since August 1940 it had become a strategic choice, when the Commander of the British Forces in Egypt, General Henry Maitland Wilson, agreed with Idris on the formation of the Libyan Arab Force. At the same time, the British appointed a Political Officer for Sanussi Affairs, Norman Anderson, a lawyer and Christian missionary, who had been living in Cairo since the early 1930s.

Being familiar with classical Arabic, Anderson's job was to liaise on a daily basis with Idris, who spoke no English. In April 1942, Anderson prepared the outline strategy that was to be pursued in the coming years. In essence, this urged the British government to promise 'a native administration in Cyrenaica under the guidance of a foreign power'

---

[10] See A. Baldinetti, *The Origins of the Libyan Nation: Colonial legacy, exile and the emergence of a new nation-state*, Abingdon, 2010, pp10–20. The subject is explored even more fully in Jason Pack's forthcoming book, provisional title *Britain's Informal Empire in Libya? The Anglo–Sanussi Relationship, 1882–1969*, Hurst & Co, 2017.

and to give Idris 'a practical share in the administration'.[11] Given this background, it is highly likely that both Norman Anderson and Duncan Cumming played a role in drafting General Montgomery's historic declaration of November 1942.

With Anderson staying behind in Cairo to keep in close touch with Idris, Cumming moved to Cyrenaica in December 1942 to put the BMA into operation, initially from the Sanussi heartland of al-Bayda (known by the Italians as Beda Littoria), high up in the Jebel Akhdar region. Here, his first deputy was Hugh Foot, later Lord Caradon, a highly effective political operator who had gained experience in Palestine at a difficult period in the 1930s and who went on to become a leading player in preparing countries for self-rule and independence. His name would later be particularly associated with Cyprus, Nigeria and Jamaica, but his brief time in Cyrenaica was a significant step on his road to prominence in the British decolonisation efforts of the 1950s and 1960s.[12]

Also at Cumming's side in the early days was Edward Evan Evans-Pritchard, a groundbreaking anthropologist who had undertaken significant research into different tribes in the Sudan and who, from the outset, advised Cumming on the tribal and religious allegiances of the Cyrenaican Arabs. His work with the BMA helped him assemble a mass of data for his major study of the Sanussi order, *The Sanusi of Cyrenaica*.

Other key members of the circle around Cumming in the early days included Ralph Hone and R. D. H. Arundell (both based at HQ in Cairo), J. F. P. Maclaren, Charles Oulton, Bill Bailey, Sholto Douglas, C. A. Collard and K. D. D. ('Bill') Henderson (who was on loan from Sudan for a brief spell in 1943) and the BMA's controversial Information Officer John Reid. Several of these were so-called 'Arabists' with experience of Sudan or elsewhere in the Middle East, and some had intelligence affiliations and had undertaken earlier missions in Cyrenaica. Cumming sought to put their experience to use in different ways.

Colonel Maclaren, previously a District Commissioner in Sudan, was initially in charge of negotiations with the Bedouin tribes before becoming Cumming's deputy after Foot's departure. Bill Bailey, who was Chief Civil Affairs Officer in Benghazi in 1943, and Peter Synge's boss for some months, had the task of liaising with the urban political elite in the city. However, having had earlier experience of Iraq, where

[11] J. N. D. Anderson, background notes to CPO, 10 April 1942, WO 230/151.
[12] H. Foot, *A Start in Freedom*, London, 1964.

Figure 3. *Sayyid Idris with British and Libyan Arab Force (LAF) officers and troops shortly after the formation of the LAF in 1940.* By kind permission of Faraj Najem Collection.

he had suffered harsh imprisonment during the May 1941 military rebellion led by Rashid Ali (which briefly threatened to create an Iraqi alliance with Nazi Germany), Bailey was possibly oversensitive to the potential for hostility among the citizens of Benghazi.

When the BMA settled in for a longer stay after the war than was first intended, most of its staff moved on to other jobs, but some stayed with it throughout its existence. After 1947, few remained who had been involved since the beginning, but one of these was Cecil Greatorex, whose fluency in Arabic helped him to move effortlessly upwards in the hierarchy, becoming one of the key points of contact with Idris in the late 1940s and well into the 1950s. His career is a good illustration of how, over the years of Britain's temporary administrative presence, the basis was laid for a connection and an alliance with Libya that survived through the growing turbulence in the Middle East until Muammar Qadhafi's takeover in 1969.

Most of those in the BMA were either on temporary secondment from the armed forces or had, like Peter, simply been conveniently available in Egypt, bringing with them a random but possibly useful set of attributes, which Cumming and his closest colleagues sought to apply as effectively as they could. Some had enough legal experience to help set up a basic system of justice. Whatever their background, all members of the BMA were entering an arena in which there was the potential for surprises from any number of sources.[13]

## A DEVASTATED LAND

First among the challenges facing this supposedly temporary administration was the sheer devastation that Cyrenaica had suffered over its two years of heavy bombardments and the alternating military advances and retreats involving innumerable heavy tanks, vehicles and aircraft. A region that only three years earlier had been a showcase for Italian fascist organisation and architecture, with state-of-the-art roads, water and power installations, had been reduced to little more than a wasteland. Worse, it was littered with unexploded munitions and land mines that would continue to kill and maim significant numbers of rural inhabitants for years to come.

The strategic port cities of Benghazi and Tobruk suffered more damage during the war than anywhere else in North Africa. The British air raids against Benghazi had begun in September 1940, with almost nightly attacks on its port and military compounds until Australian mechanised units entered the city in February 1941. Further destruction ensued as the Axis armies occupied it from April to December that year, followed by the brief Allied return of early 1942 before German reoccupation. To escape the bombings, most of the population had moved out to the surrounding countryside.

In late 1941, war correspondent Alan Moorehead wrote that Benghazi 'was no a longer a city any more. The plague of high explosives had burst on the place and left it empty, apathetic and cold. The shops were shuttered, the markets closed and ruin succeeded ruin as we drove along. … Blasts had pockmarked every building, direct hits had ploughed the waterfront and dashed the anchored vessels onto the seabed. For nearly a year the RAF had gone on and on, night after night, and here we were looking at the scoresheet – a ravaged, ruined city.'[14] Another reporter, John Gunther, estimated that it had suffered as many as 1,680 air raids in all, adding, 'Benghazi is a miserable city. I think the most miserable

---

[13] In addition to the formal account given by Lord Rennell of Rodd in *British Military Administration of Occupied Territories in Africa during the years 1941–1947*, another key summary of the period is provided by Anna Baldinetti in *The Origins of the Libyan Nation: Colonial legacy, exile and the emergence of a new nation-state*, Abingdon, 2010, pp113–5.
[14] A. Moorehead, *African Trilogy: The North African Campaign 1940–1943*, London, 1944 and 1998, p258.

we saw in Africa. ... It was half destroyed by bombing.'[15] In the harbour, nearly a hundred ships had been sunk, and the long moles that protected it from storms had been breached in several places, making access tricky during the frequent sudden squalls that are a feature of this stretch of coast.

Many buildings remained unrepaired for years afterwards. In the 1950s, US diplomat Henry Villard wrote that Benghazi's 'gaping wounds are unhealed', and added: 'Shattered homes, hollow shells of buildings, piles of rubble in empty lots are grim testimonials to the bombardment.'[16] A few of the key buildings near the waterfront miraculously survived, although with varying degrees of damage, the most prominent among them being the Italian Governor-General Rodolfo Graziani's palace, the twin-domed cathedral, the Berenice Hotel, the railway station and a cinema.[17]

Another clearly visible result of the conflict was the abandonment of 1,800 or so newly built farmhouses for Italian peasant settlers in the fertile Barce Plain, a two-hour drive from Benghazi where the Italians had planned a major irrigation scheme in an effort to recreate the area's legendary reputation as the 'granary of Rome'. After the first British occupation, the new settlers had remained, if somewhat nervously, but by 1943 absolutely every Italian in Cyrenaica had fled. As the first Secretary to the BMA, Hugh Foot, described the scene:

> In those days in early 1943 one could walk into any farm and see the pathetic evidence of sudden departure – food on the tables, toys on the floor and all the possessions of the Italian settlers, except those already looted, still there. And outside in the stables and fields there were cattle, the magnificent long-horned cattle of Tuscany, and flocks and fruit trees and vineyards. The Arabs well knew the boundaries of the lands from which they had been evicted, and they returned to take over not merely grazing lands as they had been before but farmhouses and cultivation and cattle.[18]

The Italians' ambitious irrigation scheme lay abandoned, with no money likely to be available for its completion, and the BMA had to figure out some way of reviving the agricultural potential of the area by using any talents and resources that might be available. According

---

[15] J. Gunther, *Inside Africa*, London, 1955, p177.
[16] H. S. Villard, *Libya: the New Arab Kingdom of North Africa*, Ithaca, 1956, p5.
[17] H. M. Bulugma, *Benghazi Through the Ages*, Tripoli, 1968, p55.
[18] H. Foot, *A Start in Freedom*, London, 1964, p79.

to Foot: 'The Arabs were incapable of cultivating the Italian farms and our efforts to teach them to care for the cattle and prune the vines and prevent the goats from eating the fruit trees were only very slowly effective. Usually they would pitch their tents alongside an Italian farm and use the farmhouse as a store or a stable.'[19] In time, however, the BMA took direct control of some of the biggest agricultural estates around the Jebel Akhdar region, using managers brought in initially from Sudan.

The wholesale departure of the Italians left both the modern economy and the local administration in tatters. This was in contrast to Tripolitania, where many Italians had been settled for a generation longer and had no desire to leave in the face of the British advance, and where their presence enabled the new administrators to keep things running much as before. But in Cyrenaica, where the Italians had almost totally monopolised the machinery of government, there were no clerks, no technicians or even telephone operators available to provide administrative support for the BMA.

Perhaps the trickiest task for the new administration was to engage with the population of both the towns and the countryside without stirring up new rounds of tension. Among the senior BMA officers, Cumming, Maclaren and Bailey were those mainly responsible for first assessing the social realities of the urban populations and the nomadic Arab tribes, and then finding ways of working with them. To help build a local civil service, few suitable recruits could be found; it took the first two years to recruit and deploy around 350 officials in the districts and 100 in the towns. The most prominent appointment of a Cyrenaican was that of Abu al-Qasim al-Sanussi, a cousin of Sayyid Mohammed Idris, as *qaimaqam* (governor) of Benghazi municipality. The BMA helped to set up the city's municipal council, which quickly became an important part of the embryonic political process in Cyrenaica.[20]

Under the Italians, Benghazi had been a sharply divided town, where the Arabs were pushed to the margins. The travel writer Freya Stark visited it shortly before the war and found it full of Italian families and apparently empty of Arabs. 'I began to feel a quagmire beneath this gay little town, a deadening substratum of fear. "There must be Arabs somewhere," I thought and spent what remained of the daylight trying to find them, and did eventually, in a little ghetto of squalid streets far back from the sea.'[21] In his memoir, Peter Synge wrote: 'Benghazi was a

[19] H. Foot, *A Start in Freedom*, London, 1964, p82.
[20] M. Khadduri, *Modern Libya: a Study in Political Development*, Baltimore, 1963, p45.
[21] F. Stark, *The Coast of Incense: Autobiography 1933–1939*, London, 1953, p162.

modern Italian city and the Arabs were excluded from the centre, but Jews – descendants of those from the dispersion after the fall of Jerusalem in AD 70 – had been allowed to live and own shops in the city, and when I arrived in January 1943 they were the only inhabitants of the city except for the Army.'

Jews were an integral part of the historic commercial structure of the urban areas of Cyrenaica. In Benghazi, although they had managed to survive Italian fascism, they were gravely threatened once the Germans took charge. Around half of the 5,000-odd Jews in the territory only narrowly escaped extermination by the Axis forces. During their last occupation, the Germans removed about 2,500 of them from

Figure 4. *LAF officers saluting Idris, March 1941.* By permission of the Australian War Memorial: negative 006180.

Benghazi, Derna and Barce and sent them to concentration camps in Tripolitania, but in early 1943 Hugh Foot succeeded in locating these camps and arranging their return. 'It was an extraordinary convoy which set out for Benghazi, but the Jews sang as they set out. Some five days later they sang again as they approached Benghazi. The Arab leaders of Benghazi came out several miles along the road to welcome them home again.'[22]

On the whole, life in the larger towns was dominated by the merchants, retailers and traditional artisans, who were often a mix of Arabs, Jews, Maltese, Turks and Greeks. The most prominent of the Arabs in the towns were those with recognised administrative and Islamic functions, including *qadis* (judges enforcing shari'a law) and *mukhtars* (responsible for the general management of their areas, including the registration of marriages, births and deaths).

For managing the rural areas, where a variety of Arab tribes led a largely nomadic existence, the BMA used the services of its anthropologist, Evans-Pritchard. The administration apparently hoped to replicate the type of local government that prevailed at the time in Sudan and so his tasks included identifying the main tribes and defining the outlines of a system of administration that catered for different categories of sheikhs, depending on whether they had recognised status among the larger tribal federations or only within single tribes or their subgroups, and to work out the tasks appropriate for the leading local officials, such as *mudirs* (administrators) and *mustashars* (advisers), who might be appointed to run the different rural districts.

For Duncan Cumming and his senior staff, a constant source of concern was the risk that members of the administration, or those in the Allied armed forces stationed there at the time, might cause offence to the Arab population, whether through ignorance or sheer stupidity. For this reason, Cumming was quick to set out a list of 'do's and don'ts' in uncompromising style: 'Do not treat Arabs as if they were aborigines. They are in fact a highly sensitive people who very quickly recognise anything which they consider lack of good taste and react accordingly. Show discretion in topics of conversation. These Arabs belong to the Sanussi confraternity which is puritanical and which teaches hatred of the infidel. They feel strongly about Europeans, particularly after their experience with the Italians, and there is no reason to believe that they have a great liking or respect for us.'

---

[22] H. Foot, *A Start in Freedom*, London, 1964, p80.

40

Cumming stressed that 'in general the Arab likes and responds to a European who is patient, restrained, sympathetic to his interests..., who speaks his language and does not offend his susceptibilities and who keeps his temper and his word. Efficiency, learning, good judgement and reliability, merits which have their own value in a European community, are all measured by these standards.'[23]

A close reading of Peter Synge's diaries and the official records reveals that he and other BMA officers may not always have followed such high-minded ideals. As a lifelong believer in the Empire and in the superiority of traditional British values (deriving largely from the Victorian age), Peter was not given to showing much sympathy to people of other cultures, and yet his diaries do occasionally reveal a measure of respect for several of the Libyans with whom he had dealings. At the same time, he was honest enough to admit to losing his temper under various job-related stresses.[24]

From the way Peter recounts some of his experiences, the causes of stress were not hard to find. In the conditions prevailing in early 1943, there were few certainties. For its part, the BMA was trying to bring about a semblance of stability in a country that had been devastated by successive invasions, with many of its cities and sections of the road infrastructure in ruins, and with little guarantee of acceptance by the local population. In the early stages, the essence of the mission was to win support by providing food, supplies, the basis of an economy and acceptable forms of administration and justice, and the pages that follow show how the BMA set about achieving this with a uniquely British approach and style. Much of the time, this involved the observance of clear social separation between the occupying force and the population. And throughout 1943–44, at the high point of a heavily mechanised war, the separation was paralleled in the technological sphere, with the British and American forces able to deploy their vehicles, equipment and men rapidly and comprehensively to ensure effective control.

---

[23] D. C. Cumming to CPO, 27 October 1942, WO 230/151.

[24] Peter MacDonnell Synge was born on 4 October 1905 in Herefordshire, where his father, Rev. Francis Peter Synge, was a country parson. On leaving school he joined Eastern Telegraph Company, working in Portugal and Gibraltar before being posted to Alexandria in 1926. From 1929 to 1942 he worked for the cotton company Carver Brothers at factories based in Upper Egypt. After his departure from Cyrenaica in 1947 he served the British Military Administration in Eritrea until his demobilisation in 1949, whereupon he managed a government cotton ginnery in Port Sudan until 1955. From 1956 to 1962 he served as a District Officer in Northern Nigeria, retiring to live in Somerset until his death on 11 February 1987.

Initially commissioned as a first lieutenant but anticipating an early promotion to captain, Peter found himself deployed to tasks that were both demanding and varied, as dictated by the prevailing need to improvise in the early months while the BMA was still settling into Cyrenaica in 1943. Although he was a willing worker, Peter Synge had come from a privileged social position in Egypt and clearly hoped for higher status in the system than he was given at first – but the postings and promotion he was promised remained elusive. As his personal experience shows, the BMA was a collection of competitive individuals, who spent much of the first year finding their balance and gaining a measure of confidence. It was only after these rather unpromising beginnings that more coherent policies could take shape.

# chapter 2

# DEVASTATION AND INSECURITY
## BENGHAZI, JANUARY–MAY 1943

IN THE MIDDLE OF 1942, the ever-expanding theatre of war had loomed menacingly close to the hitherto impregnable doors of Egypt. For Britain, the challenge was to hang on to its control of the Suez Canal in order to maintain unfettered access to the Indian Ocean and beyond, while for those British citizens who had made their home in Egypt since before the war, the gathering storm in the Western Desert was forcing serious decisions about the future.

Inevitably caught up in the so-called 'flap' that was spreading like wildfire through Egypt following Rommel's advance in July as far as al-Alamein – a mere 60 miles from the port city of Alexandria – Peter Synge and his family were among those who began to fear the worst. They had only recently spent a few weeks in Alexandria, where their holiday had been punctuated by air raids and the bombing of ships in the harbour. Working at the time as a cotton ginnery manager in the Upper Egyptian town of Minya, in September 1942 Peter said farewell to his wife and two children as they headed to South Africa for safety. 'We considered the perils of the sea voyage to South Africa less than the risk of a concentration camp in Egypt,' he wrote later. At the time, all ships travelling to South Africa were under threat from sporadic Japanese submarine attacks in the Madagascar Channel, but the family arrived unharmed at Durban and they were to spend the next two years at a remote mission station in East Pondoland, Natal Province.

Amid the uncertainty in Egypt, Peter set about looking actively for some way to join the war effort. His employer, the long-established Carver Brothers cotton trading company, was supportive; low cotton prices threatened its own future. Now aged 37, Peter's first application to join the Royal Navy Volunteer Reserve was unsuccessful but, once

British fortunes began to look more favourable in the wake of the decisive victory at al-Alamein at the end of October 1942, he was soon interviewed by the Civil Affairs Branch of the General Headquarters in Cairo and offered a commission for service in freshly liberated Cyrenaica, which was nominally under Occupied Enemy Territory Administration (as it had already been on two occasions since 1940).

The appointment would have taken into account Peter's ability to speak Arabic and his managerial record, but it came with the condition that he first had to undergo a month's training as a private soldier at the Infantry Training Depot at Fayid in the Canal Zone. Lasting over the Christmas period, this was an ordeal that was both harsh and badly organised and he was hugely relieved when it ended. After receiving his commission as first lieutenant on 18 January 1943, Peter said farewell to his circle of friends in Cairo before departing for Cyrenaica by train in the early hours of 23 January. On reaching Amriya, near Alexandria, the train, full of officers and troops, then set off along the coastal line leading to Mersa Matruh and Sollum and on into Libya.

As they passed the al-Alamein battlefield, Peter noticed that recent heavy rain had pushed up green shoots and flowers around the shattered remains of tanks and aircraft that were still being salvaged. Eventually, at around 6.30a.m., on 24 January, the train reached the end of the line, a few miles short of Tobruk, and he took a truck into the town where he briefly met the resident Political Officer, Major Alastair McIntosh. 'Tobruk is a city of the dead,' Peter noted in his diary. 'Not a house is whole and most are either rubble or roofless and the place is deserted. No Arabs are yet allowed to live in the town though a few come in to work.'

The next day, Peter joined a carload of naval officers to drive along the coastal road, which at the time was congested with military convoys travelling in both directions. After stopping for the night in Derna, which unlike Tobruk was hardly touched by the war – it had both electricity and water, and he noticed plenty of people about – they continued on towards Barce [the old section of the town known in Arabic as al-Marj], where he was required to report for duty.

Peter's memoir, written up later in his life, sets the overall scene, while his diary, compiled amid the events as they happened, provides the essential grit of his story. The following passages introduce us to the key characters in the British Military Administration at the outset, particularly Brigadier Duncan Cumming and Colonel Hugh Foot, and to the realities of life in Benghazi in the early months of the occupation. With very few trained clerical staff in Benghazi to help them with managing either office work or daily financial transactions, those in the team were under pressure to keep up with very mundane duties, even as they were expected to manage the trade in food supplies, attend to war-related security concerns, make the acquaintance of local political personalities and act as magistrates in court.

So-called 'general military courts' were improvised to handle civil cases involving killings, assaults and thefts. It is clear from Peter's succinct accounts of the broad outline of the proceedings and from his discussions with his colleagues that judgements were swiftly delivered and sentencing could be harsh. This was a time when nearly everything was similarly improvised, whether in pursuit of the war or to establish a semblance of order. As a result, Peter's tasks and experiences were highly varied. He reports investigating the cutting of telephone lines outside Benghazi, when he notes the expanding presence of American forces, and he inspects land that is to be cleared to make a new airfield. With mentions of air raids, offshore naval battles, drunken American troops molesting local women and the occasional drinking party in his own living quarters, these extracts reflect the prevailing mood of uncertainty and insecurity.

There is also a flavour of the determination of some members of the administration, including Peter himself, to maintain a very British sense of normality. This is evident in his regular references to the accommodation ('the Mess') and to the social activities within the small occupying team, especially the almost nightly games of bridge, where the stakes were measured in Egyptian piastres (PTs – PT100 = £1). By May, we learn that there was also an Officers' Club, providing a point of contact within the overall British military community.

During these early months, the principal figures in the BMA appear and disappear with regularity, those most visible at this stage being Duncan Cumming ('Brig'), Hugh Foot, Bill Bailey and J. F. P. Maclaren.

## FROM THE MEMOIR

*On through Beda Littoria [al-Bayda] and Luigi Razza and down into the deep Wadi Kuf by a zigzag road with many hairpin bends and the graveyard of many military vehicles whose drivers had lost control and plunged over the side. Previously the Italians had built a fine road carried high along one side of the valley with many bridges across the ravines and an easy gradient, but the bridges had all been blown during the first Italian retreat and now the road wound along the valley bottom. Here were the first fine trees which I had seen in Africa, and it is in fact practically the only place in Cyrenaica where trees of any size are to*

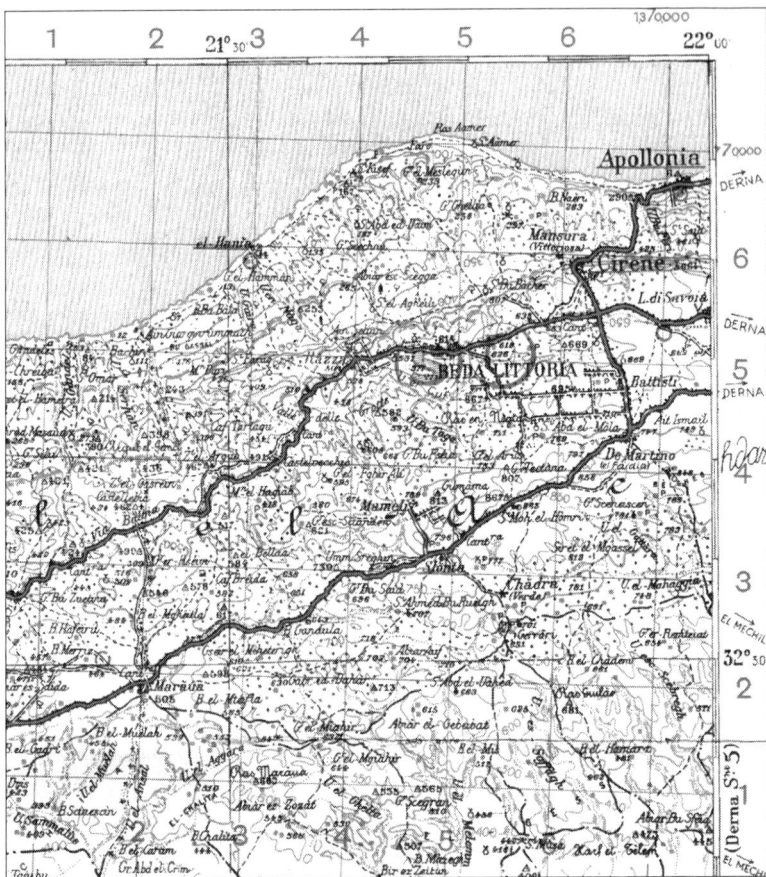

Figure 5. *Apollonia/Beda Littoria in 1942.* Detail of British Ministry of Defence (MoD) map of Cyrenaica (based on Italian sources, with grid divided into squares of 10 km).

*be found. Elsewhere the trees have a never-ending struggle to survive at all against drought and the depredations of man and goat.*

*Eventually the road came on to the eastern end of the Barce Plain, which is a vast shallow dish some 10 miles long and 2 miles wide and was the granary of colonial Cyrenaica. This plain when I first saw it was growing nothing but a fine crop of grass. The soil here is the colour of the rich red soil of Devon, and towards the end of January 1943 with a little imagination one could imagine oneself looking at a vast meadow in April in Devon and one got the impression of tremendous fertility, but this was a false impression. The winter of 1942/43 had been the wettest winter for many years. Immensely heavy rain had fallen in the desert where it had hardly been known in living memory, and all over Cyrenaica. Rain had saved Rommel from complete destruction when the New Zealand Division had made a huge sweep southwards into the desert, to come up behind Rommel as he retreated from Benghazi, to cut him off at Mersa Brega. Had they succeeded, Rommel himself might have been in the bag but heavy rain bogged the vehicles down before they were able to reach the coastal road, and in 1945 when I was in Agedabia District the deep furrows made by the bogged down vehicles were still visible and may even be visible today unless covered with blown sand.*

*Barce was at that time the HQ of the Military Administration as Benghazi, the capital of Cyrenaica, was still an important army base from which*

Figure 6. *Barce in 1942.* Detail of MoD map.

*the troops which had just captured Tripoli were supplied and it remained the base until Tripoli harbour could be re-opened. ... Next day I was told to report to the Political Officer, Barce District, but, almost as soon as I had done so, High Authority changed its mind and I was told to go on to Benghazi and report to the Controller of Civil Supplies there, and I got a lift in a staff car with a Major Collard [Political Officer, Agedabia] and Lt Col H. Foot, Chief Secretary Cyrenaica ... [Foot] had donned uniform more recently than I but had not had to suffer the indignity of a period of army service as a recruit, although two years younger than I. As we were driving through the Plain, he suddenly turned to me and said: "What would you do about the Plain, Synge?" Though flattered by the question, I was rather taken aback*

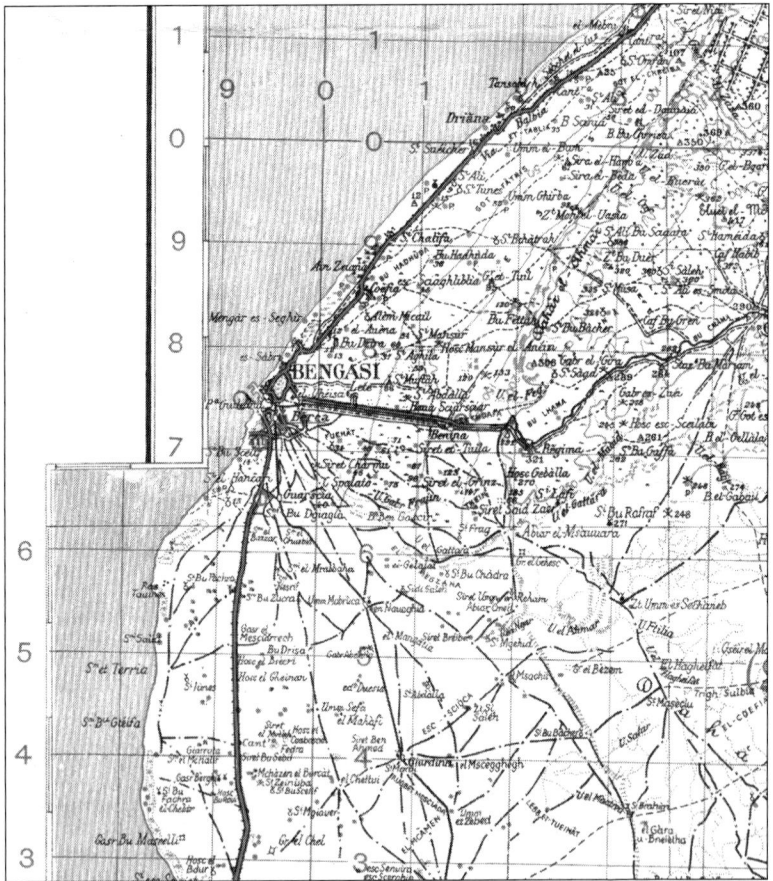

Figure 7. *Benghazi in 1942 (note the Italian spelling).* Detail of MoD map.

*as I had had no opportunity to think about it and was certainly no agricultural expert but I managed to stammer out a reply that there must be many farm labourers in the forces who should be released to plough it up and sow a corn crop. This was probably as good an answer as any because at that time there were no Italians left and the Arabs had made themselves scarce in the fastnesses of the desert which was "blossoming like a rose" owing to the unprecedented rain, and growing crops where none had been seen for years; and with all available shipping being utilised to pour men and war materials into North Africa there was no question of importing tractors and farm machinery. In fact, nothing could be done until the autumn, as corn must be sown immediately after the first rains in November to do any good, and it proved impossible to do anything on a large scale until the autumn of 1944 when the Mediterranean was clear and shipping could be used for more peaceful purposes.*

*Benghazi was the most dreary place imaginable when we arrived there. It had suffered severely from bombing and although debris had been cleared from the streets there were no shops open and no civilians to be seen, and it was raining. Although I was to spend the next four years there – off and on – and came to like the place, it always mystified me as to why it had ever come into being there, and why the Italians developed it into the capital of Cyrenaica.*

*Major Robertson, the Controller of Civil Supplies, was a dark volatile little man with a very fiery temper. He had lived in Italy before the war and spoke Italian fluently. He had installed himself in a first floor flat in the main square and had invited four other officers besides myself to live in his mess as well as an Italian Jew civilian who was his adviser and general factotum. It was an extraordinary set-up but I suppose as no military security was involved it was allowed.*

*Supplies of flour, sugar and tea had to be drawn from the army base supply depot and distributed to merchants who were responsible for doling it out, in accordance with a strict ration, to the populace who registered with them, and the merchants had to pay cash down before drawing their supplies. My job was to work out how much each merchant was entitled to and how much he had to pay and to receive the money and issue a voucher, which he took to the store. The lira had been devalued to the rate of 500 to the £ whereas it had previously been 100 to the £ so that the public was paying five times the price for their supplies, but it was amazing how they could always produce enough cash. Sterling was also in circulation and almost every merchant would produce both currencies and slap down a wad of each without apparently any idea of how much he had or how much he was required to pay, and frequently I had to hand back a wad of notes after calculating the amount due.*

# FROM THE DIARY

[Benghazi]

## 8 February
*Brig [Cumming] and [Major] Luesley found some [British] soldiers looting a store this a.m. and had them run in. Discipline in this town shocking and nothing and nowhere is safe. A large area of the town is roped off for street fighting practice with live ammo and grenades and it is all close to the inhabited parts of the town so I suppose the soldiery thinks that nothing belongs to anybody. Lovely day with cloudless sky.*

*Brig left after lunch and I had two words with him and he told me that this job is only temporary and that as I was taken on as an APO [Assistant Political Officer] I should be one. I'm not sure I want to be one now, seeing what a life [Captain] Woods, the APO here, leads.*

## 9 February
*Excitement over arrest of a man dressed in naval uniform accompanied by a genuine NO [naval officer] who is running a big racket of bringing tea etc from Egypt and going on to Tripoli and buying stuff there etc. Maj Robertson responsible for getting him arrested and hopes they will be tried and put into clink, but they are trying to wriggle out by saying that trade was a mask to their real activities of secret service work. What twaddle! Fine day again. Played cutthroat bridge [i.e. bridge with three rather than four players] this evening as Luesley refuses to play any more.*

## 10 February
*Supply situation very bad and there seems to be nothing for us at all. An idiot of an officer at Transit Section signed an HB10 on Saturday on his own saying that we had received 151,000 lbs of flour when in fact we had only 41,000 and signed for that quantity and we cannot get the balance. ... This is the fourth day we have drawn practically nothing but we have managed to get S&T [Supplies and Transit] interested and are collecting sugar and flour tomorrow.*

## 11 February
*Another wet night, after a gale from the south in the first part of the night. Wind veered to west and it looked very rainy early. Cleared up a bit in the morning but some very heavy storms p.m. Sent two lorries to collect sugar and flour and at midday went in the truck to see how they were getting on. Found the store shut and the guard said nothing had come. Went to the*

50

*Depot and was told they were drawing from Transit. Went there and found nothing and later Bishop came and said they had been sent from place to place and only began loading at noon. After lunch went round to store and got lorries unloaded and they went away about 3p.m. and loaded the whole 10 tons allotted but nothing more. Maj Robertson and Nahum went to Sidi Khalifa to settle a dispute about ration cards. Played cutthroat bridge after dinner and lost heavily.*

**12 February**
*Weather a bit clearer today but noise of the sea very loud. Spent all the morning in the office receiving money from merchants etc. New system means a lot of calculation as each merchant has different number of customers instead of each having 500. Went for a walk along front for ½ hour after lunch. Sea very rough and huge breakers on the beach but wind has backed to SW and is almost off the shore and blowing spindrift off the tops of the waves. 3 steamers riding outside harbour as impossible to anchor inside owing to breaches in the walls. Wondered what protection they had against possible sub attack. Busy all afternoon. Collected 15 tons of flour but supply situation very bad still.*

*Much colder this evening. Played cutthroat again and Robertson had amazing luck. Held all the cards and always found dummy with aces and kings. He won PT27 playing at ¼ PT per 100.*

**13 February (Saturday)**
*Busy in office all morning. Sent supplies to Agedabia last night and giving rations to Benghazi people today. No supplies coming in but we are promised 70,000 lbs of flour when we have lorries but only one is working. Went for half an hour walk after lunch and saw about 15 small ships outside the harbour as it is too rough for them to come in. Also a large hospital ship. Heard gunfire this evening. Luesley says he was told that 3 Hun planes were over this morning. If true, which I doubt, I hope they won't attack the ships but presumably there is minefield protecting them from the sea.*

*Busy afternoon again and took 220,000 lira in about 20,000 notes. Value only £450, which would mean only five notes in Egypt. Played cutthroat again after dinner; Robertson was not quite so lucky, but he won again.*

**16 February**
*Very busy day taking money from merchants and I did nothing else all day … Took ½ million lira (£1,000) and my balance was OK. Managed to slip out of the office at about 3p.m. for a quick walk. Went into docks and along the west mole. Wrecks everywhere and it will take years to clear the harbour and*

*rebuild sea walls, which are breached in many places and let in the sea so that the harbour is almost unprotected from westerly gales.*

## 17 February

*Not quite so busy in the office and merchants brought bigger notes so not so much counting and I have now got a list of calculations which saves a lot of work. ... Air raid at about 8.15p.m. tonight. Lights went out and then we heard planes and shooting began. Very few bombs. Watched part of the fireworks from downstairs. Green and red tracers and star shells. Raid lasted about ½ hour. Planes very high.*

[Peter was told to expect a job as Political Officer at Soluch, 50km from Benghazi, although this never materialised.]

## 4 March

*Shall be glad to have a change of job as this cashier business is too much of a good thing with no staff to do the donkeywork and no ordinary office facilities.*

## 6 March (Saturday)

*Dreamt last night that Brig Cumming had resigned owing to lack of support from GHQ. Had a restless night and my cold seems worse. Fleas crawling all over me.*

## 13 March (Saturday)

*Went off to Soluch in the 15cwt truck this morning to arrange about rationing and for me to see the place. Made a false start and owing to one way roads had to come right back thro' Benghazi and out on Tripoli road and got onto a terrible track across flat stony country, all covered in flowers and very poor barley. Nice enough now but must be a howling desert in summer. Hood of truck pressing on my head all the time and we found a piece of iron to hold it up but because it fell down once Nahum threw it away and I was very angry. Arrived at Soluch, only 50 kilos, at 12.15 having started at 9.30 [a.m.] or so. Arranged about rationing and then went for a stroll with the Waheed el Mudir [local government administrator] who showed me that all offices were inhabited by troops. An American sergeant asked me how to deal with a native boy who had stolen his clothes and I was able to settle that by telling the Mudir the story and I hope it will be settled satisfactorily. Mostly Americans there and a pretty poor town but a good water supply. American aerodrome outside with dozens of Liberators. Left about 1.30p.m. and lunched on the road. Got back via Giardina in under 2 hours, driving on a better road, and found work to do, which kept me busy until late.*

## 14 March (Sunday)

*Was prepared to celebrate my last day in Supplies but had a shock when I went to see [Colonel] Oulton this morning to tell him about Soluch and the Mudir's office being inhabited by troops, and he told me that it was impossible for me to be replaced at once and Woods was required until the end of the month. I asked him about my sitting on the court this week and he said that it was just too bad for Major R[obertson]. I told him that it was impossible for the office to carry on unless I was replaced and he said he couldn't help it. Had a fairly easy morning and went and sat on beach for half an hour.*

## 16 March

*Hoped to get off to Sidi Khalifa early this morning but the chauffeur had to get oil and he took so long that I began to wonder if I should ever get to the place. Just as we were starting we heard that the Mudir [of Sidi Khalifa district] was in the Political Officer's office and so I went and hauled him out to take with us. Found to my amazement that he was only a boy in an old suit and might have been someone's servant. No business to be a Mudir at all. Found when we got there that he had obviously forged the [identity] cards as they were in his handwriting, and he had at least two handwritings to which he admitted. He would not admit the forgery so I brought him back to Benghazi and after lunch he confessed to Major Robertson and was arrested.*

## 17 March

*Went and sat in my first court and was duly sworn in as a magistrate. Case of a boy of 14, who had killed a girl of 8 with a rifle. Case lasted till 6p.m. and we found the accused not guilty as he had obviously attempted to make the gun safe and the accident had happened while his friend had been trying to take the rifle out of his hands. I was glad to be able to ask the various witnesses some pertinent questions and to be asked my opinion by the President of the Court. A great change from the drudgery of counting cash.*

## 18 March

*As is it Mulid el Nebi [the Prophet's birthday] today we sat at 8.20a.m. in order to finish the case by midday and we actually finished at about 2.15p.m. Another accidental killing of two people by a man with a rifle entering a tent. He had it over his shoulder and as he stooped to enter it went off. We found him guilty of gross negligence and gave him 2 years. I would have liked to have give[n] him more but according to precedent he couldn't get more. He had neither inspected it to see if it was loaded or that that the safety catch was on or the accident could not have happened.*

*I asked Capt Shackleton, defending counsel, to dinner and we had a good one although both cook and* sofraggi *[house servant] were off for the evening. Played bridge after dinner.*

### 19 March

*Court sat at 9.0a.m. today to hear the last case, which is a complicated murder case with completely different stories. Am inclined to believe the mother of deceased, as if it had been a pure accident during a feast, as defence pleads, she would not have been so antagonistic and would have forgiven the accused. Very rainy and stormy today and wind changed round from SW to N this afternoon and blew a gale. Very big seas and heavy squalls this evening.*

### 20 March (Saturday)

*Court didn't sit till nearly 12 [noon] as we wanted some more witnesses. 3 defence witnesses turned up then and they all told the same story but were not present at the actual shooting which was fishy, as accused said there were between 15 and 50 witnesses. I was more and more convinced that the accused killed his niece on purpose and made out it was an accident but as deceased's mother's evidence was proved faulty on several important points we could not convict on the evidence before us. I summed up my views of the case to Evans and he was in agreement and brought in a verdict of gross negligence and gave him 5 years, which is a good stretch and the most we could do on the charges. We sat until nearly 8p.m. before the case was completed and it was quite dark in the courtroom and Evans had only one tallow candle to write his judgment by.*

### 21 March (Sunday)

*Back to my old job again, worse luck, and I wish I could sit on a court again.*

*The Arab quarter where street fighting was practised has been wired off and certain streets closed. The wiring off is good but not across some thoroughfares. Went on to roof and sat in the sun with a book for nearly an hour and then went back to office.*

### 29 March

*Col Foot was here yesterday and my relief is arranged for and I hope soon to be changing over but hope I shall not be long under Oulton. He is about the most unpopular man in Benghazi. Col Foot was very impressed by the success of our price fixing and closing of the vegetable market to troops. S&T can now buy for the troops cheaply and all prices are down and it is the only country in the world where prices are falling. Heard that 8th Army had pierced the Mareth line [in Tunisia] and is advancing northwards … and onwards.*

**4 April (Sunday)**

*Major Fisher arrived from HQ and brought my relief Capt Greatorex, an Alexandria man.*

**5 April**

*Played bridge after dinner and playing with Renato [Robertson's assistant] I called and made a grand slam and also a little slam doubled and redoubled vulnerable. Total rubber 3,500 points. A mine went off about 10p.m. and shook the whole house, and nearly blew the windows in. Cold and windy tonight.*

**6 April**

*Greatorex took over from me but was so slow that I had to help him or he would never have finished. Brigadier [Cumming] and General Hone[1] here staying in Civil Affairs mess where I heard they had hardly any dinner and had to borrow eggs and marmalade from us. Went for a walk with Greatorex in the harbour where they are salvaging a lot of the odd scraps of metal lying about and repairing one of the quays.*

*Went to see about taking over in Civil Affairs Office as Robertson had said that Bailey had told him he couldn't spare Woods and agreed to take over next morning and Bailey wanted me to go off and investigate a line cutting case at a village not far away.*

[Peter is now working as an Assistant Civil Affairs Officer (CAO), Benghazi region, reporting to Major Bailey, CAO Benghazi.]

**7 April**

*Greatorex took over from me first thing and I went over to Civil Affairs Office soon after 9a.m. and found that the place where line had been cut was south of Soluch and too far away, so I was put on to interviewing petitioners without being given any instructions as to how to proceed. Met Col Maclaren who seems a nice easy-going man, and he apologised for having to keep me in the office here for a bit. Went for a walk after lunch with Greatorex. He had an easy day and only had five merchants in. No lights again.*

**9 April**

*A storm blew up from the worst possible quarter for this harbour, which is almost open to west owing to huge gaps in the Mole. The last storm from*

---

[1] Major General Herbert Ralph Hone, Chief Political Officer for the conquered Italian colonies 1942–43, and based at the Middle East Headquarters in Cairo.

*this direction soon after we captured the place caused the loss of five ships, one of which is hard ashore, one was floated just before the swell began last week and is now on the bottom again, and another is getting the full force of this storm and waves break clean over her. There were six men on board this afternoon and I watched them coming off by a knotted rope on to a tug, which was rather hazardous.*

## 12 April

*Office crowded with petitioners and I was only able to deal with half. Mostly destitute women wanting free rations.*

## 14 April

*At 10a.m. Col Maclaren called me in to his office to say that he wants me to go and investigate the cutting of the telephone line at Tailimun. He wanted me to leave as soon as possible and stay a night or two if necessary. Major Rice [Defence Security Officer] arranged for a car to be at my disposal as it was thought that a 3 ton truck would not look as good and a car would be better for prestige, with which I heartily agreed.*

*I left about 2.45 [p.m.] and picked up the Sergeant who asked me if I had been in Minia and when I said I was he said he had come to see me last summer about somebody in Minia. I remembered the incident but not him nor the man concerned and it was clever of him to recognise me as I was a civilian then. We got to Ghamines about 4p.m. and I met the Mudir and he called a Sheikh Saad el Kammar and we went to see the place where the line was cut. We found five cuts and I took a very serious view of the business because it was deliberate sabotage as no line had been taken away. I told the two men that it was very serious and that I would hold them responsible and that they must send a stern warning out to everybody and try and bring in the culprit and I would call back next evening or the following morning to see what they had done, and I went on to Magrun, which is a village on a hill. A very compact little place and very clean looking and nice. It is a shocking road from Ghamines. Capt Baldry of the LAF [Libyan Arab Force – acting as gendarmerie] was away having left for Benghazi the same time as I left for Magrun but has a staff sergeant there and he told me to make myself at home. A telephone message had come from Major Bailey to me asking me to see about some barley, which needs cutting at the nearby aerodrome, so after a cup of tea I went out there … I said (to the CO) I would see the Mudir and get him to get the labour, and I went back to Magrun and found the Mudir who promised to have it done at once but he said it did belong to the local inhabitants.*

## 15 April

*I went to the Intelligence officer (American) at Soluch and asked him if he had anything to report and [he] told me about the cutting of a line in the town and other small incidents. I went to the Mudir and found him in the throes of registering ration cards and told him about the incidents which he said were nothing. I then took Mustafa el Arfar and we went to Tailimun and after finding the line which had been cut we went to visit some of the Bedouin encampments. The first was a small one and they were shearing sheep and we went into a tent and had tea and boiled eggs, and Mustafa told them what we had come for. He is much respected and they all greeted him affectionately and of course said they knew nothing. We went on to the next camp and were asked to stay to a meal and although I didn't want to I felt I ought to accept though we had plenty of food with us. It took a long time to prepare and we had more brewed sweet tea and then some mint tea and eventually eggs cooked with semolina, hot bread and lumps of tough boiled mutton. There were some good carpets in the tent and the owner is a merchant. A dust devil hit us while we were having lunch, which covered everything in dust. We got no information there but warned the people about the line and then went on to three more encampments which has [had] been nearest the cuts on consecutive nights, had moved south to Magrun and we were told the name of the chief. We decided to appoint a ghaffir [watchman] for the line and cost to be borne half by us and half by them and we went back to Soluch.*

*After a cup of tea I went down to look at the water point which has an engine and a sapper in charge and I got the sapper to agree to repair the animal watering trough as the animals would need water from now on.*

## 16 April

*Up at 7.15a.m. and no signs of life. At 8a.m. went to look for bkfst and found all the lazy devils in bed. Baldry must be a queer chap as everything is filthy and he has as many Arab servants as he wants and yet nothing is done for him, apparently, as his dirty water was still in his basin. We got away soon after 9a.m. and arrived at Ghamines at 10 where I saw the Mudir and Sheikh Saad again and they brought me the owners of the tents and houses near the line. I told them they must guard the line and after several complaints it was agreed they would take it in turns. There was an unexploded bomb in the village (American) which I promised to have removed and we looked at the school which lacked doors and windows and benches but I told the Mudir to start with the pupils sitting on mats.*

*Got back to Benghazi at noon and reported to Col Maclaren and Major Rice. Completed my report and gave it to be typed and heard from Rice that the line had been cut at Tailimun the night I went out, but it must have been repaired quickly as we saw no signs of it. Capt Woods had to go over to the Supplies Office as Maj R[obertson] is off to Tripoli on Sunday so I am left again and Major Bailey refuses to hand over cash or make any transactions until a sub-accountant is appointed.*

## 17 April (Saturday)

*Signal from HQ that Bailey can hand over to me so I have to count cash and square accounts all morning. Thought I was short but find all OK. Sent a lot of money away to field cashier, and sent all petitioners away till Monday. I really know nothing about my job yet and Woods hasn't handed over anything to me. Bailey is a nice fellow but quite scatter-brained. I wanted to see him about various subjects and he asked me over to tea to discuss them but we talked about other things with Bertram the fishing expert from Palestine. Bailey told me he would go back to the office at 9.0p.m. and would send over for me to discuss the estimates but he didn't send for me.*

## 18 April (Sunday)

*Went out to Fuweihat [al-Fuwayha] to pay the gardeners, and saw over the vegetable gardens etc. There is a lot of land there and the earth is good but water is a problem. Walked a bit after lunch and saw Col Foot on his way to Tripoli and asked him about my 3rd pip [i.e. captain's insignia] and he said he would see when he came back. Roberston left a.m. with Howells and is meeting Foot in Agedabia.*

## 20 April

*Wind round to south and weather more like summer. Decided to go out to Lete [Lethe] this morning and settle the dispute about the gardeners and took the 3 ton lorry. Was rather disappointed when I saw the place, which looks nothing from the road. When I arrived I was surprised to find I was expected because they had rung up to ask me to come out after I had left. I smoothed things over and arranged to take on the gardeners again and then went down to the grotto where the waters of Lethe are. … It is a water point for the RAF now. Called at Fuweihat on the way back to see the headman. Very warm today so I changed into KD [khaki drill] after lunch.*

## 21 April

*Went to Tokra by truck, two hours away. Arranged with Mudir to collect beans and we would send lorry on Saturday morning, but Mudir told me price in Benghazi for beans is PT4 and Army were only prepared to pay PT1. I settled on PT2.5 and found when I got back that the army had bought for PT2. Difficulty is to get on to Tokra and tell them.*

*Tokra is a pleasant place close to the sea and there is plenty of vegetation about with the escarpment in the background and it appears to be cooler than Benghazi. Left about 5p.m. and was back just before 7p.m. 2 American nurses to dinner.*

## 22 April
*Very warm today. … Walked with Greatorex and explored Graziani's palace which is in a hell of a mess but it must have been magnificent before the war. Full of marble and mosaics.*

## 27 April
*Sent off a lot of money with Col Maclaren and during morning went out to Fuweihat to see about an electric motor for Lete gardens. Had a bigger crowd than ever for passes to Misurata. After lunch went for a walk and inspected a Fascist cinema on Cathedral mole, which must have been a fine place before the war. Full of filth now.*

## 30 April
*Lunching with Omar Kanun, a well-known merchant at Berka, but at 1.15p.m. in walked Col Foot and Thackrah who had only left Tripoli on Wednesday and had broken down at Magrun (Bailey had just had news and was arranging breakdown gangs). Kanun's house is quite a pleasant one and well furnished. We arrived at 2p.m. and sat till 3p.m. before having lunch, which was quite a good one, far too much but it was well cooked and not cold. Yusuf Lenghi[2] and the Qadi were other guests. Finished at 4.30 and arrived back to find Col Foot just leaving for Barce. He is a hustler and I wasn't able to see him about my promotion. Went to Officers' Club again in the evening with Greatorex.*

## 1 May (Saturday)
*Sounds of a battle going on at sea at about 8p.m. Later saw flashes of guns and went on to the roof and watched pompoms and other stuff about 25 miles out. No signs of a ship being sunk but evidently a convoy being attacked.*

## 2 May (Sunday)
*Heard that a troopship was sunk last night but that we brought down 7 enemy planes. It was a large convoy and they were Indian troops but most of them were saved. Part of the convoy came in here and some ships went on this afternoon escorted by corvettes.*

---

[2] Yusuf Lenghi was one of the foremost merchants in Benghazi at this time.

*About 4p.m. went and bathed at Juliana mole. Found a place where one could dive into deepish water and though a bit rocky it was not bad at all. Sun very hot but sea just right. Quite a nip in it but pleasant. Woods and Greatorex came with me. Had tea at Officers' Club and after dinner had a bit of a party as Luesley is off on Tuesday.*

## 5 May

*Changed over to Civil Affairs mess while keeping on my room in Civil Supplies mess. The food is not exciting but much more to my taste than the stuff served in the other mess. Major Bailey goes off to Beda today for CAOs' meeting. He sent me off with W/Cdr Hargreaves to inspect the new site for an aerodrome at Bersis this afternoon. ... The site is all barley and wheat and will have to be cut.*

*Felix Carver [Peter's former employer in Egypt] turned up and after dinner I went over to the other mess to talk to him. Both messes absolutely full and people sleeping all over the place.*

## 6 May

*500 refugee Jews arrived today but I'm glad I hadn't got to look after them.*

## 8 May (Saturday)

*I had to get LAF to mount a guard for the show this afternoon. We had news early that Tunis and Bizerta had fallen and the Qadi wanted to give a party to celebrate at 5p.m. in the Municipal Hall. Had to dress up and we got a flag out and I had to receive the Area Commander, SNO [Senior Naval Officer] and SHO [Senior Health Officer]. The Qadi made a speech from the balcony and Bailey replied but the microphone failed in the middle of his speech. ... A large crowd gathered and there was a lot of cheering and handclapping. We had tea and the party dispersed about 6p.m.*

## May (Sunday)

*Sat on a court trying a murder case. Accidental shooting and quite straightforward but he was sentenced to 3 years as a deterrent though I am afraid too big a sentence may have the effect of making it more difficult for the police as these shootings may be hushed up and the police are understaffed as it is.*

*More trouble in the square over American troops drunk and molesting women. American MPs [Military Police] useless and afraid to touch them.*

## 10 May

*Oulton arrived at 7.30p.m. and the Brig and [Colonel Norman] Anderson came in with Bailey about 8.45 having been at Omar Mukhtar Club and later at Officers' Club. We had dinner in two parts.*

**11 May**

*At dinner, Brig said he had been told by SNO [Senior Naval Officer] that there were 87 sunk[en] ships in the harbour and 103 at Tobruk. He said the only reason any are visible is that they are sitting on top of others. There are only 14 visible! The forging Mudir of Sidi Khalifa was sentenced to 5 years today [see the entry for 16 March].*

**12 May**

*Major Rice here. Brig left p.m. Greatorex came to take over duties of ACAO. Court sentenced a murderer to death, 1st death sentence passed to date, and caused a sensation. Light came on today, and we actually had electric light for the [a] time after dark for over a month.*

**14 May**

*Very simple case [in court]. A quarrel over a sheep and a fight ensued in which one of accused shot and killed one man and wounded another. Not very conflicting stories but rather a tedious case.*

*Had tea at Brahim Kadiki's shop where there were some good cakes.*

**15 May (Saturday)**

[Court case continuing] *Judgement was delivered about 6p.m. and we gave him 20 years. I wanted death penalty as I considered the 1st accused a dangerous and bad type, but [Major] Lindsay pointed out there was provocation and death sentence would not be upheld. When sentence was given accused grinned and thanked Lindsay, and I thought afterwards that it must be because he was afraid for his own life from the family of the murdered man and was only too glad to be in gaol. Shackleton thought it a savage sentence. Had tea again at Kadiki's.*

**21 May**

*Was woken up about 12.30 last night by another drinking party up in the sergeants' mess. At 1a.m. I went upstairs and saw Sgt Walton who grinned and said he had no control. I went inside and saw CSM O'Brien and he said he would tell Capt Woods. It then turned out that Woods, EJ [Evans-Jones] and Greatorex were all there so I had to retire, as they are all Capts. They didn't quiet down until 2a.m. or later but, with an aspirin and some cotton wool, I got to sleep and was woken at 6.30 by the servant furniture-pushing upstairs. Wrote a curt note to Sgt Walton about it.*

*Three Sudan agriculturalists have come to stay with us. They are huge men who just make themselves at home without worrying about anybody else. They each weigh about 16 stone and look as if they drink like fishes but they can't do that in our mess as there ain't any.*

*Went to the "flicks" this evening to see "Eagle Squadron". The cinema was opened last night. It is a fine place but it was badly knocked about by bombs and has been repaired and is very rough but the seating arrangement is excellent. It was a very good film and good acting in it.*

### 22 May (Saturday)
*Maj Bailey went off to Agedabia yesterday. ... Greatorex in charge and I find the position rather galling. He is a decent chap but he is ten years younger than me and with no real experience comparable with mine and yet he is senior to me. Lay down after lunch and had a short nap, then went for a walk along the front. The sea thick with black oil, evidently from the tanker sunk 3 weeks ago. No bathing possible by the prison, if one wanted to. Bailey came back about 6p.m.*

### 28 May
*About 10.30p.m. last night a terrific storm blew up and it poured in torrents with brilliant lightning and loud thunder. ... 5cm fell last night. The oleanders in the town are in full flower and are weighed down with blossom. Very pleasant to see among so much devastation. There are European swallows and martins flying about and singing too. Lights came on tonight.*

### 30 May (Sunday)
*Another lovely day. Intended to try and get to church but impossible. Col Foot came and talked about refugees etc. Went out to the Blue Lagoon at Coafia [Kuwayfiyah] after lunch to bathe. Crowds of men there. ... Col Foot left after lunch.*

### 31 May
*Up early and went for a walk before breakfast and noticed that a building between the RAF and Navy house was open for the first time. Went in and found that Howells of Customs had taken ground floor flats as offices. Went upstairs and found six good flats. Modern, light, and with good windows and doors and not needing an awful lot of repairs. Came back and told Bailey and persuaded him to come and see them after breakfast. He agreed that they were good and the best yet. ... After lunch went and stuck "out of bounds" notices on the four top flats and arranged for a contractor to make necessary repairs. Col Maclaren came back tonight.*

# chapter 3

# SETTLING IN AND WINNING SUPPORT

## BENGHAZI, JUNE–SEPTEMBER 1943

F ROM THE OUTSET, Duncan Cumming's British Military Administration in Cyrenaica had foreseen working closely with Sayyid Mohammed Idris and his Sanussi network. It was a practical alliance based
on the help that Idris had given since the formation in 1940 of the
Libyan Arab Force (LAF), which was led by a combination of British and
Cyrenaican officers and had participated in desert actions against Axis
forces. The LAF was now busy establishing itself as a permanent gendarmerie, to be known as the Cyrenaica Defence Force (CDF).[1]

Cumming and Norman Anderson kept in close touch with Idris
over plans for an early visit that would mark the end of his long exile
in Egypt. The hereditary head of the Sanussi order, Idris had once also
carried the title of amir, with nominal control of the desert regions of
Cyrenaica (shorn of the coastal region that had been in Italian hands
since their invasion in 1911). But since his dramatic departure on horseback into Egypt in 1922 – as a new war flared between the Sanussis and
the Italians – he had tried to maintain his profile as a key flag-bearer of
independence, preferably for both Cyrenaica and Tripolitania.

Strategically, by mid-1943, thanks to a string of victories against
Germany and Italy, the British could take their time to nurse the political process in Cyrenaica on their own terms. For now the military
priorities were still paramount. The area around Benghazi was increasingly well stocked with functioning airfields, introducing a significant
American presence, which attracted retaliatory attacks from Italian

---

[1] 'Formally an arm of its paymaster the BMA, the CDF was a governance institution fabri-
cated by the British yet descended from a force loyal to Idris and raised under his banner.'
J. Pack, 'British State-Building in Cyrenaica during the War Years (1941–1945)', MSt dissertation, Oxford University, 2011.

fighters dropped in by parachute and by submarine, with the result that several – mainly British – aircraft were damaged or destroyed.

Benghazi was at this point playing a key role in the wider war effort, and on 1 August 1943, from the airfields around Benghazi, the United States Air Force launched its largest air raid across the Mediterranean to date. Code-named Operation Tidal Wave, it involved sending more than 150 B-24 Liberators from Benghazi to destroy a number of oil refineries in Nazi-occupied Romania. Although they inflicted severe damage on some of their targets, the bombers came under intensive ground attack and over 50 of them were lost, with the deaths of at least 300 aircrew members and the capture of over 100 by the German forces.[2] Peter Synge's account of seeing a fleet of bombers depart from the major airfield at Benina and his noting of the depleted number that returned after their 12-hour ordeal leaves a memorable image of the ebb and flow of the war at the time.

The diary entries also include the wild celebrations on 9–10 September following the capitulation of Italy: 'Great rejoicing everywhere and nobody doing any work. ... There were a lot of drunken parties.' But such events were highly exceptional, as Peter also provides plenty of evidence that the BMA was beginning to function with more focus than it did at the outset. However, bad management, combined with the demands of bureaucracy, could prove irritating to those who wanted to keep things moving, as Peter and his close colleague Cecil Greatorex clearly did. Both men were reprimanded in August for composing and sending letters without the signature of their boss Bill Bailey, the Civil Affairs Officer for Benghazi, whom Peter had already dubbed 'scatterbrained'. Given the lack of clear preparation for their multitude of tasks, such procedural arguments and personality clashes were perhaps inevitable but, for a while, the clash between Bailey and his juniors became a central drama in the micro-world of the BMA.

At the senior level of the BMA headquarters in Barce, there was a seemingly smooth consolidation of authority around those who were on loan from, or recommended by, the Sudan Political Service (SPS) in Khartoum, which at the time was considered the foremost British colonial elite in Africa. Duncan Cumming was himself one of their number. Following the recall of Hugh Foot to Palestine in July, the role of Chief Secretary went to another SPS man, Colonel J. F. P. Maclaren, who had been a district commissioner in different parts of Sudan in the 1920s

---

[2] 'Operation Tidal Wave', US Air Force Fact Sheet, Air Force Historical Studies Office, Joint Base, Anacostia-Bolling, DC, USA.

and 1930s. At the same time, John Reid, a former Governor of Sudan's White Nile Province, became the BMA's Information Officer; he was clearly unpopular and often caused offence to others. Among those also drawn from SPS ranks were Major E. G. Evans, Major P. Evans-Jones, and Major D. H. Weir.[3]

The underlying principle of 'indirect rule', pioneered in Nigeria by Lord Lugard and subsequently applied in experimental form in many parts of Sudan, was no doubt seen as particularly appropriate for Cyrenaica as well.[4] Since December 1942, Cumming had been in touch with Douglas Newbold, the influential and powerful Civil Secretary of the Khartoum government at this time. Although Newbold could not meet Cumming's request for the loan of some of his highly valued Sudanese *mamours* (police magistrates), he did send trusted colleague K. D. D. ('Bill') Henderson, who spent a couple of months in mid-1943 helping and advising the BMA.[5] Among other things, Henderson was fully alert to the risk of any deterioration in British relations with the Arabs. One of his letters to Cumming drew attention to the fact that British troops were being accused of setting fire to fields and causing damage to local farmers' crops and, as a result, he recommended that the BMA make swift payment of compensation to any valid claims of this kind.[6]

The anthropologist Edward Evan Evans-Pritchard had worked closely with the Khartoum government since the 1920s, helping to define the distinctive characteristics of various tribes, and most recently in 1942 by leading a group of irregular Sudanese forces in guerrilla warfare against the Italians on the borders of Ethiopia. In Cyrenaica, Cumming wanted him to describe and identify the key elements of the Sanussi history and socio-political structure, and to help clarify the role of the different kinds of sheikhs with authority in Cyrenaica, whether recognised by the Sanussis or by the tribes. It was a task Evans-Pritchard set about with extraordinary energy and enthusiasm and the resulting book, *The Sanusi of Cyrenaica*, helped to secure his future academic career as Professor of Anthropology in Oxford.[7]

---

[3] The full membership of the exclusive SPS is listed by Harold MacMichael in *Sudan Political Service, 1899–1956*, Oxford, *c*. 1958.

[4] 'Based upon inexact comparisons with Northern Nigeria and the pseudo-scientific prescriptions of Lord Lugard, Indirect Rule in the Sudan was stridently proclaimed but haphazardly enforced.' M. W. Daly, *Imperial Sudan: The Anglo–Egyptian Condominium, 1934–56*, Cambridge, 1991, p5.

[5] D. C. Cumming to D. Newbold, 14 Jan 1943, WO 230/151.

[6] K. D. D. Henderson to D. C. Cumming, 5 July 1943, FO 1015/972.

[7] Evans-Pritchard referred to the tribal system in Cyrenaica as a 'segmentary structure' and one of his key assertions was that 'every section of a tribe, from the smallest to the largest, has its sheikh or sheikhs.' E. E. Evans-Pritchard, *The Sanusi of Cyrenaica*, Oxford, 1949, p59.

To maintain the appearance of an efficient Sudan-style government, Cumming stressed to the Commander-in-Chief of the Middle East Command, General Henry Maitland Wilson, during an early July visit to Benghazi, that he hoped that he could at least have a minimum of nine 'expert Arabic speakers' around him.[8] There was still a shortage of good Arabic speakers on the BMA staff, although the total number of officers at his disposal must by now have risen to more than the 27 he started with (but it is not possible to verify the numbers of BMA staff at any one point).

The first collective meeting of Cummings' more senior CAOs had taken place in May at the Sanussi heartland of Sidi Rafa in al-Bayda. One of their decisions was to recognise the more senior tribal *omdas* (chiefs) and sheikhs, and that these should be supported by *mustashars* (advisers representing the government). The idea was to try to engage with the tribal system, while also keeping elements of the inherited Italian administrative system, by appointing new *mudirs* (local government administrators), though not as many as the Italians had done before them. Several of the new *mudirs* were recruited from the Cyrenaica Defence Force (CDF).[9]

Norman Anderson was taking the greatest possible care to ensure that Sayyid Mohammed Idris was kept informed about, and stayed supportive of, the BMA's work. He relayed the CAOs' decisions at Sidi Rafa for final consultation with Idris in the hope of receiving his approval.[10] Undertaking his own tour of the country, Anderson had a long discussion with a leading personality in Derna, Ali Pasha al-Obeidi, who was of the opinion that Idris should come as soon as possible. When Anderson told him that Idris did not want to travel with the large retinue of sheikhs who insisted on accompanying him, and that the BMA was in no position to provide accommodation for such large numbers, Ali Pasha said that it would not matter if Idris came with a small group because 'the Sayed's personal and religious prestige stood so high that a visit from him even if he were riding on a donkey would evoke adequate enthusiasm.'[11]

Now promoted to captain and subsequently feeling 'more like someone', Peter Synge gives an insight into the mood on the streets of Benghazi ahead of an anticipated visit by Idris at the end of July. There was heated debate about the official status of Idris in the newly

---

[8] R. D. H Arundell to CAB, GHQ, ME, 12 July 1943, WO 130/151.
[9] Conclusions of CAO Meeting, 6 May 1943, FO 1015/972.
[10] Conclusions of CAO Meeting, 6 May 1943, FO 1015/972.
[11] N. Anderson to CCAO, May 1943, WO 230/151.

Figure 8. *Benghazi, British Military Administration officers with Grand Qadi and the Mufti, Benghazi, 1943; Peter Synge seated second from left next to the Grand Qadi.*
Peter Synge Collection.

liberated country. Under international law, Cyrenaica still belonged to Italy and so the BMA was in no position to declare that Britain regarded Idris as the country's actual or potential ruler. Although people commonly referred to him as *semu al-amir* (His Highness the Amir), the BMA insisted, on Anderson's advice, that the administration should not use the same formula, but call him *sahib es-siada* (roughly translates as His Eminence).

After a few days of heightened expectations, the planned visit was postponed to a more propitious time, whereupon the threat of violence on the streets seemed to ease. A few well-informed insiders knew that the reason for the deferment was that Idris was 'doubtful of his status and had no "assurance" of the future in his pocket to proclaim'.[12]

---

[12] Letter from D. Newbold to R. C. Mayall, 30 October 1943, in K. D. D. Henderson, *The Making of the Modern Sudan*, London, 1953, p344.

Figure 9. *Group of Benghazi notables with British officers, 1943.* Peter Synge Collection.

This version is confirmed by the correspondence between Idris and the British Minister of State in Cairo, Richard Casey, in which, in June, Idris had initially asked for clarification about the future that the Allies intended for Libya. After much debate among British officials in Cairo and London, it was not until late September that Casey sent the agreed response, stressing that the Libyan nation did not really exist under international law, that the matter would have to wait for the decisions of a post-war peace conference and that, in the meantime, the BMA was only trying to assist the local populations to re-establish a normal way of life.[13]

Peter's daily record of these crucial four summer months of 1943 in Benghazi contains many vivid and revealing moments. After his initial visits to the villages of Magrun and Ghamines in April, where he had stayed in the quarters of Captain Baldry of the LAF/CDF, we come across Baldry again, this time being 'forbidden to have anything more to do with the Arabs' for interfering with an award to a man who had provided crucial information that led to the capture of 15 Italians. We also encounter a complex court case involving a long-running blood

---

[13] Idris to R. Casey and multiple draft responses, June–Sept 1943, FO 371/35661.

feud between two tribes and there is a performance of a memorable play about Italian misrule by a theatrical troupe from Derna.

Fleetingly, we get glimpses of the BMA's chief ideologues Evans-Pritchard and Norman Anderson, the former holding outspoken opinions that seem shocking to Peter and the latter making a long speech in formal and literary Arabic to give the BMA's public explanation of the non-appearance of Idris. And not for the first – or last – time we find the BMA being made welcome by the Omar Mukhtar Club, an institution that commemorated the foremost Cyrenaican national hero (executed

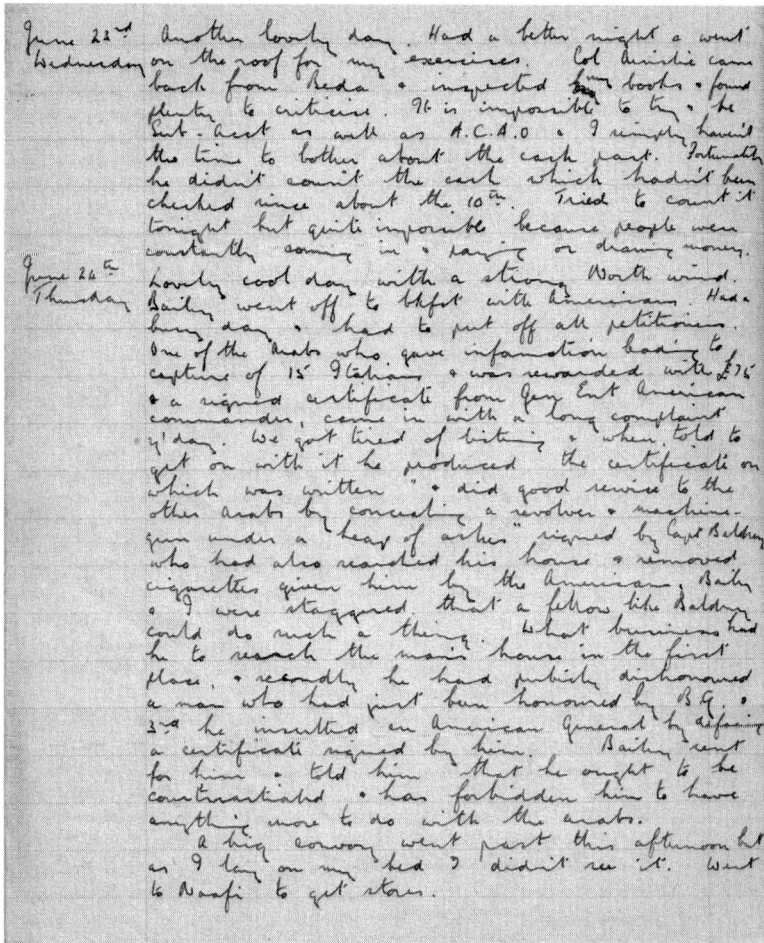

Figure 10. *Peter Synge's diary entries of 23–24 June 1943.* Peter Synge Collection.

by the Italians in 1931, see Chapter 5), but which would evolve politically over the next four years to become increasingly alienated from both the BMA and Mohammed Idris. With its headquarters in Benghazi, it spawned branches in the main towns, and most notably in Derna.

We also get a glimpse of the more arduous physical work of the administration, including collecting jerrycans for the war effort and the tricky task of organising labour to bring in the barley harvest just as the fasting month of Ramadan begins in September.

The diary well conveys the continuing uncertainty and the sudden changes in circumstances facing a group of people from different backgrounds with little clear preparation for their varied tasks. For the time being, Peter continues to work under the Benghazi CAO, Bill Bailey. The work gives him interesting insights into the main issues facing the BMA and puts him in contact with several of the leading political figures in the city, but in early August he falls foul of Bailey dramatically.

A row about responsibilities and planning, triggered by an apparent failure to prepare for the third anniversary celebrations of the 1940 agreement between the Sanussis and the British government[14], quickly deteriorates into an outright confrontation between the CAO and his juniors. Bailey's delicate mental state is now fully apparent to those around him; it is attributed to his earlier experience of being handcuffed to a prison wall for five days in Iraq in May 1941 during Rashid Ali's month-long rebellion in that country. (Arrested for distributing leaflets in Arabic on behalf of the British cause, Bailey had spent the month locked up alongside convicted murderers).[15] Bailey remains highly valued for his skills in communicating with the notables and citizens of Benghazi, but he is soon given less stressful duties, going on leave at the end of September to return with the status of Senior CAO and a promotion to colonel.

## FROM THE MEMOIR

*Major Bailey, my new chief, was not an easy man to work for and he had a habit of telling me to do something and then doing it himself, which was hardly conducive to good organisation. He had been in Iraq at the time of Rashid Ali's revolt in 1941 and had been locked up in the local jail under horrible conditions and he had had a nervous breakdown, the effects of which*

---

[14] Thereafter celebrated every 9 August as 'Sanussi Day'.
[15] F. Stark, *Dust in the Lion's Paw: Autobiography 1939–1946*, London, 1961, p112.

70

*were still apparent. He had no administrative experience and had no idea how to delegate duties to his juniors.*

*I was given fairly interesting assignments, which took me out of Benghazi. The first was organising the collection of jerrycans, which littered the desert, and the second was the purchase of barley from the Bedouin who had harvested the biggest crop almost within living memory.*

*Sugar and tea were commodities which were in very short supply amongst the Bedouin and were very much sought after by them, and troops could buy as many eggs as they wanted for a handful of tea and two handfuls of sugar. When it was announced that so much sugar and so much tea would be given in exchange for 10 jerrycans, they poured into the collecting centres in thousands.*

*I spent a lot of time buying barley. There was a narrow gauge railway which ran from Benghazi south eastwards to Soluch, about 30 miles away, which was the principal centre of the barley growing area, and I would go out armed with several hundred pounds and see the barley weighed and loaded onto the train – sometimes travelling back to Benghazi on the top of an open loaded truck. The track was none too even and on one occasion the engine driver went a good deal faster than was safe and the truck on which I was travelling lurched alarmingly, and I spent most of the journey trying to prevent the top sacks being thrown off and was in some danger of being thrown off myself. At collecting centres not on the railway the barley was weighed, paid for and stored in buildings requisitioned for the purpose and collected later, when transport was available.*

## FROM THE DIARY

### 10 June

*Apparently there was a huge sensation and almost a riot because Mr Reid refused to allow the words Semu el Amir Sayed Idris to appear in the paper.*[16] *The people got to hear about it and went mad and wanted to shoot the editor, Abdel Jawad, and break up the offices. A deputation saw Maj Bailey and he smoothed them down. I didn't realise there was so much fanaticism about, nor did I realise there was any trouble. It was very tactless of Reid. Oulton arrived about 10.45p.m. on his way to Tripoli.*

---

[16] 'The first newspaper was *Jaridat Benghazi*, set up under the supervision of the BMA through its Information Officer John Reid. This was later superseded by *Barca el Gedida*, which was also controlled by the government.' M. Khadduri, *Modern Libya: A Study in Political Development*, Baltimore, 1963, p45.

### 11 June

*Oulton went off by air this a.m. Bailey and I and Abdel Jawad walked up to the bazaar to show ourselves and we stopped and had tea with Qweri Pasha, a nice old Turkish officer. Called at Yusuf Lenghi's [the richest merchant in Benghazi] and were given Turkish delight. No signs of any crowds or unfriendliness. ... Packed up my clothes and moved to the new quarters and slept there tonight.*

### 12 June (Saturday)

*At 4.30p.m. Bailey came and announced that my promotion with effect from 1/6/43 had been confirmed and he gave me two pips to put up. ... I am a Captain at last and feel more like someone.*

### 14 June

*United Nations Day. A ceremonial parade ... General Collier inspected the troops. ... Arab notables very annoyed because the General didn't speak to them and no arrangements were made for them to mix with the officers.*

### 17 June

*On Monday and Tuesday [14/15 June] Italian parachutists dropped south of Benghazi and elsewhere. Nearly all were at once rounded up by Arabs, or information [was] given which led to their arrest. Paid rewards today.*

### 18 June

*Heard at lunchtime that Italian parachutists got at Benina [Benghazi's airfield] last night and put bombs on six Wellingtons and another in a hangar. Two Wellingtons were actually destroyed and also 2 Hurricanes in the hangar. It looks as if there were more than two men still at large and those who gave themselves up were a blind, to lull us into a false sense of security.*

### 19 June

*[Bailey] tells me I am to be in charge of Regina and Tokra, which is good news, but there is still no sign of the cashier for T&S [Supplies & Transit Dept.] to relieve Jones. Had a disastrous evening at bridge and lost 5,000pts.*

### 24 June

*Bailey went off to bkfst with Americans. Had a busy day and had to put off all petitioners. One of the Arabs – who gave information leading to the capture of 15 Italians and was rewarded with £75 and a signed certificate from General [Uzal Girard] Ent, American Commander – came in with a long complaint yesterday. We got tired of listening, and when told to get on with it, he produced the certificate, on which was written 'and did good service to the other Arabs by concealing a revolver and machine gun under a heap of ashes', signed by Capt Baldry, who had searched his house and removed cigarettes given him by the Americans. Bailey and I were staggered that a fellow like Baldry could do such a thing. What business had he to search the man's house in the first place, and secondly he had publicly dishonoured a man who had just been honoured by BG [British Government], and 3rd he insulted an American General by defacing a certificate signed by him. Bailey sent for him and told him that he ought to be court-martialled and has forbidden him to have anything more to do with the Arabs.*

### 27 June

*Inspected Sharia Court and girls' school with Bailey, the Qadi, Sheikh Senussi [possibly Abu al-Qasim Sanussi, cousin of Mohammed Sayyid Idris and* qaimaqam *of Benghazi] and Mr Reid, and drank mint tea and ate cakes, which I don't like in the morning. Girls' school quite well run and most of the girls are quite clean and well dressed.*

*Very big convoy went past going west this evening. Two or three ships came in here. I counted 41 ships including about 10 destroyers and escort vessels. Feel that big things are about to begin.*

### 8 July

*The CinC Sir Henry [Maitland] Wilson is paying a visit here and there is a reception for the Arabs at 12.30p.m. The court is rising at 11.30 for it. I hurried back to the office to find no expected crowds, and obviously the show was off and we are sitting again at 2.30p.m., but the sitting had to be put off till 4p.m ... Was told to accompany Gen Collier and introduce him to the notables, while Bailey escorted Gen Wilson. Not a very large gathering of people but quite enough. Gen Wilson shook hands all round and then sat down and everyone was served with tea.*

*Arrived in court at 4.15p.m. and we sat until 8.15. It is a tribal killing case and the evidence is very unsatisfactory though all the facts appear to be clear enough. A man of one tribe quarrelled with a man from another and killed him and was taken to Tripoli with the Italians. Blood money was refused by the tribe of the murderer, who repudiated him, and he was therefore fair game for the tribe of the murdered man and when he returned from Tripoli he was ambushed and killed. I feel that it was almost justifiable homicide but we must pass a heavy sentence to enforce the law and then reduce it if a settlement is made.*

73

**9 July**

*Court sat at 9.0a.m. and we heard a mass of lies. Maj Collard wanted an acquittal and [Major] Lindsay had to consider our findings and we were to see him at 5p.m. to discuss sentence. ... Eventually we agreed on 10 years with a reduction if peace is made by the tribes.*

**10 July**

*Heard today that we have invaded Sicily.*

*Went to an Arabic play about Italian misrule. Wonderfully acted and a really 1st class performance all done by Libyans from Derna.*

**16 July**

*Bailey went off early to Tokra and as usual took the key of his cabinet with a pile of files inside. My clerk got bolshie about some work I told him to do. He is a hopeless fellow. ... Sat on roof after lunch and surprised a couple of Italians doing some burgling. They had collected some books and cotton wool from a house. ... It is scandalous that they are allowed to go climbing all over the place without being stopped.*

*Bailey came back at about 6p.m. and had an interesting day with Arabs shooting off their rifles and a huge lunch. He said they talked about an earthquake last night and I remembered feeling my bed shake violently.*

**22 July**

*Evans-Pritchard arrived today. He is amusing but has a shattering tongue and a controversial mind. He announced at dinner that Winston [Churchill] was "narrow-minded and ignorant"!!!*

**23 July**

*Supposed start at 7.30[a.m.] for Soluch to have lunch with Sheikh Nasr el Kizza paramount Sheikh of the Awaghir. ... Arrived at about 12.45p.m. and were given a welcome with horsemen firing off their rifles. We were ushered into the guest tent and sat down on the floor and drank tea while all the elders came in and after an hour or so we had lunch which consisted of terribly greasy soup, lamb and chicken and melon, which we ate with our fingers – except the soup. We left about 4p.m. ... At Shledina we saw signs of battle and there were minefields on both sides of the road and tank traps across it.*

**26 July**

*On the appearance of the local paper printing a curt official announcement of Sayed Idris' visit without the title of Semu el Amir people gathered outside the offices of the paper and shouted. The notables met Maj Bailey and we all went to the offices and Bailey made a speech in Arabic in which he said that officially the BG didn't use the title but* they *could, and he announced that the title would appear in the paper the next day. The Editor was to blame for not doing what he was told.*

### 30 July
*A lot of mystery about Sayed Idris not coming after all and Anderson is investigating the demonstration on Monday.*

### 31 July (Saturday)
*Tea party this evening in the Municipal Hall. Col Anderson made a long speech in Arabic which he speaks very well, but much too well for ordinary conversation.*[17] *Maj Mackay and I sat and talked to all and sundry.*

### 1 August (Sunday)
*Saw 28 Liberators start off on a raid this morning. … Had lunch at Omar Kanun's in Berka. Large crowd there. About 12 officers and 15 notables. A good lunch and fairly quickly served, but we didn't finish until 4.15. Four of us went and bathed afterwards. … Sat at officers club afterwards and saw Liberators returning and only counted 12. I wondered where they had been, as they had been away 12 hours.*

### 2 August
*Heard on the news that a large force of Liberators had attacked Ploeiesti oil refineries [in Romania] yesterday and 30 or more had not returned.*

*Bailey had it out with Reid after lunch about his servant and the running of the mess and I'm glad to say put Reid in his place. He paid his mess bill in the evening.*

### 3 August
*Managed to go out to Coafia with Mackay to inspect some gardens, which have been pillaged by troops. … Sat and talked a bit and were shown the place where 20,000 troops captured at Tobruk were kept for some time. Went and inspected the gardens, which are really patches of wild grapes growing among dunes. The grapes are very good and quite a lot still there, but I thought it best to ask for claims to be settled on a generous scale as the amount involved*

---

[17] There is a marked difference between the *fushaa* (literary) and *'ammiyya* (vernacular) forms of Arabic; Peter's comment aptly conveys that Anderson's scholarly training apparently equipped him best for high-level theological discussions in *fushaa*, but that he lacked the ability to speak colloquially in *'ammiyya*.

*is so small. Had arranged to call at Yusuf Lenghi's house, but drove all over the desert before we found it, because people gave us different directions. Got there at 7p.m. and ate fruit galore till 7.45p.m. and then came home. Yusuf worried because a policemen came and said they were going to bomb the district tomorrow. Can't be true and we think it must be that they were going to explode some useless ammo.*

### 4 August

*Heard p.m. that 27 Italians had been caught at Suani Ternia landed from a submarine with explosives etc to attack aerodromes.*

### 5 August

*Col Maclaren left after giving Greatorex and me a lecture on our duties. Apparently HQ hasn't approved of some of my letters and so we are not to sign any, but must put up drafts to Maj Bailey. This is not going to be easy because he is often out and his tray gets so full that letters will be held up for days.*

### 6 August

*At about 7.30 Major Robertson rang up to say goodbye to me and Bailey, and I thought we had parted friends. 5 minutes later he rang up and asked me to prepare a movement order (as tomorrow is a standstill day) and get Major Bailey to sign it. I said "I will try, sir" whereupon he said "Look here Synge I won't have any impertinence from you. I shall report you to HQ." I tried to say that Major Bailey was out and I might not see him but he got more worked up and said "It is an order from your superior officer and this is the third time you have been impertinent to me." It was no use my saying anything so I just kept quiet and when I eventually said that I might not see Maj Bailey till late he said "Very well I will get the Area Commander to sign it." A most unpleasant incident and a most unpleasant man and I still do not know when or how I have been impertinent to him.*

### 7 August

*Bailey took me along to the slaughterhouse walking this morning and we had a couple of sheep weighed, slaughtered and cut up so that we could see the weight of waste. The carcass weighs 40% of the live weight so that if a man buys live weight at 8PT per kilo he has to sell at PT20 to be even square, and controlled price is PT15. The whole business of the meat contract has been mishandled from beginning to end. Nahum has the contract for skins, heads and offal. He pays the butchers PT3, the army PT2½ and he gets skins, which he can sell for at least PT5. Half the heads at PT6 each which is PT3 and the stomachs and uneatable offal, which he can sell for* another PT6 so he makes about PT10 per head of sheep or £25 a day, on the contract of 250 sheep.

Walked back via the vegetable market and grain market and got some interesting information. Bailey insisted on walking all the way home and wanted to go back via the bazaar but I thought I had walked enough and as there was work to be done I took a gharri [horse-drawn cart] home. Did nothing much p.m. except write a report on education and schools here.

### 9 August

Today is the 3rd anniversary of the agreement between BG and Sayed Idris to fight the Axis together and it is a great day for the Senussi, who had been very depressed until Italy declared war on us. Reception at 11a.m. at the Mustarrafiya.

I went to the mess to go off with Bailey at 10.40[a.m.] and got chewed up because I couldn't be found and had done nothing. I was told nothing about the affair [the anniversary celebrations] until the programme was handed to me last night and had every right to imagine that everything was arranged, but I was blamed for the fact that no police officers could be found and that Reid was still in bed at 10a.m., and was accused of having no initiative. As anything which I have done on my own has always been reversed, out of cussedness, it is not surprising. However, the show was quite a success and finished half an hour too soon. No loudspeaker was laid on and speeches had to be made with the natural voice.

There was a tea party in the Omar Mukhtar Club at 6.30p.m., which lasted till 7.45p.m. Colour photos were taken by an American war correspondent. The Area Commander came back to drinks. At 10p.m. there was supposed to be a showing of the Arabic version of "Desert Victory" [1943 film focussing on al-Alamein] in the square. Huge crowds turned out but the projector wouldn't work and all sorts of excuses were made and Reid as usual said 'It's nothing to do with me'. Everybody had to be sent home disappointed and it was definitely not the MOI's best day. Reid did nothing and nothing was done and he disclaimed all responsibility for a complete failure.

### 17 August

Got sugar sent out to villages south and at 3p.m. I collected jerrycans from the office and took them to salvage where I was appalled by the rough treatment they get. Egginton turned up while I was there with his second load, so we delivered 900 today. I went off to Sidi Khalifa to complain about the state of the cans which were mostly rusty and found that he hadn't collected any from there so I brought back a load.

## 19 August

*Sent off two lorries to collect jerrycans from Sidi Khalifa and Coafia this morning early and they came back about 12.30[p.m.] having only brought about 300 between them when each should carry 250.*

*Had an annoying morning with the usual criticism of everything from Bailey. Since 9/8 he has criticised everything I have done and I don't know what he wants.*

## 20 August

*Bailey started off at bkfst by criticising my distribution of sugar in the districts and then asked what I had done about distributing sugar to the poor. I said "Nothing as it is not my job" and he said "I asked you about it yesterday". He had but he hadn't told me to do anything as it was supposed to be delivered on 9 Aug, and presumably someone else had been told to see about it. He is a bully when he wants to be and a very clever one because he puts one in the wrong whatever one says. If I have failed in my duty I expect to be rated but it is very galling to be rated when I haven't failed.*

## 26 August

*What a day! Arrived in the office with Greatorex at 8.30 having been to inspect doors and windows etc and were called into the presence [of Bailey] and slanged for everything. We were not allowed to say anything and were accused of every possible or impossible thing. ... Must be in office at 8a.m. because he was. ... I was told that I would be transferred as I make no attempt to cooperate or do anything right, to which I agreed and was told I was impertinent. I was called for several times later, and the same thing went on, so I wrote a letter to him asking for my transfer, to which there was no reply. He went off bathing at 5.45p.m. and I decided to go to the cinema and had an early dinner with Allen and he was not back when we left and I went straight to bed after the flick, which was an amusing one with Ginger Rogers and Ray Milland called "The Major and the Minor".*

## 27 August

*Got up early and in to bkfst at 7.40a.m. and to office at 8a.m., but no Bailey. Found that the warehouse did not open at 8.0a.m. and anyhow Mohamed and Regeb did not turn up till 8.20. Got away nearer 9a.m. with 4 bags of sugar and two 3 ton trucks to pick up jerrycans at Ghamines. Got there soon after 10a.m. and collected all they had and then came back to Salvage by 1.45p.m. with 438 cans.*

## 28 August (Saturday)

*Got to office at 8.0a.m. and were called in to be shown how the files are to be dealt with. Everyone was found fault with and, if one [a file] hadn't come to either of us with a letter in it, it was our fault. I left the office at 1p.m., and Bailey was out with Col Pitcairn. Nobody knows where he has gone and he was not in for lunch or tea. Went to Club with Shackleton and Greatorex and found when we got back that Bailey had returned and gone to bed. They had been at Soluch and Magrun and Ghamines all day. Bailey had a fever.*

## 29 August (Sunday)

*Bailey got up about 10 and when I went to see him about 11.45 he stopped me and said that he had received my note and was sorry I was unhappy but that he could not apologise for what happened on 9 Aug because it showed a complete lack of responsibility on my part.*

*Went to the Club at 7.30p.m. and about 8p.m. Felix Carver[18] walked in and asked me to stay and have dinner with him. He had looked in at the office and seen Bailey and when he had started dinner he said that he was worried about what I had told him on his way thro' last week and had talked to Bailey. He told me a lot of things and talked good hard sense, the core of it being that I must swallow my own pride and sink my own feelings and attempt to do what Bailey wanted. It would do me no good to be moved nor would it do Bailey and it was up to me to see that we could work together.*

## 30 August

*Decided to go to Benina with FEC [Felix Carver] this morning to take sugar and bring back jerrycans and we started at 8.30. Saw him off at the airfield and then went to find the jerrycans.*

## 1 September [coinciding with the start of Ramadan]

*Bailey didn't appear at all today and when we went to see him at lunchtime he said there was nothing wrong with him, but he was going to do nothing until he had leave. He looked awful and we told him we were sending for the doctor, which annoyed him. He went out about 4p.m. and didn't appear until 6.30p.m. having ordered a mess meeting at 5.30 and we had a bogus meeting. When he came in we were all present but he refused to hold the meeting, and insisted on playing bridge. Greatorex and I went to the club at 7.30p.m.*

---

[18] Felix Carver was a member of the Carver Brothers cotton trading company, for which Peter had worked in Egypt until 1942, and his occasional visits to Benghazi suggest that he may have had some kind of business relationship with the BMA.

### 2 September

*No plans made for my purchase of barley tomorrow and, when I try to discuss it, he [Bailey] goes off at a tangent. I have done all I can but I don't think I shall have either money or transport. Got a truck after lunch and purchased 1,000 sacks but couldn't get labour to unload it.*

### 3 September

*Got up early in order to get off by 8.30a.m. but of course nobody was up to load the truck and I didn't get off till 9a.m., and as the road is bad it took nearly 2 hours. As it is Ramadan I had great difficulty getting any labour and they only worked about 4 hours. I weighed about 25 tons but only got about ten transported to the station. All labour very unwilling to work. Mustafa el Oufor insisted on giving me lunch tho' I wanted to eat on my own and he also asked me to eat with him at night and he produced most awful greasy stuff and I did not enjoy it and hoped I should be able to get away tomorrow.*

### 4 September

*Got about 25 tons weighed by 1p.m. and decided that I must stop and concentrate on getting it shipped otherwise I should never be able to check and would not finish today. Labourers very slow and unwilling and by 6p.m. it became obvious that we couldn't finish tonight so I stopped at 7p.m. Invited to dine with Saad Busweer, son of a merchant, and dreaded it but actually it wasn't a bad meal. Quite good soup, rice pilaff and mutton and stuffed vine leaves and an omelette and camels' milk to drink. Sat till 9.30p.m. and then came to bed but couldn't sleep because of the heat and the dogs, and I had drunk too much coffee and tea.*

### 9 September

*Got back to Benghazi at 11.0a.m. and heard that Italy had capitulated. Great rejoicing everywhere and nobody doing any work. … There were a lot of drunken parties last night and Woods' mess was turned upside down and so was the Club. I'm glad I wasn't there. … I went to the Club about 7p.m. and got a beer. Collard arrived from Agedabia. EJ [Major Evans-Jones] arranged a tea party at the Municipality at 10p.m. to which Army, Navy and RAF representatives were invited and speeches were made. Reid was supposed to have spent a lot of money on sheep and flour, sugar and tea for the poor but it ought to have been distributed in the square but wasn't.*

### 10 September

*Couldn't get any transport till about noon to fetch barley from stores and take it to Red Lodge for the horses, which Bailey had said were starving. He also said his partridges were starving and needed barley, but they don't eat barley. At 2p.m. had to go out and fetch sacks for tomorrow's expedition to Magrun.*

*Went to the office after tea and to the Club with Shackleton and decided to stay to dinner there as there was an RAF sister Shackles liked the look of. Had too much rum and was a little bit tight. Went back to mess about 10p.m. and Greatorex came in soon after and said he had had no dinner and while I was getting him some bread and cheese he and Shackles suddenly fell on me and tried to debag me. Unprovoked aggression and very unfair. I escaped upstairs once but fell on the stairs and they caught me again and intended to take me into the ante room where the others were playing bridge but desisted outside the door. I was allowed to go eventually without being completely stripped.*

## 17 September

*Got off in the 3 ton before 9.0am and arrived at Ghamines at 10.30am. … Went on to Magrun where there was a huge crowd and a lot of barley, all from small people, and I couldn't pay them all myself and gave the money to the Mudir and left soon after 1pm.*

## 19 September (Sunday)

*Got to the station at 9a.m. [to go to Soluch] and found that there had been an accident last night due to sabotage and the two passenger coaches had been involved and so there were none today and I had to sit on the brakeman's seat on an open wagon. Very uncomfortable and very jolting because the train went so fast. At Giardina I found a mess again but not as bad as last time, but at Soluch all was well. … We only stayed ¾ hour and there was no covered truck to sit in so I sat on top of the sacks in an open one, but we went so fast and wagons swayed so, that several were in danger of falling off and I just saved one in time with the aid of a guard. At Giardina I changed and sat on the brakeman's seat again but the smoke and dust and jolting were awful and I arrived back absolutely covered in dust.*

## 27 September

*Bailey not going till Wednesday but he went to Tolmeta today. … Went to see Maj Weir, who is a nice, understanding, sensible man and I hope we shall get on. He agrees that I should not go on with this buying indefinitely.*

## 28 September

*Up early and off to Magrun. Lee left early for Beda [al-Bayda]. All went well today and everything was easily settled. Got back at 4.30[p.m.] without incident. ... Trouble in the town [i.e. Benghazi] because a search was made in Sabri for paraffin, and notables' houses were entered and the people roughly handled and upset. Haven't heard the full story but it sounds a most tactless and unnecessary business and so damn silly to go upsetting everyone.*

## 29 September
*Usual busy morning and Bailey still here and dashing about madly as usual. He left after lunch with Little and Adams and we heaved a sigh of relief. Weir didn't leave the office till after 3p.m. owing to a meeting with the Grand Qadi about yesterday's affair. Apparently there is some doubt about whether the Eid [end of Ramadan] will be held or not which is rather childish. ... Riley, the SIB [Special Investigations Branch] man responsible for the raid, came in and said he had done his duty and it wasn't his fault. After dinner we went to the Sharia Court for a meeting to take witnesses accounts of whether they saw the moon and decide if the Eid was to take place and Weir made a short speech apologising for the method of the raid. The moon was said to be seen and it was decided to hold the Eid after all, and everybody was pleased.*

## 30 September
*Called on the Qadi at 11.0a.m. and then Hussein Pasha Buseikri[19] and drank lots of tea and ate sweets.*

---

[19] A former politician from the days of pre-1911 Turkish rule.

# chapter 4

# HARVESTS, FARMS, LAW AND ORDER
## BENGHAZI, OCTOBER–NOVEMBER 1943
## BARCE, DECEMBER 1943–MARCH 1944

APTAIN PETER SYNGE continued to work in Benghazi until late November 1943, with a full regime of duties. These included buying barley and distributing seeds in the rural areas, overseeing the repair of school buildings and making transport arrangements for local people wanting to participate in the hajj pilgrimage to Mecca. After the quarrels of recent months, the *esprit de corps* within the British Military Administration was seemingly improved, with the notable exception of its habitually hard-drinking and often obstreperous Information Officer, John Reid, who continued to irritate just about everyone with whom he had dealings – at least until he moved out of the Mess and took up residence outside Benghazi.

The management of the available food crops was a priority for Cyrenaica's survival at this time. Every effort was made to collect barley and other crops from local Libyan farmers to the south of Benghazi. Peter was fully engaged in this exercise and spent much of this period arranging for the purchase and transport of barley from the area around Soluch, Ghamines and Magrun.

At some of the larger farms on the more fertile slopes and plains of the mountainous Jebel Akhdar, the British had put in new managers, several of whom had previously worked in Sudan. On the large Barce Plain, the Middle East Supply Centre organised a team of officers and a working company of prisoners of war to organise the cultivation of wheat and barley over 4.85 ha in the first year, rising to 20,000 in 1944. All available Italian farming machinery was collected and repaired for the effort.[1]

---

[1] Rennell of Rodd, *British Military Administration of Occupied Territories in Africa, during the years 1941–47*, London, 1948, p260.

It was to Barce (al-Marj) that Peter was sent in November as Assistant Civil Affairs Officer. Here he found the workload much lighter, managing to take three weeks' leave in Egypt over Christmas. He got on well with his new boss, Major Sholto Douglas, whom he described as 'much more human and understanding' (i.e. than his former boss, Bailey). Both Douglas and Peter were interested in sailing, which they occasionally undertook in nearby coastal waters at Tocra [Tokra] and Tolmeta, and in their spare time they built themselves a new boat.

When Peter first arrives in Barce, a delegation of Sanussi family members are being shown around some substantial farming properties with a view to taking them over. Peter is clearly aware of the importance of the visit, but has no idea at the time of the extent to which he will later become involved in the issue of the Sanussi occupation of these and other farms. Barce lies in an upland valley some 300 m above sea level. Over this area of the Jebel, Peter is impressed by the efforts made by the Italians to establish modern farming, and especially their experiments with larger farms. He provides a possibly unique description of a massive 23,000 ha show estate that had belonged to a man called Jung, an Austrian Jew and friend of Mussolini. Some time later, we find him lamenting the destruction of the initial modernisation efforts of the Italian colonists, who he says 'had done a fine job of work and it is a tragedy that it is all wasted'.[2]

He also describes another substantial farm at Abiar, halfway between Benghazi and Barce, which had been developed by an Italian General called Borghi, and in time will be offered for the use of Mohammed Sayyid Idris as one of several rural hideaways for the reclusive ruler-in-waiting. As regards the more marginal land to the south being grazed by nomadic herders, Peter has occasion to meet and be greeted by the chiefs and sheikhs of the local tribes, including the Barasa, with whom he will have much more extensive dealings at his next posting in al-Bayda.

In February 1944, the diary happens to note the first two instances of capital punishment that took place under British rule. The official records show that this was seen as a major test of the new system of justice and thus a cause of anxiety for the BMA, not least because the main accused was a Barce policeman. From the files it emerges that, at the end of a relatively extensive trial by the standards of the time, the policeman, Anwar Habib, and his second wife, Nissiya, were both found guilty of the murder of Habib's first wife, Zeinab. After death sentences were

---

[2] Such views suggest a form of 'solidarity among colonisers' that was probably not unusual among expatriate communities in the region at this time.

84

Figure 11. *Civil Affairs Officer Major Sholto Douglas meets tribal sheikhs in the Barce region.* National Library of Australia, Frank Hurley Collection, PIC FH/5963 LOC Cold store PIC HURL 179/7.

announced on 20 December, an appeal was heard by Lt Col Maclaren (acting for Duncan Cumming who was on leave). Maclaren proceeded to confirm the sentences on 24 January; shortly after Peter's diary notes that the weight of responsibility made Maclaren 'look older'. Meanwhile Major Douglas, as Civil Affairs Officer of the town, was making his own inquiries into local opinion and finding that people were 'unanimous' in support of the sentences, as 'the case had aroused great interest and had been thoroughly conducted.'[3] Both executions – by shooting   went ahead in the early morning of 26 February. After this landmark Habib case, the administration was noticeably less nervous about subsequent death sentences; the archives also hold papers concerning the case of those accused of murdering an RAF sentry at Berka in March 1945: seven men were convicted and executed at the end of that year.[4]

---

[3] Papers relating to the case of Anwar and Nassiya, 1943 and 1944, WO 230/140.
[4] Papers relating to the murder of the RAF sentry, 1945, WO 230/140.

# FROM THE DIARY

[Benghazi]

## 2 October (Saturday)

*My birthday, but no letters and not much difference in the day. Went to Berka to see about schools again and decided the Bank of Rome better than nothing. Municipal Council [and] took tea with Weir and the Brig.* ... [Went to Club for dinner with Shackleton and found Evans-Jones and Jones, Woods and Abbott] *It was EJ's birthday too and he is 10 years my junior! Got very tight on rum and lime and all joined up for dinner. The Sgt in charge allowed us to sit on after hours and brought us beer, which is officially non-existent. Got to bed at midnight well lit up.*

## 3 October (Sunday)

*Woke up not feeling too bad but headache came on later. ... Went to church. A new padre who had an awful coughing fit and could hardly finish the service. Very few men there. ... Went bathing and it was perfect. Sea clear and blue and smooth and temperature of sea and air perfect. Still no light in the mess and very few candles.*

## 4 October

[to Ghamines and Magrun and back by truck, bringing a load of barley]

## 5 October

*All sort of interruptions, including a delegation by the Qadi and Sheikh Senussi, Khalil Gelal and Salim Ben Amar to get schools going and extend date for the payment of deposits for the hajj. They came to me and I took them into Weir and the talk lasted well over an hour.*

*Tried to collect sacks to load onto the train to Soluch but phone out of order and no transport. A Sudanese lorry smashed into the Bedford in the square and put that out of action, so Soluch is without sacks.*

## 9 October (Saturday)

[In the evening] *Reid came in and was extremely offensive to Hawkins, who exercised admirable restraint.*

## 10 October (Sunday)

*Determined not to work today but had to go to station at 8.45[a.m.] to inform people of Soluch and Giardina about additional expenses of the Haj, and at 10.0a.m. arranged to go out inspecting schools with Forman. Got back at 12.15 and got through a few files. Went bathing with Weir and Greatorex.*

### 13 October
[Trip to Soluch and back] *Got back about 1.50p.m. and was informed that Hamid, the black* sofraggi *[servant working for Reid], was blind drunk and had to be put to bed before lunch. Reid had informed me earlier that he had asked him [i.e. Hamid] to go with him to Quarry Farm and he had agreed but, knowing how he hates Hassan, I could not believe he agreed but was forced. Anyhow he came to me and said he wanted to go, so that settles it, and it will be better so. He [i.e. Hamid] also denied he was drunk and said he was filled with emotion.*

### 14 October
[To Ghamines and Magrun and back] *Reid left today with his b [sic] servant and the mess breathed a sigh of relief. He goes to Quarry Farm when he comes back from his tour.*

### 19 October
*Found an enormous quantity of barley at Magrun and unable to pay for a quarter of it, though had paid out £1,100 yesterday. All went well with the convoy and it was off by 11.0a.m. but only took and average 7 tons [in each 10-ton truck].*

### 20 October
*Went to Soluch by train. Steam locomotive "Jessie Madden" which was built locally and named after the wife or daughter of the OC Railway [i.e. a former manager of the railway under Italian rule]. Only took ½ hour longer than the diesel going, but was slower on the way back and got in at 2.45. Had lunch on the train.*

### 24 October (Sunday)
*Off by train to Soluch with the old 'Jessie Madden' again. Hoped to be home earlier but she wasn't running so well today and couldn't get up enough steam and I wasn't in till 3p.m. … Played bridge with Phillips against Webster and Stretton. Had good hands and lucky distribution and won.*

### 28 October
*It poured with rain about midnight last night but quite fine this morn. Went thro' the market today and found it full of a crowd of Arabs and Jews. All the shops full of stuff and people auctioning articles up and down the street. Very*

*picturesque scene with all the bright colours and no smells like the bazaar in Jerusalem for instance. Went to Torelli school and found that nothing had been done yet. Qadi came in and said that that the school wasn't suitable and the children's fathers didn't like it. I said if they could find another and do it up we would change, but it was impossible to please everyone.*

### 10 November
*Shackles [i.e. Shackleton] said there was a game of rugger at Barce and would I play. I didn't want to but was persuaded though I haven't played for 15 years. ... After dinner went for a walk with Shackles and dropped in at the Oriental café where there was a lot of trouble through people having too much to drink. I think the place should be closed as it is going to cause more trouble.*

### 11 November
*Capt Henry picked me up at 12.45 and took me to his workshops where we assembled for the journey to Barce. South wind but a clear sky and not hot. ... Got to Barce at 3.15p.m. It was pleasant to get up on the hill again and see the hill farms at Baracca. I had no idea that there were so many farms and had a big surprise when we came to the Barce plain and saw farmhouses dotted about – hundreds of them – for as far as we could see. It must have been a fine sight for Mussolini three years ago, but now most is neglected and all the houses are empty. The game was not such hell as I expected and, although I played 2nd row and couldn't get my head in and nearly had my neck broken in every scrum, I was able to keep going. The other pack were hefty men and pushed us off the ball every time but our backs were good and never got through, and the game ended without a score at all. ... Had tea in the mess and two RAF sisters from Benghazi sat next to me. Had hot showers and then went to the Club where we drank poison till 7.30 when we collected for dinner. Three more RAF sisters came along so we were five girls to 15 men, which is a pretty good average. Had quite a pleasant evening though I would like to have got home sooner. Left at 12.30a.m. ... Got home at 3a.m.*

### 20 November (Saturday)
*Anniversary of the capture of Benghazi a year ago. A public holiday and a march past to be arranged at 11.0a.m. Saluting base [on] the steps of the cinema and spectators sat in the square in front of the Officers Club. Very warm in winter clothes as the wind is still in the south. Parade not too bad with the SDF [Sudan Defence Force] playing marching tunes but the Senussi contingent were all out of step. Had drinks afterwards and sat at the club until 1p.m. A tea party in the Municipal Hall at 6p.m. and Madam Fhifla brought some*

*girls all dressed up in beautiful robes to present flowers to Bailey. Speeches made complaining of lack of help from the Govt and giving the impression that the Senussi with our help turned the Italians out of the country. Went to bed fairly early.*

### 21 November (Sunday)
*Got Bailey's car and went to Giardina and Soluch to settle up the outstanding barley purchases and had lunch on the way back near a lake where there were hundreds of duck and one could have some good shooting if one had a gun and some cartridges. Everybody wanting more rain but ploughing still goes on. Went for a walk in the harbour and sat on the roof for a bit.*

### 23 November
*Went to Magrun in Bailey's utility with Lawson. Strong south wind again and dust blowing off the aerodromes on the Tripoli road. Settled up at Ghamines and spent a good long time at Magrun. All the damaged barley cleared up and all the rest secure and we have bought large quantities in merchants' stores.*

### 24 November
*Wind round to west at last and looks as if might rain in a day or two. Bailey called me in to his office and said that I had been transferred to Barce and must go at once!!*

[Barce]

### 25 November
*Got away in Reid's car at about 2.30[p.m.] and had an uneventful drive and arrived [at Barce] about 4.15. It looked like rain and there were a few showers about but nothing near the road. Found that the Senussi party of six Sayeds were being entertained at Douglas' house so had to keep away. Went to the Club before dinner and then went round again to watch the dance for a bit. Douglas is on leave but staying here and his relief – Raven, from the Sudan – seems like a nice chap. Maclaren is here too as he is escorting the Senussis round the country.*

### 28 November (Sunday)
*Raven and Douglas went to Abiar with the Senussi Sayeds and Maclaren went back to Beda [al-Bayda].*

### 29 November
*Brigadier left with Senussis for Benghazi.*

## 30 November

*Wind round to the south and clear again. After lunch went off to Jung's farm on the way to Abiar with Raven and the Mudir. The farm is a big estate taken over by the Agric Dept and is on rolling down land and is a fine place. Jung was an Austrian Jew and a friend of Mussolini and it was a show estate, 57,000 acres, of which about 14,000 is being farmed and sown under wheat and barley.*

## 5 December (Sunday)

*Strong south wind and clear sky today, with fog over the Jebel. Left for Tolmeta with Raven for the day and got there at 10.15a.m. Sleepy little place cut off from the world. ... After lunch we tried rigging the boat which was leaking and while getting it rigged it heeled over and nearly sank so Raven got out and D [Douglas] & I took it out but it went to leeward so badly that we had to row and then it went so far off the wind that when we went about to come back we couldn't even make the harbour although we ought to have been running before the wind. Not a very satisfactory boat but it could be improved. Had tea with the Mudir and then returned to Barce getting back about dark.*

## 8 December

[Departure for Egypt on leave, returning to Barce on 8 January]

## 9 January (Sunday)

*Several officers took part in a foxhunt with a mixed pack of hounds.*

## 10 January

*Back at work. The accounts clerk is on leave and things are in a pretty mess and December accounts are not yet in and not likely to be for a long time. Took over the cash and spent the day trying to get up to date.*

## 14 January

*Rainy day. Spent all day on the accounts and in the end was no nearer finishing them. The Arab clerk is very willing but it is very tiring having to explain technicalities in Arabic. Lights failed tonight and so did the pressure lamp. Had to eat by candlelight and sit in the dark afterwards but there was a grand fire.*

## 19 January

*Most of HQ moved from Beda [to Barce] today.*

### 22 January (Saturday)

*Transferred some of my cash to HQ as my safe was full and had to have two officers to guard the transfer. Col Maclaren arrived to stay with us over the weekend. He looks older.*

### 26 January

*Went to look at the Fonduk this morning. Not much doing there and only a few animals being sold. After lunch went with Douglas toward Tecnis on the south road to look at areas selected for cutting wood. Found a man cutting on the wrong side of the road and ran him in. Lovely view from the top of the pass over the plain and it was a lovely day with cumulus clouds throwing shadows over the country. Col Maclaren left this afternoon.*

### 28 January

*A series of thunderstorms last night and very heavy rain, which continued most of the day. Went out with Douglas to Filzi and it poured with rain. Huge lakes in all the hollows and rushing streams on the slopes, of red foaming water. Damp patches appearing everywhere in the house and the stone walls of Barce mortared with mud are falling down.*

### 29 January (Saturday)

*It was a year ago on 26th that I arrived in Barce and a year ago yesterday that I left for Benghazi, and the time has gone pretty quickly.*

*At 2p.m. Abdelkarim announced that part of the town was flooded so we went out to look at it and found several streets flooded and a rushing torrent running through the town and over the main road to the west of the town. The torrent was coming from Sidi Gibrin direction and had washed away a lot of the hutments and causing lakes all over the place. The floodwater was running out over the Barce plain, a lot of which is now flooded. We have had over 8in of rain this month.*

### 4 February

*Fine but cloudy. Visited the market and the meat market, and ordered uniforms for the Municipal Police. Douglas went riding and I went and sat in court and heard two minor cases. The interpreter is very bad indeed and doesn't know enough Arabic or English. Left the office about 5p.m. and did some tree cutting in the garden.*

### 5 February (Saturday)

*I went for an inspection of the town and Douglas went to collect agricultural implements. After lunch I went out in a lorry to collect harrows and cultivators at Oberdan. Very cold wind but a lovely afternoon and country very attractive. The more one sees of the Italian colonisation the more one regrets the foolhardiness of Mussolini in entering the war and losing it all. They had done a fine job of work and it is a tragedy that it is all wasted.*

### 6 February (Sunday)
*A dull rainy day. The rain began last night and poured through our ceiling, which was supposed to have been repaired last Sunday but it is much worse now. … Douglas busy on the mast of his boat and after lunch I went and worked on it and it was pleasant to have sharp chisel in one's hand again and do some work with it. I cut the key at the foot of the mast to fit into the socket in the boat, and we considered we had done a good day's work. Pouring with rain again tonight and rain still coming through.*

### 16 February
*Gave the first instalment of the rating book to Municipality and hope to collect first rates in March. Will bring in £1,000 a year and make the Municipality self-supporting.*

### 25 February
*Webster went off to Benghazi after lunch for the execution of Anwar Habib and his wife tomorrow.*

### 26 February (Saturday)
*After lunch went with Webster in the 30 cwt [truck] up the south road to the foot of the hill and walked up to the monument. A grand view over the Plain. I squeezed through a window and climbed the tower but Webster wouldn't risk getting stuck. The monument is for Italians killed in Cyrenaica and there is a special road leading to it. Had to walk most of the way home as the truck was late.*

*Webster got back from Benghazi at 1.45[p.m.]. The execution took place at 7.0a.m. and without a hitch.*

### 29 February
*[Visit to Abiar] Left about 10.0a.m. and arrived there at noon. A complete Italian town with barracks as well and it is tragic to see so much waste. The Arabs are beginning to come into the town and it is hoped they will desert their own hovels in time. Went out to General Borghi's house about 3 miles away. A fine Swiss-type house which has been badly looted and spoilt. Thousands must have been spent on the buildings and outhouses and all wasted. He had a large estate but not much production, mostly for show and he is*

*supposed to have spent £10,000 a year on it. Had quite a good lunch with the Qadi and left about 3p.m. Stopped at Sidi Mahines and inspected the orchard damaged by fire. Some trees still alive but all badly damaged and the loss is terrific. Fire took place last June. Over 10,000 fruit trees involved. Got back at 5p.m. Col Bailey to dinner.*

### 7 March

*Mulid el Nebi. A public holiday and Douglas, Webster and I went to Bu Gassal, in the desert south west of Marana, to a sheikh of the Barasa. … A big crowd of sheikhs there and it was rather picturesque. Lunch of chicken and lamb – the latter very nice and tender. We left at 3[p.m.] with a young lamb as a present, and got back about 6 after stopping and inspecting a salvage dump on the way. Found lice and fleas in my clothes. Quite a good day.*

### 8 March

*Budagagia said that the Municipal Council reject the scheme for rating the town…*

# chapter 5

# TRIBAL ISSUES, AND PREPARATIONS FOR THE SAYYID
## AL-BAYDA, MARCH–JULY 1944

IN MARCH, Peter Synge became a Civil Affairs Officer (CAO) in his own right, being posted to al-Bayda (known at the time as Beda Littoria) to manage the substantial district that stretched to the north and south of the ancient city of Cyrene. This included the coastal port of Apollonia (also known as Susa), Shahat (next to the ruins of Cyrene) and al-Bayda itself (600m above sea level). Peter was clearly very pleased to have achieved this promotion, not least because it was a sign of Brigadier Cumming's confidence in his ability to speak adequate Arabic for the task. However, from the outset it was not an easy posting. Peter was in some ways starting the local administration in the immediate area around al-Bayda from scratch, as the British Military Administration had hitherto made the small town its headquarters for the whole country, before moving fully to Barce in January 1944 and then to Benghazi by the end of the year. As if through oversight, it had so far paid scant attention to the complex affairs of the surrounding locality.

In the Cyrene/al-Bayda district, 'the people are less nomadic and have more inclination to be settled peasants than their countrymen to the east and west, though they also prefer the Arab tent as a dwelling to the Italian cottage,' wrote the BMA's Colonel Maclaren at this time. 'Three main tribes, the Hasa, Barasa and Dorsa inhabit the district, though half the Dorsa tribe are in Barce district.'[1] Peter immediately found himself having to deal with the competing demands of these tribes and their sheikhs.

It is clear from his accounts that Peter was by now perfectly fluent in Libyan Arabic and the archives confirm his efforts in communicating

---

[1] J. F. P. Maclaren, BMA Annual Report, 25 February 1944, AIR 23/6753.

with the tribal sheikhs. After identifying tribal hierarchies and introducing processes of mediation and communication, BMA policy involved granting official recognition to different levels of sheikhs. A difficulty inherited from the Italian period was the excessive number of sheikhs whom the Italians had recognised and who had come to depend on official support, and this made it hard for the more 'legitimate' sheikhs to establish their authority.[2]

During 1944, the BMA was particularly concerned to maintain harmony among, and between, the Hasa and Barasa tribes before turning to the Dorsa and the Masamir. On 10 April, Peter wrote to his superiors: '1. Herewith Sheikh Bu Bakr Bu Dahn-Dorsa and Sheikh Mohamed Bu Shdeik Hazig-Barasa for presentation of their letters of appointment as Mustashars [advisers] of their respective Qabilas [communities]. 2. I understand from Major Laurie that the latter was also to be appointed Omda but Hussein Taher [the *mudir*] views this with alarm as he says that the Barasa expect to have an Omda for each of their sections and will not accept Sheikh Mohamed Bu Shdeik as Omda of the whole Qabila.'[3] Reports of this kind from the tribal districts were intended to help Maclaren and others at headquarters to decide exactly how many sheikhs needed to be recognised.[4] The practical work of the CAOs in this field was at the same time obviously of great value to the sociological and anthropological research being undertaken by Edward Evan Evans-Pritchard who, according to the diary, visited al-Bayda in mid-May.

There was also a huge amount of court work to get through in this period, with Peter estimating that he handled 700 cases in six months. The pace being set in the courts of Shahat, al-Bayda and Apollonia was astonishing, often involving more than ten cases a day. He gives little detail of individual cases, but most of them must have been of a fairly trivial nature and easy to resolve quickly. On one sensitive case in particular, Peter does go into some detail both in the memoir and the diary; this involves the blatant abuse of power by a key member of the Cyrenaica Defence Force (CDF) known both as Sanussi Kaddum and Sanussi Effendi.[5]

---

[2] Rennell of Rodd, *British Military Administration of Occupied Territories in Africa during the years 1941–1947*, London, 1948, p253, J. F. P. Maclaren, BMA Annual Report, 25 February 1944, AIR 23/6753.

[3] P. M. Synge to Chief Secretary, 10 April 1944, FO 1015/972.

[4] J. F. P. Maclaren to CAO Beda, 21 August 1944, FO 1015/972, and Rennell of Rodd, *British Military Administration of Occupied Territories in Africa during the years 1941–47*, London, 1948, p253.

5 Sanussi was (and remains) a common surname in Cyrenaica and throughout north-eastern Africa, and has also been adopted in other Islamic regions of the continent.

Figure 12. *Hussein Taher,* mudir *of al-Bayda, 1944.* Reprinted from *Geoffrey Keyes of the Rommel Raid,* 1956, by Elizabeth Keyes.

General military courts had been established by the BMA in early 1943 to handle both so-called 'war crimes', such as trespassing in prohibited areas or handling military equipment, and ordinary civil crimes. The records show that throughout Cyrenaica in the first year, there had been 28 convictions for 'wilful killing', 90 for assault and 388 for theft.[6]

---

[6] J. F. P. Maclaren, BMA Annual Report, 25 February 1944, AIR 23/6753.

In 1944, CAOs like Peter Synge became even more involved in running these military courts until, at the end of the year, the responsibility was transferred to a more regular civil court service. According to the official history, the reopening of civil courts in late 1944 involved adapting the previously prevailing Italian court system, while using a (British) qualified lawyer to act as president of the court with unlimited jurisdiction, albeit with the support of either governmental or other socially prominent arbitrators.[7] At the same time, shari'a courts continued to operate under the management of a Grand Qadi and a number of both senior and junior *qadis*.[8]

Over the summer months, the emphasis of Peter's responsibilities shifted towards the long-expected visit of Sayyid Mohammed Idris. After the tour of Cyrenaica by six Sanussi leaders in November 1943, the plans had been firmed up in May, and Peter was involved in the preparations for a prolonged stay by Idris in al-Bayda before and during the fasting month of Ramadan, starting in August. The town of al-Bayda was particularly significant as the original heartland of the Sanussiyya fraternity, of which Idris was the current head, but it had also played a part in the campaigns of the German Afrika Korps, with Field Marshal Rommel basing himself there for much of the time while in control of the territory.

The building that the BMA first used as its own first headquarters in 1943 was the very same house that Rommel himself had used as a command centre, when it had been the site of a daring but unsuccessful attempt by British commandos to assassinate Rommel in November 1941. After landing from a submarine, Lieutenant Colonel Geoffrey Keyes and his colleagues had managed to break into the heart of the house, killing four of the Germans there, but Keyes himself was shot and killed while most of his companions escaped. It was only later discovered that Rommel had been away in Derna at the time of the attack. However, on Rommel's orders, Keyes was buried with full military honours in the local Catholic cemetery alongside his German victims.[9] In June 1942, Keyes was posthumously awarded the Victoria Cross. Peter's memoir notes that in 1944 the Rommel House still bore the scars of the hand grenades and bullets used in the raid.

---

[7] Rennell of Rodd, *British Military Administration of Occupied Territories in Africa during the years 1941–47*, London, 1948, p469.

[8] J. F. P. Maclaren, BMA Annual Report, 25 February 1944, AIR 23/6753.

[9] A full account of the raid was written by Elizabeth Keyes, in *Geoffrey Keyes of the Rommel Raid*, London, 1956, pp218ff.

Figure 13. *The Rommel House, al-Bayda, 1944.* Reprinted from *Geoffrey Keyes of the Rommel Raid*, 1956, by Elizabeth Keyes.

The choice of the Rommel House as a potential residence for Sayyid Mohammed Idris was based on the symbolism of its location; it had been built (by Italians) adjacent to the site of the very first Sanussi *zawia* (lodge) set up over 100 years earlier, in 1841. The Zawia al-Bayda ('the white lodge'), incorporating a mosque and a shrine dedicated to Sidi Rafa, a companion of the Prophet Muhammad, was the first among at least 50 such *zawias* around Cyrenaica established by the founder, Sidi Muhammad ben Ali al-Sanussi, who became known as the 'Grand Sanussi'. His fraternity soon held sway in a vast region of north-eastern Africa at a time of a general Islamic revival both north and south of the Sahara.

One of the more recently established such fraternities active in North Africa, the Sanussi order appeared to hold a similar appeal to that of the Tijani order in the more westerly regions of the Sahara in the same period. Each in its own way managed to be distinct from the older Islamic orders that still had influence in North Africa, such as the Qadriyya and the Ahmadiyya. However, the Sanussi order was unique in that it came into existence in a region where very little effective political control existed at the time, giving it the semblance

Figure 14 (left). *The grave of Geoffrey Keyes at al-Bayda in 1944.* Reprinted from *Geoffrey Keyes of the Rommel Raid*, 1956, by Elizabeth Keyes.
Figure 15 (right). *The cross in its present location at Tingewick church, Buckinghamshire.* Author photograph.

of functioning rather like a state.[10] Born in Algeria in around 1789, and having travelled, studied and preached throughout North Africa and Arabia, Sidi Muhammad al-Sanussi found Cyrenaica to be particularly suitable as his main centre of activity, and set about building dozens of *zawias* in every centre of population and even a university at the oasis of Jaghbub before his death in 1859.

The lodges were places for prayer, education and the dispensing of Islamic justice, and yet were also hubs of trade and agriculture, and this helped to give the fraternity a semblance of economic and political power in the face of the ineffective Ottoman rule over this region in the late 19th century. The Sanussiyya and their *zawias* played a role in

---

[10] E. E. Evans-Pritchard, *The Sanusi of Cyrenaica*, Oxford, 1949, pp91ff. Another account described how in the late 19th century the second Grand Sanussi 'became very powerful, almost like a territorial monarch from the west frontier of Egypt to Darfur, Wadai and Bornu to the south, to Bilma and Murzuk to the west and, in the north, to the coast of Tripolitania.' Gordon Casserly, *Tripolitania*, London, 1943, p111.

preventing intertribal conflict.[11] While setting out a simple and power-ful spiritual code, based on the values of moderation and self-discipline to which the Saharan tribes were already well attuned, the Sanussis also managed to establish and develop new caravan trade routes across the most barren and empty stretches of the eastern Sahara, extending their reach as far as Darfur, Tibesti, Wadai, Borku and Bornu (present-day Sudan, Chad and Nigeria), until these were interrupted by French colo-nial campaigns in Chad.

The vital element in the history of the Sanussis that still gave them relevance in the 1940s was the historic resistance they had put up against the Italian colonisers. Their struggle, initially in alliance with the Ottoman Turks and then in the 1920s under the charismatic guerrilla leader Omar Mukhtar, was widely recognised as a valiant effort against impossible odds. In 1922, the same year that Mussolini took power in Italy, the Grand Sanussi's grandson, Sayyid Mohammed Idris, chose exile in Egypt rather than continued acceptance of the Italian presence while Omar Mukhtar fought on. But the Italian Fascists' tactics, espe-cially under General Rodolfo Graziani after 1930, became increasingly ruthless, including mass deportations from the Jebel Akhdar region and the establishment of concentration camps, where thousands of peo-ple died. Eventually Omar Mukhtar was captured and executed in Sep-tember 1931, whereupon the fighting ended, only to resume in 1940 as a small but symbolically important element in the titanic struggle between the Allies and the Axis.[12]

While Peter Synge was fixing up the Rommel House in readi-ness for a long stay by Idris, it was clear that the Sayyid's treatment by the British had to be impeccable and that a successful visit could help bolster Britain's prestige and so underpin her military pres-ence. Although there was still no certainty about the role Idris might play in a new Cyrenaica after the war, it was an opportunity for Cum-ming, Maclaren and their bosses in Cairo and London to display the essence of the British 'indirect rule' model in action.[13] Above all, they wanted to ensure tight control of the tour as well as effective political choreography.

---

[11] A. Baldinetti, *The Origins of the Libyan Nation: Colonial legacy, exile and the emergence of a new nation-state*, Abingdon, 2010, p31.

[12] Among the most accessible accounts of this history are those of J. Wright, *A History of Libya*, London, 2010, E. E. Evans-Pritchard, *The Sanusi of Cyrenaica*, Oxford, 1949, and A. Baldinetti, *The Origins of the Libyan Nation: Colonial legacy, exile and the emergence of a new nation-state*, Abingdon, 2010.

[13] I am grateful to Jason Pack for pointing out how the tour could be analysed as a demon-stration to the populace of the British preference for indirect rule.

## FROM THE DIARY

### 18 March (Saturday)

*[Major] Fisher rang up this evening to say that I must go to Beda [al-Bayda] first thing on Monday, as Allman has been recalled and must leave on Tuesday and I must take over from him. Rather a shock as I hoped that he at least would still be there to show me the ropes but now there will be no-one.*

### 20 March

*Got to Beda about 11.30 and found Allman looking awfully lugubrious and worried. Started to take over his cash before lunch and met Lewis the policeman who informed me that* he *was going in a day or two and Skelton Smith was taking over and arriving today so I tried to ring up HQ to stop that. It would be fantastic if he left me to run the place without anybody who knew anything about the district – but I couldn't get Barce, line out of order. Took over the cash after lunch and then got on to Maclaren, who promised to do what he could to stop the transfer and gave me a few tips about the tribes.*

### 22 March

*Spent most of the day talking to sheikhs about one of the Hasa/Bakheit tribe who killed a man about 18 months ago and who is still at large. Their rations have been stopped until they produce him and they are rather anxious about their food. They suggest that we put their relations in clink until he is produced, and ask for their rations. I have promised to give a decision tomorrow when I have talked to Weir. The Mudir Hussein[14] arrived tonight and I had a short talk with him.*

### 8 April (Saturday)

*Col Maclaren went off to Derna and I had an awful morning trying to do some work but being interrupted by visiting sheikhs all the time. Had ordered my horse for 2p.m. but wasn't ready so I went to the office instead and had more visits from sheikhs. I am now [so] completely 'moidered'[15] with them all that I don't know who is who. Talked to the two* mustashars-elect *of*

---

[14] Hussein Taher, the new *mudir* of the district, had also served as a *mudir* under Italian rule, despite remaining loyal to Idris and the Sanussis; in 1941 he had played a crucial role in facilitating the British raid on Rommel's headquarters. E. Keyes, *Geoffrey Keyes of the Rommel Raid*, London, 1956, pp209ff.

[15] An Irish pronunciation for 'murdered' – implying 'upset' – that was regularly used by Peter's Irish-born father.

*Dorsa and Barasa who are going to Barce on Monday to meet the Brig and be appointed. Went out riding at just before 6p.m. ... I got some more practice at trotting and began to feel more at home.*

## FROM THE MEMOIR

*Cyrenaica was very tribal, and in spite of the fact that the Italians had driven the Arabs out of the Jebel and had tried to suppress the tribal system, the old jealousies and feuds remained and the tribes were constantly at loggerheads over the ownership of wells. There were four main tribes in the Jebel and three of them inhabited my new district. They were: the Hasa who lived mostly round Cyrene and were despised by their neighbours for having collaborated to a certain extent with the Italians; the Dorsa who inhabited the wild country between Beda and the sea; and the Barasa who inhabited the southern slopes of the Jebel and the desert areas beyond. All were descended from a common ancestor but they were as jealous of their tribal boundaries as any of the European nations. The Dorsa and the Barasa were comparatively easy to deal with as they each recognised one man as their paramount chief or Sheikh m'Sheikh but the Hasa were quite a different kettle of fish. Their hereditary chief was a shifty and weak man who had no authority and was not recognised by any of the divisions and sub-divisions of the tribe, each of whom had their own claimant.*

*It was necessary that there should be a spokesman or mouthpiece for the tribes, especially someone to whom government policy could be explained and who could put it across to the rest of the tribe, so after much discussion and thought I chose a man who seemed to have the necessary qualities of leadership and who was the recognised head of a section of the tribe, and I recommended him to the Chief Administrator, who in due course came up to Cyrene to make the announcement to a gathering of representatives of the sections. To have appointed him Sheikh m'Sheikh would have caused serious trouble, so it was decided to appoint him Mustashar or Adviser. There was mild opposition from the hereditary chief but when I threatened to put him 'inside' for a breach of the peace he subsided and I had no trouble of any sort while I was in the District, and I found the Mustashar very helpful.[16]*

---

[16] Despite all these efforts, an anthropologist later concluded that 'the British experimented unsuccessfully with the idea of representatives nominated by the people of the tribes and their sections themselves. ... Among the Bedouin, the tribal structure did not provide a framework to which administrative positions could be attached.' E.L. Peters, *The Bedouin in Cyrenaica: Studies in Personal and Corporate Power*, Cambridge, 1990, pp112 and 119.

## FROM THE DIARY

### 3 May

*Went off to Shahat for a court, which I finished by 12.45. ... Went for a walk to the Zawia. ... Quite interesting up there and traces of some very ancient ruins. Butler says there is a bit of mosaic pavement but I couldn't find it.*

### 4 May

*After lunch went off to Faidia to talk to the sheikhs and stayed there till about 5p.m. and then back to Shahat where I looked at the building going on and talked to the ass who claims rent for the shops. Skelton out after Brahim Bu Ali, who was seen in Shahat and shot at two of his men* [possibly the man mentioned in the diary entry of 22 March; he was still at large on 25 May].

### 5 May

*Talked to the Mudirs about assessment from 11.30 to 1p.m. ... Went up to the Zawia and found the bit of pavement and wanted to go down towards the sea but found it too steep. ... Continued the meeting of Mudirs afterwards and finished about 6.15p.m.*

### 10 May

*Another lovely day – absolutely cloudless. Had a court at Susa and tried 10 cases there and then back to Shahat for four more. At 6p.m. met several of the sheikhs of the Hasa who have started quarrelling over the commission for the assessment of the crops. I was quite deadbeat and didn't feel capable of dealing with the situation at all and just walked out on them after a bit.*

### 11 May

*I learned that the Hasa would quarrel whoever was appointed so it doesn't matter much.*

### 12 May

*[A] festival and people came from all over the place for a visit to the tomb of Sidi Rafa and there was a lot of firing of rifles from horseback and a pictur-esque gathering of sheikhs. Went off to Cyrene to see the Mudir and also to ring up Barce and Derna as my telephone is out of order and has been since yesterday morning. Signals today found the line cut in the village and are at last putting it overhead.*

**13 May (Saturday)**

*Decided to go and look for the Mudir of Mamelli and find out how he was getting on as he was due back on Thursday. Found Sheikh Senussi Bu Beidan who said he would go with me to some place where the Mudir was said to be. We went to Marawa where we were told they had been. … After lunch went to Bir-something and found the policeman who was supposed to go with the Mudir who had been told to wait there while the Mudir went south for a few days and he had not returned. As it was then after 5p.m. we came home and came back to Marawa and across to Kasr el Lybia. A very bumpy and slow road and my back was very sore. Got back about 8.15.*

**14 May (Sunday)**

*Went over to Wadi Kuf to explore the original road, which has been blown in several places, and walked down it to the first demolition, where there is no sign of the original bridge but the concrete pillars were being built and don't look as if they had been destroyed. I don't understand it at all. Took a short cut over the hill and at the top came on an old man with a "Naja" [camp] close by and he asked me in to tea and I was given goats milk again – out of a teapot this time, and raw broad beans to eat. When I left I found I had guessed my direction so well that the truck was only 50 yds away.*

**15 May**

*Had a court this morning and tried 8 cases, though I was told there were only four. … Brig and Col Maclaren passed on their way to Cairo.*

**16 May**

*Evans-Pritchard and Evans looked in a.m.*

**17 May**

*About 6p.m. a lot of Barasa Hussein sheikhs came in to object to the [crop] assessment boards. I sent them away and decided to accede to a request for one more Hussein member but they wanted a complete Hussein board. After dinner Hussein Taher came in a suggested agreeing one more and I said I would talk to them in the morning and sat up thinking out what to say.*

**25 May**

*Strong south wind and hot. Couldn't stay in the office so went to Mamelli by a new way via Gareega Battisti road and branch right to Sidi Mohamed Homra on the south road. Saw a man with a rifle on the road who ran like a hare and hid when he saw the car. I wasn't armed so could do nothing. Suspect it was Brahim Bu Ali. Came back via Mamelli.*

**30 May**

*Went out about 10a.m. after being held up by sheikhs wanting to see me and went to Slonta to get news of Qwedir [the man in charge of assessment of crops] and his commission. Found the policeman there who said that the commission was south of Gerdis but that Qwedir wasn't with them so I took Ibrahim Bubakaer and went to Gerdis where we found some people at a well who said Qwedir had gone to Mamelli so I came back and went to Mamelli but no news of him there so went to Faidia to try and find Hussein Maziq. The road is terrible and it took an awful long time but we met the lorry on the road and also Hussein, so I talked to him and then came back across country. Got back about 3.30. Rode between 6 and 7. Cold dull day with a kind of drizzle.*

**31 May**

*Court at Shahat and I started just before 10 and sat with one break of 5 mins until 1.45p.m. and tried 14 cases which wasn't bad. Got back to lunch at 2.15 and went to the office afterwards and rode between 6p.m. and 7p.m.*

**17 June (Sunday)**

*A bad day. Plans to be made for reception of the Senussi family and Sayed Idris himself very soon and I am without a Mudir. One in Cairo, one in hospital and one alternately sick or out doing the assessment.*

*The Barasa are up in arms because the Aulad Hamad have said they want to be assessed by the Dorsa and I agreed. The Barasa say that the Aulad Hamad are living on Barasa land and no Dorsa can come and interfere. All sorts of things to be done and no-one to do it with and I feel completely flummoxed.*

**2 July**

*Fletcher arrived at 10.30 to see Rommel's house, where Sayed Idris will stay when he arrives on 20th.*

**8 July (Saturday)**

*Was met by Abdulla Dweili, who I thought was going to make further complaints about his farm and my judgment, but he brought a serious complaint against Senussi Eff[endi, of the Cyrenaica Defence Force] at Shahat, who had beaten up a man and a girl and put them in clink for a night without a cause. Wanted to go over to Shahat in any case so called for Skelton and went. We heard both sides of the story and then went and saw the girl who is quite good looking and almost certainly a whore but there is no excuse for Senussi's action.*

## FROM THE MEMOIR

*One of my duties was to sit as a magistrate and dispense summary justice at Beda, Cyrene and Apollonia. ... and during my six months in the District I disposed of some 700 cases. The police had been formed out of the Cyrenaica Defence Force which itself had been formed in Egypt from deserters and exiles from Cyrenaica towards the end of 1940. One of the first Libyans to be commissioned [i.e. Sanussi Effendi] was now in charge of the Cyrene detachment and he was a very smart and zealous officer. Every time I sat in court at Cyrene I noticed that a certain man or his wife was charged with being in possession of war material of some kind of other – generally army rations. Each time they appeared, the fine was heavier, but one day a woman was charged and her address was the same as that of the couple. She however did not appear in court and I was informed that she was sick. When the court rose I decided out of curiosity to go and see where these people lived and I was taken to a rather squalid two-roomed house on the outskirts of the village. The accused was in bed but she did not look ill. She was in fact a girl and a very good-looking one – in fact the nicest looking North African girl I had ever seen, and she was surrounded by illustrated English newspapers, such as* Picture Post *and* Everybody's, *and it slowly began to dawn on me why her parents had been appearing in court so often. There was a small unit of the RASC [Royal Army Service Corps] stationed at Cyrene and the girl was either visiting the camp or being visited by the soldiery, and was demanding or accepting payment for her favours in kind as well as in cash. The smart police officer had taken a fancy to her but he could not give her what she wanted in the way of payment and in any case she had not time to pay any attention to him, so he decided to take it out on her parents, hoping in this way to blackmail her into accepting his advances. Having started in this unethical way of bringing cases to court it was not long before he got himself into more serious trouble and eventually he was dismissed from the force.*

## FROM THE DIARY

### 9 July (Sunday)
*Watched the first half of a soccer match between Beda and a combined team from Susa and Shahat. Very poor play and bad refereeing. Beda lost.*

### 10 July
*Brigadier arrived for lunch on his way to Derna. Looked at Rommel's house which is being done up.*

**11 July**
*Had a difficult morning with dozens of people to see me. Complaints from the Dorsa that the Sayed was not having a meeting of the Dorsa in this District as well as in Barce. Felt quite overwhelmed today with everything.*

**12 July**
*Off to meet the Brig at crossroads at 4.0p.m. A crowd of sheikhs and others came to hear Bakar being appointed Mustashar and a lot of them raised their opposition although they had previously agreed to his appointment and there was a disgraceful scene. Brig went off about 5p.m. and I stayed with the Mudir and got back about 6.*

**13 July**
*After lunch went to Apollonia to collect furniture etc for the Sayed's visit. Feel less harassed now that Hussein Taher [the* mudir] *is back to make arrangements for the Sayed's visit. Very cloudy weather, damp and cool and some rain in Apollonia.*

**14 July**
*Getting Rommel's house cleaned up for the Sayed and army of workers in it, but a lot of the work wasted because people's boots make such a lot of mess. Water doesn't run upstairs.*

**15 July (Saturday)**
*Col Maclaren arrived about 6p.m. After tea we went and looked at Rommel's house and he was quite pleased with it. More furniture is needed though. Quite chilly tonight.*

**16 July (Sunday)**
*After bkfst at 9a.m. went and looked at Rommel's house and decided to get more furniture.*

**19 July**
*No court at Shahat today and busy putting finishing touches to the Sayed's house and getting furniture etc. The house looks very nice now and plenty of carpets are forthcoming from all over the place.*

chapter 6

# KEEPING IDRIS
# TO HIS WORD
## AL-BAYDA,
## 20 JULY–7 SEPTEMBER 1944

SAYYID MOHAMMED IDRIS arrived in Cyrenaica from Egypt on 17 July 1944. After an initial stop in Tobruk, he travelled from town to town throughout the territory for a full three weeks, and so it was on 20 July that he first arrived in the original Sanussiyya capital of al-Bayda, high up in the Jebel Akhdar, for a stay that lasted four days. Here Peter Synge reports that Idris was greeted by horsemen firing their rifles and was ceremonially feted; he made speeches and received numerous visitors wanting to kiss his hand, before his cavalcade moved on to his next destinations of Barce and Benghazi.

The crucial symbolism of this first wartime visit by Idris was encapsulated by one of Libya's leading historians, Majid Khadduri, as follows: 'When he visited Benghazi city on 28 July 1944, after an absence of almost a quarter of a century, he was presented with a sword, representing the country's struggle against Italian domination for more than thirty years. Two days later he gave an address in which he thanked the people for their welcome, promising a prosperous future and urging them to unite as one family and avoid dissension. Finally, he paid tribute to Great Britain and called for cooperation with her until the country received independence.'[1]

Idris had not set foot in Cyrenaica since his decision to go into exile in Egypt in November 1922, leaving Omar Mukhtar to lead the armed struggle against the Italians while he himself tried to sustain the international legal case against colonisation (although he was not necessarily accepted by the other Libyan exiles as a candidate for

---

[1] M. Khadduri, *Modern Libya: A Study in Political Development*, Baltimore, 1963, pp55–6.

leadership).[2] Now, in 1944, Idris hoped to use his return to promote the case for full independence for Cyrenaica (and potentially the whole of Libya) in any negotiations that might follow the ongoing world war (at this stage entering a decisive final phase following the Normandy landings in June). On this first exploratory trip, he was accompanied by several close personal advisers and some of his Sanussi relations, who brought with them a variety of views, hopes and ambitions.

After three weeks of noisy gatherings and ceremonies across the territory, Idris returned to al-Bayda on 6 August. He was expected to remain there for a prolonged private stay that would include the fasting month of Ramadan, which that year was due to start on 20 August. Some on the British side may even have hoped that he would stay there permanently, but it is clear from Peter's account that the intentions of Idris could never be taken for granted – as, for example, when he threatened to return to Cairo, complaining of feeling cold and unwell. Throughout his time in Cyrenaica, there were signs of a high degree of nervousness – as much within the British Military Administration as among Idris's entourage – about the way in which the mutual relationship might develop in future.

Duncan Cumming was quick to announce the positive gains of the visit, although he was not averse to criticising both Idris and his associates. 'The people showed unqualified enthusiasm wherever the Sayed went,' Cumming declared in his official report, written in mid-August. 'If any doubt may have existed about the Sayed's popularity, it has been emphatically removed.' He even suggested that 'there will not only be discontentment but also armed resistance in Cyrenaica if the Sayed is not given at least the titular leadership of the country after the war.' At the same time, Cumming was less than impressed by Idris's public persona. 'His rhetoric is unlikely to rouse the excitement of his hearers,' he noted. 'He is a poor "showman."'[3]

With his superiors in the War Office in mind, Cumming also took the opportunity to boast about the BMA's own achievements. 'A satisfactory feature of this tour was the evidence it gave of the friendly relationship between the people and officers of the Administration, which is the result of the close personal contacts our Arabic speaking

---

[2] E. A. V. De Candole, *The Life and Times of King Idris of Libya*, published privately 1990, p45. For a full discussion of the politics of Libyan exiles in the 1920s and 1930s, see A. Baldinetti, *The Origins of the Libyan Nation: Colonial legacy, exile and the emergence of a new nation-state*, Abingdon, 2010, pp69ff.

[3] R. D. H Arundell to CAB, GHQ, including D. C. Cumming's Report, 22 August 1944, FO 371/41511.

Figure 16. *Sayyid Idris's triumphant return: Sayyid Idris welcomed by British officers and shaking hands with Colonel Norman Anderson.* By kind permission of Faraj Najem Collection.

officers have cultivated since the occupation,' he declared. 'Less satisfactory was the confirmation of our belief that the Sayed's personal staff is discreditable.'[4]

Contemporary reports suggested that public reactions to Idris's visit varied among the different tribes and towns that he visited. While the tribes regarded him as a symbol of religious faith and the political tradition, in the towns he was seen as 'a religious non-political leader'.[5]

---

[4] D. C. Cumming's Report, 22 August 1944, FO 371/41511. The 'discreditable' epithet seems very likely to have referred to one of Idris's secretaries, Omar Sheneib, whom Cumming would describe later as 'an ignorant, hot-headed, agitator who, before the war made a living as a propagandist against the Italians', who in turn 'bought him off during the Italo–Abyssinian war.' Cumming wrote that Sheneib was hired by Idris in 1940 and 'the only reason he has not been discharged is that he would at once transfer his custom to the Sayed's opponents in Cairo.' Commentary by D. C. Cumming, 1946, undated, FO 1015/91.

[5] A. Baldinetti, *The Origins of the Libyan Nation: Colonial legacy, exile and the emergence of a new nation-state*, Abingdon, 2010, p122.

Figure 17. *Sayyid Idris on his arrival in Soluch, July 1944.* By kind permission of Faraj Najem Collection.

For his part, Cumming noted that 'the rural Arabs behaved in the traditional manner: their main preoccupation was to touch the Sayed's person, and one would have liked the Sayed to have given more attention to the section of the populace which deserves the whole of the credit for resisting the Italians.' Cumming was at the same time dismissive of those members of the urban population who 'tried to make amends for their collaboration with the Italians by showing the same manifestation of hysteria as they used to show the Duce and his representatives.'[6]

From the perspective of the predominantly rural al-Bayda district, the evidence from Peter Synge's diary is that Idris did indeed engage only minimally with the different tribes, whom Peter had by now come to know extremely well and among whom there were several continuing disputes that it was his job to try to resolve. By this point in 1944, the activity level of the BMA had reached full pitch, especially in its complex dealings with the tribes[7] and in its ongoing management of numerous civil court cases.

At this stage of the war, the outside world took little notice of what was happening in Cyrenaica and the official correspondence reveals

---

[6] D. C. Cumming's Report, 22 August 1944, FO 371/41511.
[7] The diary entries cover the tribal issues and disputes in much greater detail than is included in these pages.

that any publicity given to Idris's visit was carefully censored.[8] But there was one apparent glitch in the pre-planned international coverage. Over two months later, the London-based weekly *Picture Post* published a double-page illustrated account of the visit in its issue of 7 October 1944, entitled 'Britain Restores an Arab Ruler to His Country'. Using high-quality photos of the visit, supplied by the Ministry of Information, this was no doubt intended as morale-boosting propaganda in the midst of the war, and yet the subsequent correspondence between officials at Middle East Headquarters in Cairo and the Foreign Office in London reveals that Colonel Norman Anderson, in particular, was outraged by the *Picture Post*'s headline, which at a stroke seemed to have given away the entire British game plan for Cyrenaica.

'The title of the article … inevitably implies that Sayed Idris not only returned to his country permanently (which is not true) but returned as Ruler,' Anderson complained. 'It is true that the writer admits in his penultimate paragraph that the post-war position of the Sayed in Cyrenaica has not yet been decided, but … [this] may escape the notice of the casual reader.' The author of the *Picture Post*'s text, Professor Hamilton Gibb from Oxford, had undertaken an extensive visit to Cyrenaica some months earlier and was well briefed about the true situation. When informed of the annoyance the headline had caused, Gibb apologised and pushed the blame for 'a few breezy and unimportant inaccuracies' onto the sub-editors, who 'supply the pep which the academic style notoriously lacks', but denied that anything he had written was factually misleading.[9]

The *Picture Post*'s photos of the visit included a view of a five-storey building in Benghazi, with people waving from every balcony, the windows draped with tapestries and Sanussi flags (later incorporated into the Libyan national flag). Other photos showed Bedouin horsemen pressing close around Idris, their rifles in the air, and cheering crowds being controlled by police. One showed a smiling Idris seated in front of expensive hanging carpets, with two rather anxious-looking British officers on each side of him, above the caption: 'The End of a Happy Day: British officers entertain the Arab ruler in Arab style at their club.'

---

[8] *The Times* in London reported (from Cairo, on 16 July) only that the visit was beginning, adding that it was 'private in the sense that the Grand Senussi is not returning as ruler of Cyrenaica' and that it was 'certain that he will receive a great and enthusiastic welcome'. *The Times*, 17 July 1944.
[9] Correspondence between J. N. D. Anderson, CAB, GHQ, and H. A. R. Gibb, November 1944, FO 371/41511.

The Grand Senussi Arrives
*He comes ashore and passes through an Arab guard outside Agedabia.*

Rifle-Fire Salutation
*Tribesmen raise their rifles and fire as he passes through Soluch.*

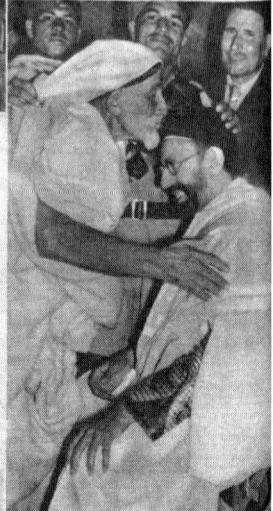

The Traditional Greeting
*An old man, who remembers the coming of the Italians, kisses his long-exiled chief.*

# BRITAIN RESTORES AN ARAB RULER TO HIS COUNTRY

**The end of Italy's African Empire means the return of the Grand Senussi as leader of Cyrenaica's Moslem puritans.**

AFTER 22 years of exile—years of painful waiting while a foreign conqueror played havoc with his people—Sidi Mohammed el Idris, the Grand Senussi of Cyrenaica, comes home.

His car drives westward into Libya, following that famous desert route on which three British armies have fought since this war began. He rides past the wreckage heaped up in their campaigns. He sees the little graves of his tribesmen, who fell in the long struggle against the Duce's ruthless empire-builders—mounds of sand with simple wooden poles, to which a shred of cotton that was once a flag still clings.

But he sees also the hopeful signs of the new British Military Administration. He sees walls on which some Arab hand has scrawled: "Long Live the Emir." And as he drives into Tobruk and Derna, white-robed desert horsemen, their rifles aloft, cheer him through the streets, press close around him, and must be beaten off by police cordons to prevent them from tearing open the doors of his car and planting the traditional kiss on his forehead.

How is it that these men retain their loyalty to him, after his absence during 22 eventful years? For Mohammed el Idris is not a warrior chief whose exploits could be woven into legends for entertainment at camp fires. He is a spare, shy man of fifty-three, graceful and courteous, with a scholar's spectacles and interests, and a note of gentle sadness in his voice. He has spent his exile living unassum-

ingly in a Cairo suburb, surrounded only by a few Senussi refugees. But the Senussis of the Libyan Desert never ceased to look to him for guidance in their faith and politics, and they still see in him a symbol of their former glory, when the name Senussi stood for fanatical dervish zeal in the defence of Islam against unbelievers.

It was his grandfather, a century ago, who founded their religious confraternity. His name was Mohammed - ben - Si - Ali - ben - Senussi - el - Khembi-el-Hassani-el-Edrissi-el-Midjahiri. His followers called themselves "Senussis" after their leader, as did the Franciscans or Dominicans in Medieval Europe. Their creed was one of abstinence and Puritanism, and throughout Cyrenaica they built a network of Zawiyas, or monasteries, in which to practise it.

In those days the Senussis were growing into a powerful people. They sent their missionaries and traders east and west, from India to Morocco and, through the Sahara, into Equatorial Africa. Wherever they went they made and proselytes until, in 1902, after a protracted war with France, they were forced back into Libya. Nine years later Italian troops landed on their northern shores. The Senussis joined with their Turkish overlords in defence of their lands, and when Turkey acknowledged defeat, the Senussis still fought on and almost drove the invaders back into the sea.

Their war raged on until 1917, when Sidi Mohammed el Idris succeeded his warlike cousin as Grand Senussi and concluded formal agreements with Britain and Italy. Six years later Mussolini scrapped the treaty, accusing the Grand Senussi of still encouraging rebellious subjects.

Sidi Mohammed crossed into Egypt. His people

Fourteen Desert Tribes Have Sent Their Men to Welcome Him to Agedabia
*It was from here that he set out on his journey into exile 22 years ago. The future of the country has still to be decided, but it won't be under Italian rule.*

Figures 18 (above) and 19 (opposite). Picture Post*'s coverage of Idris's visit.* (October 7, 1944 edition)

Peter's diary and memoir allow us to look behind the scenes and show the somewhat neurotic nature of the figure whom Hamilton Gibb's article described as 'a spare, shy man of fifty-three, graceful and courteous, with a scholar's spectacles and interests, and a note of gentle sadness in his voice'. Peter's record reveals Idris's aversion to noisy celebrations and shows of enthusiasm. It also focuses on a dramatic threat to the BMA's careful diplomatic choreography on 19 August, when Idris claimed to be feeling ill and wanted to return to Cairo immediately. At this point, he was only persuaded to stay on by Peter Synge's personal

114

Picture Post, October 2, 1944

**Benghazi Puts on Festive Dress for the Return of its Ruler to His Capital**

*Every balcony and window is draped with tapestries and the Senussi flags. Inscriptions and portraits of the Grand Senussi show the inhabitants' loyalty to their spiritual and temporal head.*

were driven from the fertile "Green Mountain" strip along the coast, and into the desert. Since then much has changed in Cyrenaica. Though to-day every Senussi tribesman still carries his rifle, the enormous losses they have suffered have turned their minds from war to the urgent tasks of reconstruction. They must re-form their scattered and depleted tribes, their herds of camels and sheep. They must re-sow their scanty barley and, within a land of little natural wealth, try to create some form of regular economy.

These are the problems with which the Grand Senussi has gone back to deal. And they will not be easy ones. For the land of the Green Mountain lies fallow; the ports are idle; trade has stopped long ago; Benghazi and Tobruk are in ruins.

Perhaps the most difficult problem will be that of the Italian settlements. Fascist governors seized all the good land to plant on it Italian colonists, stripped from Italy. To-day there is not a single Italian left in Cyrenaica. They scampered off in Wavell's day. But their derelict farms still occupy the landscape. What is to be done with them? There is no world market for Cyrenaican wheat, almonds and wines. So the farms will have to be turned to some other use and some of the tribesmen will have to return to settled cultivation.

Fortunately, Sidi Mohammed el Idris is a man who has seen a great deal of men and affairs during his long exile, and has acquired greater breadth of view and wider experience than his predecessors. The actual future of Cyrenaica has still to be decided by the United Nations, but the British Foreign Secretary has given a pledge that the Senussis shall not be put under Italian domination again. If the people of Cyrenaica have a voice in the disposal of their country there is no doubt of their unanimous desire that Sidi Mohammed el Idris shall be their ruler.

But he himself knows that he will need help from outside, financial help in the first place. It will cost as much as the entire revenues of Cyrenaica could produce in ten years to clear up the debris of war and set the country on its feet again. Even after that, something must be done to enable the country to find its own niche in the political and economic life of the world. Cyrenaica will never be a rich country. It will not need large numbers of highly-paid officials, and its tribesmen, after their bitter experience, will resent any foreign control. But there will be room and a welcome for a few qualified men who can give tactful and expert advice and assistance in municipal and agricultural services.

H. A. R. Gibb

*The End of a Happy Day*
*British officers entertain the Arab ruler in Arab style at their club.*

loan of a woollen scarf and warm underwear (long johns, according to his verbal account).

Afterwards, Peter was convinced that his action had prevented a crisis developing by making it possible for Idris to keep to his agreed schedule. At the time, however, there were others who would certainly have challenged such a statement. The diary itself reports that some members of the BMA – particularly John Reid – were quick to blame Peter for not looking after Idris properly. And even more tellingly, the diary catches the moment on 12 August when, after a long meeting with Idris, Duncan Cumming suddenly offered Peter the remote posting of Kufra, almost as if it had been decided that he should be sent as far away as possible.

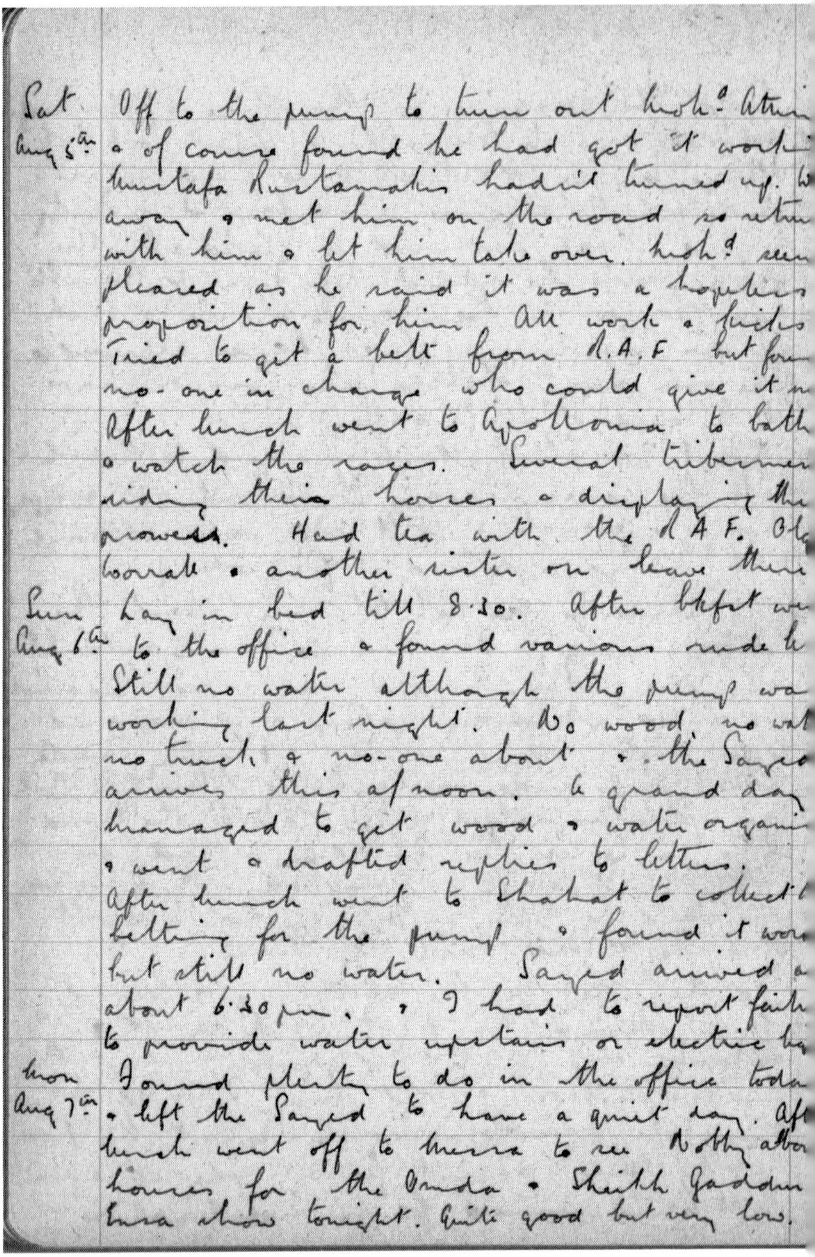

Sat
Aug 5th

Off to the pump to turn out hosh? Althou of course found he had got it work... Mustafa Rustamatis hadn't turned up. W... away & met him on the road so retu... with him & let him take over. hosh? see... pleased as he said it was a hopeles... proposition for him — all work & ... Tried to get a belt from R.A.F but fr... no-one in charge who could give it m... After lunch went to Apollonia to bath... & watch the races. Several tribesmen... riding their horses & display... the... prowess. Had tea with the R A F. Old... Boorah & another sister on leave ther...

Sun
Aug 6th

Lay in bed till 8.30. After bkfst we... to the office & found various rude le... Still no water although the pump wa... working last night. No wood, no wat... no truck & no-one about... the Sayed... arrives this afternoon. A grand day... managed to get wood & water organi... & went & drafted replies to letters.... After lunch went to Shahat to collect t... belting for the pump & found it wor... but still no water. Sayed arrived a... about 6.30 pm. & I had to report fail... to provide water upstairs or electric lig...

Mon
Aug 7th

I found plenty to do in the office toda... & left the Sayed to have a quiet day. Aft... lunch went off to Messa to see Nobby abo... houses for the Omda & Sheikh Gaddin... Ensa show tonight. Quite good but very low.

Figure 20. *Peter Synge's diary entries of 6-10 August 1944.* Peter Synge Collection.

Called on the Sayed this morning, to my surprise found Ibrahim Shelhi back, heard that he had returned last night with the Sayed's family. Found out the Sayed's requirements & went, phoned Bruce. Went to Cyre with the Omda to get his photo taken, my hair cut & distribute sugar for the poor. & as I had a lot to do tried to come back to lunch. The Dodge stopped at Shahat & wouldn't go at all. Got a lift to x rds & rang up for a truck & came back myself in E.h.S. & lunched about 3 pm. Made arrangements for tomorrow's holiday.

Went & saw the Sayed again & asked him to lunch on Saturday. & spent most of the morning in the office but went to bed after lunch & then prepared my speech for the tea party at the Omar Mukhtar Club. a football match & riding display were arranged for 6 pm & 7 pm & at 7.30 the tea-party. My speech went all right, the Sayed replied, & by 8 pm we were away & I saw him home.

Foggy like all mornings recently. Off to Cyre for a court but unfortunately have to be back for a lunch party at 2 pm in Beda. Got 5 cases done & came back & managed to leave again soon after 3.30 pm & got 10 more cases finished by 6.30 pm & got back by 7.30 pm. Lewis still here investigating the case against Senussi Eff.

In terms of what the 'long johns incident' tells us about Idris, it confirms Cumming's earlier observations in a confidential letter of December 1942, describing Idris as 'a childless hypochondriac with an acute political instinct but few of the attributes of an administrator.'[10] In fact, it emerges from repeated circumstantial evidence that Idris often used his hypochondria to further his political negotiations. He was not just looking for sympathy, he liked to play on his susceptibility to illness to underline his personal importance to the bigger issues of the day. He apparently found this to be an effective way of influencing those he was dealing with as well as testing the limits of their goodwill.

From his own personal acquaintance of Idris in 1944, Peter's later memory was of 'a pale, delicate and ascetic little man with great charm'. This accords with the view of those who attributed to Idris an immense personal charisma and an unworldly, almost mystical, aura, which sometimes seemed to give him a hypnotic hold over those he met. The well-known Middle East travel writer Freya Stark recalled an encounter in Egypt in 1934, when Idris was staying in a modest house on the edge of the desert, west of Alexandria. Observing his 'beautiful breeding, the sheer ignoring of a material world', she went on: 'He sat and talked in a gentle voice, unhurried and detached, with his long slender fingers resting on the arms of his chair as in some Elizabethan portrait; the narrow face and pointed beard and dark eyes might also have belonged to that time, and the outward gentleness run, as it were, on a thread of steel, unpitying and unflinching.'[11]

As time went by, Cumming and his closest colleagues developed an almost limitless tolerance in handling Idris's tactics of delay and surprise, as will be seen in Chapters 9–11. British calculations in terms of the value of their alliance with the Sanussis always had to accommodate the unpredictable character of Idris himself.

The diary extracts included here contain plenty of clues relating to Idris's activities and interests during his supposedly 'private' stay in al-Bayda between 6 August and 7 September. Water and electricity supplies to the Rommel House were unreliable, but 'his family' (probably his wife and her relatives) arrived unexpectedly to join him on 8 August. In the following days, Peter hosted his own formal welcome to Idris at the local Omar Mukhtar Club and also hosted a lunch for him. Subsequent visitors included Brigadier Duncan Cumming, Colonel J. F. P. Maclaren

---

[10] D. C. Cumming, 'Summary of factors relating to the administration of Cyrenaica', 10 December 1942, FO 1015/71.

[11] F. Stark, *East is West*, London, 1945, p79.

and leading members of the Sanussi clan including Abu al-Qasim al-Sanussi, Sayed Safi al-Din and Sayed Izz al-Din. At the end of August, a large number of Benghazi notables arrived to put intense pressure on Idris to extend his stay and it was shortly after this that he decided to spend the last weeks of Ramadan in the much warmer climate of the seaside capital.

One overall point of longer-term significance arising from Idris's time in al-Bayda was that he was obviously very keen to visit and identify possible future places of residence in different parts of the territory. For the BMA at least, this could be taken as a sure sign that the visit had made him think seriously about moving to Cyrenaica on a permanent basis. The big question that no one could answer at this stage was when Idris might decide that the time was right for such a move.

## FROM THE DIARY

### 20 July

*I went off at 2p.m. to meet the Sayed at Lamluda and got there before 3p.m. and had to wait till about 5.15p.m. before they arrived and then I found I had to come back in my own truck as there was no room in the Sayed's car, and had difficulty in keeping up as they drove very fast. The horsemen at various intervals all fired off their rifles and some galloped alongside for a short distance. We stopped at Shahat crossroads and Bakar was introduced to the Sayed, and then a jam began and we only moved just in time.*

*Horsemen at intervals along the road fired their rifles in spite of the Sayed's request not to, and in Beda [al-Bayda] there was a solid line of people with rifles on each side of the road all firing. However all went well and he wasn't overwhelmed, though as soon as he was in the house a huge crowd surged up to the door and a band of fanatics with drums danced themselves silly outside. We left the house after showing him over it, and I went back about 9.30 to see if anything was wanted and found the Sayed having dinner with a large party. I stayed and talked for a bit and then left.*

### 21 July (Friday)

*People were firing their rifles most of last night at intervals and the Sayed complained when we went to see him this morning at 9.15. He didn't want to pray at Sidi Rafa today so there was nothing until the lunch at 1.30, which was held in a tent under a cypress tree on the Gareega road. All went well until the hand kissing ceremony began when there was pandemonium but the police did very well and order was kept. At 4p.m. we returned to the house and the Sayed had ½ hour's rest to let the crowd get to the square and then he made a speech from the top of the PTO [Posts and Telephones Office] building. The square was filled with horsemen and the other square in front of the office was full of men. At 5.30 we returned to the house and at 6.30 went to watch the riding display. Hussein Taher rode but fell off and had to be taken to hospital, otherwise all went well, and the show ended in a parade of horsemen headed by the mounted police and finished about 8p.m. Cinema show this evening ... an Egyptian film.*

### 22 July (Saturday)
*Still cool and pleasant. Went to the office for a bit and left at 11.30 for Battisti as the Sayed wanted to see the place. Took the Gareega road and got there about noon and it only took five minutes to see it so we were miles too early and decided to go and inspect a vineyard at Saf Saf, which made it about right and we arrived at Shahat at 1.15p.m. Great crowds and rifle firing but all very orderly. Had a goodish lunch and went up to the tent to the south of the town at 3.15p.m. Speeches first and then the hand kissing which took just over an hour. The police did well.*

*The Sayed was presented with a horse and a saddle said to cost £100 each and the horse was ridden in the display and is quite a fine animal. One man was shot by accident otherwise there were no incidents and we left about 6p.m. and were back by 6.30. Beda absolutely deserted and all has returned to normal. Had an early bed.*

### 23 July (Sunday)
*Had a bit of a lie in today but not very long. Breakfasted at 9a.m. and went to see the Sayed later. Left at 11.30 for el Gareeb for the Dorsa lunch. Much hotter today. Went through the Wadi Kuf but the driver went unnecessarily slowly and we took longer than we need have and didn't arrive till 1.0p.m. The setting was a very pretty one and the whole scene very picturesque.*

*A big reception tent was prepared for the Sayed and it was intended to introduce a few sheikhs but everybody started to crowd in so the tent had to be cleared. After a cup of coffee we went to the lunch place, which was made of beams of wood and leaves and was rather pleasant. An enormous lunch which went on from 1.30 to 3.30 and then we sat waiting for tea till 4.15. Then the Sayed made a short speech and two others followed and then he went on to Barce and I returned here, and was back in my bumpy old truck in just over an hour. The Brigadier and Col Anderson were at the lunch.*

*Hoped to have a quiet evening but am told there has been an inter-tribal fight, over a well.*

## 25 July

*Morning in the office. [Major] Laurie rang up to suggest we meet about the well dispute between Faidia and Guigab and decide whose territory it is in. Abeidat are living in it and Hasa are watering from it. Went off after lunch and picked up Mudir and Bakar at Shahat, and met Laurie who was accompanied by [Major] Thackrah and Phelps at the well. We sat down to a chinwag and tea in a house and after a lot of talk it was decided that the Hasa should continue to drink from the well between dawn and 4p.m. and the rest of the time the garden should have water. The Abeidat have been trailing their coats [i.e. been deliberately provocative], aided by the Mudir of Guigab, and have dug a pit without permission near the wellhead, and animals see the water and naturally want to drink and the pit is inside the garden area.*

## 6 August (Sunday)

*Still no water although the pump was working last night. No wood, no water, no truck and no-one about and the Sayed arrives [from Benghazi] this afternoon. A grand day. Managed to get wood and water organised and went and drafted replies to letters. After lunch went to Shahat to collect the belting for the pump and found it working but still no water.*

*Sayed arrived about 6.30p.m. and I had to report failure to provide water upstairs or electric light.*

## 7 August

*Found plenty to do in the office today and left the Sayed to have a quiet day.*

## 8 August

*Called on the Sayed this morning and to my surprise found Ibrahim Sheikh back and heard that he had returned last night with the Sayed's family. Found out the Sayed's requirements and went and phoned Barce.*

## 9 August

*Went and saw the Sayed again and asked him to lunch on Saturday and spent most of the morning in the office but went to bed after lunch and then prepared my speech for the tea party at the Omar Mukhtar Club. A football match and riding display were arranged for 6p.m. and 7p.m. and at 7.30 the tea party. My speech went all right and the Sayed replied, and by 8p.m. we were away and I saw him home.*

## 10 August

*Foggy like all mornings recently. Off to Susa for a court but unfortunately have to be back for a lunch party at 2p.m. in Beda. Got 5 cases done and came back and managed to leave again soon after 3.30p.m. and got 10 more cases finished by 6.30p.m. and got back by 7.30p.m. Lewis still here investigating the case against Senussi Eff.*[12]

## 11 August (Friday)

*Had a pretty busy day with a good deal to be done after two days away from the office. Sayed Idris went to Zaweit Beda at noon. I went for a ride this evening and had quite a good gallop.*

## 12 August (Saturday)

*Went and saw the Sayed after breakfast and then had to sign a remand warrant for Senussi Eff[endi], who has to go to prison in Derna. We are all sorry for him as he was a good officer but he has apparently made his name stink in Cyrene and he must be charged and tried.*

*Had a lot to do in preparation for my lunch party and the Sayed arrived a bit early and we had to wait for 20 mins before the food was brought, though it was all ready. It wasn't a very good meal but it might have been worse. Had Bel Gasim*[13] *and the Mudir as well, and they left almost immediately.*

*The Brig arrived about 4.30 and went to see the Sayed and stayed till after 7p.m. and I hung about waiting. He went away about 7.40p.m. He asked me if I wanted to go to Kufra. I said "No".*

## 13 August (Sunday)

*A nice lazy day. Wrote letters before lunch and went to bed afterwards and for a ride at 5p.m. Went to the cemetery to see Keyes' grave. The cross and body have been removed, and the* ghaffir *[watchman] wasn't there. We don't yet know who took them away.*[14]

## 14 August

*Held a court today p.m. as I seemed to have a lot to do in the morning, but there were very few cases ready. The witnesses were here in the morning but*

[12] Sanussi Effendi, also referred to as Sanussi Kaddum, was the 'smart police officer' whose case of abuse of power was discussed in Chapter 5.

[13] Abu al-Qasim al-Sanussi, BMA official and *qaimaqam* of Benghazi, cousin of Sayyid Mohammed Idris.

[14] Both the body and the cross were removed at the request of the family of Lt Col Geoffrey Keyes VC, who was reburied at the Benghazi War Cemetery, while the cross was taken to his family's churchyard in Buckinghamshire. E. Keyes, *Geoffrey Keyes of the Rommel Raid*, London, 1956, p263. H. Foot, *A Start in Freedom*, London, 1964, p81.

*disappeared when told to come in the evening. Sayed Safi el Din and son arrived this evening though we were warned [sic] from Derna that he wasn't coming.*[15]

## 15 August
*The Sayed has a cold today and has said he won't go to Faidia. I went there and Cyrene.*

## 16 August
*Did not go to Cyrene for a court today. Having great difficulty with the phone, which is an awful nuisance. Col Maclaren arrived about 5.30p.m. and went to see the Sayed. New landing in the south of France yesterday.*

## 17 August
*Col Maclaren feeling ill today and not coming to the lunch party at Apollonia. Started at 12 as the Sayed didn't want to be late, so of course we were early and arrived about 1.10p.m. in spite of driving very slowly. A very good lunch but much too much of it of course. Finished about 3.15 and then went up to the 'Filtro' where we sat and the Sayed made tea and we ate fruit, and about 4.45 went to the airfield where there was a riding display. The Sayed sat in his car to watch. We started back about 5.30p.m. It was quite a good day. Maclaren has a very heavy cold.*

## 18 August
*Another Sidi Rafa festival and all the Barasa here riding about and letting off their rifles. The Sayed went and watched in the evening but I didn't go with him and went for a ride at 6p.m. Maclaren stayed in bed all day.*

## 19 August (Saturday)
*Had a conference with Maclaren most of the morning. … Just before Maclaren left, the Sayed sent a note to say he would like to see him and me, so we went up and found that he was suffering from colitis or something and didn't like the cold and damp here because he had forgotten to bring his warm woollies and he wants to go back to Cairo next week. He also wanted the Borghi house at Abiar done up, and Maclaren was taking notes for an hour.*

*He wouldn't come to Faidia, so I had to go and tell the disappointed populace. I sat with the sheikhs and watched the "Meyz" [an unknown word, perhaps suggesting a display or show] and then they started telling me their troubles. The wretched well at Oweinat Gheith had been closed by order of the*

---

[15] Sayyid Safi al-Din al-Sanussi, a first cousin of Sayyid Mohammed Idris and brother of the former Grand Sanussi, Sayyid Ahmed al-Sharif.

*police and I decided to go and find the Mudir of Guigab and if necessary post police to allow the Hasa to drink but we found that the police had given the order without authority.*

## FROM THE MEMOIR

*[Idris] sent for me and said: "I must go back to Egypt." This was a bombshell and I knew that if he broke Ramadan and left Cyrenaica everybody would say that he had had a disagreement with the British, so I asked him why and he eventually told me that he had brought no warm clothes with him and he found it too cold after all the years in Egypt. I suggested that it would be easy to send someone to fetch warm clothes but he said he couldn't trust anybody and must go himself. I told him what I feared and then said that I could lend him some warm vests and pants and a woollen scarf if that was really all he wanted and I went straight back to my quarters and got them out and gave them to him. He was delighted and to my great relief he agreed to stay.*

*In due course, I got them back with many thanks but I have always felt a little disappointed that nobody ever recognised that I had prevented a crisis developing by making it possible for him to stay the full length of his visit as announced.[16]*

*Sayed Idris, later to be officially recognised as Amir of Cyrenaica and later still as King of Libya, was a pale, delicate and ascetic little man with great charm and was revered by all his countrymen. The Senussi sect was very austere and all its followers kept strictly to the tenets of Islam. It was most noticeable that they kept Ramadan as a strict fast and did not, like the Egyptians, make it an occasion for all night feasting and revels. Many of the Senussi would not even swallow their spittle during the daylight hours and, after a very ordinary meal taken soberly and quietly some considerable time after sunset, would retire to bed until the early hours, when, after prayers, they would take a light meal before dawn.*

## FROM THE DIARY

[Ramadan had started on 20 August]

### 25 August
*Committal proceedings for Senussi Kaddum.*

---

[16] Peter Synge's description of the incident illustrates how Idris would often exaggerate an illness and emphasise his distrust of those in his own entourage as a means of testing the loyalty of potential personal allies. As things turned out, Peter never became a close confidant although several other BMA officers were drawn into much more long-lasting relationships with Idris.

## 26 August (Saturday)

*Went to Faidia for the Hasa/Abeidat meeting, which started at about 11.0a.m. For one hour compliments were passed and then it was suggested we went to Sidi Sbag to see the Awakla, so we went there and sat for 2½ hours while they said they wanted the Hasa out altogether. Laurie wouldn't give in and agreed that it was just, so I had to bow, though it seemed to me all wrong. The Abeidat refused to come back to Faidia so I had to go and tell them and of course the Hasa were furious. They hadn't had a chance to state their case and were being turned out. Went to see the well at Belgis where Hasa are supposed to drink and found it was not enough for all the Hasa. … Got in at 7p.m … and was met by Butler to say that the Sayed is not now going.*

## 27 August (Sunday)

*Went to phone Laurie and he promised to do what he could.*

## 29 August

*Maclaren appeared with an American Naval Lieut who wanted to see the Sayed, so we went up about 6p.m. and saw him. He was sitting in the sun to keep warm and told us that the Benghazi notables came in waves on Saturday and told him he couldn't go because it would look bad and he was very angry. He wants to go and stay in Benghazi until he goes back because it is too cold here.*

## 30 August

*Maclaren saw the Sayed all morning and about 2.15p.m. Sayed Izz el Din[17] arrived and had to be entertained. Maclaren saw him and looked after him and he went off about 4.30 and so did Col Maclaren. Went for a ride at 6p.m. and fell off for the first time. The pony waved his head about and put it between his legs and I fell off over his head in front of a convoy of vehicles. Very infra dig. A bit bruised but nothing much. Had electric light for the first time tonight.*

## 2 September (Saturday)

*Went to see the Sayed at 10.0a.m. and he expressed a desire to see the house at Cyrene, occupied by RAF and originally [Rodolfo] Graziani's villa and then a CAO's house, so I took him along. It is a very pleasant house and well shut in and with a big garden. Rather small for him though, as it only has five rooms and no servants' quarters.*

---

[17] Sayyid Izz al-Din al-Sanussi, a distant cousin of Sayyid Mohammed Idris and one of the first of the family to begin occupying vacant Italian farms in Cyrenaica.

*Met Webster, who was tight [i.e. drunk], but he told me that people were saying that the Sayed was leaving Beda because I had not looked after him properly and Reid was saying I ought to be sacked. It did not worry me because it isn't true, but I determined to tell the Brig*

### 3 September (Sunday)
*Saw the Brig who was surprised when I told him what I had heard, but promised to take it up with Reid.*

### 5 September
*Went to see the Sayed at 9.30 and took [Major] Johnson in and said we would go with him [Idris] to Mamelli, but we didn't leave till nearly 11.0a.m. and the car had petrol trouble about 4 times but we got there via Faidia by noon, and he [Idris] did not stay long and we came back the same way and were in by 1.30p.m.*

### 7 September
*Sayed Idris left punctually at 9.0a.m., so that responsibility has been removed. Butler went with him to Barce.*

# chapter 7

# ADVENTURES IN THE DESERT
## AGEDABIA, SEPTEMBER 1944–MAY 1945

ESPITE THE FACT that Captain Peter Synge had persuaded Sayyid Mohammed Idris to continue his visit as planned, it is very hard to gauge his subsequent standing in the eyes of Brigadier Duncan Cumming. Was it a sign of increased trust in Peter's abilities that Cumming offered him the management of the remote desert oasis of Kufra? Whatever the truth, Peter turned this offer down, no doubt because of the extreme remoteness of Kufra, whereupon at the end of August Cumming proposed Agedabia (Ajdabiyya), a posting that he was happy to accept.

As a trading centre where coastal peoples and remote desert communities interacted, Agedabia had a history as an important centre for the Sanussiyya. It also connected Cyrenaica with communities along the Gulf of Sirte to the west. Only two years earlier, Rommel had demonstrated its strategic importance by sending his forces out from the town on long-distance manoeuvres that succeeded in outflanking the British forces concentrated along the coast.

On 7 September, having bid farewell to Idris, who spent the remaining ten days of Ramadan in Benghazi, before his eventual return to Cairo at the end of the month of fasting, Peter himself left al-Bayda on 12 September, reaching Agedabia on 14 September. His predecessor, Major C. A. Collard, was helpful in showing him around his new beat, and took him on the long three-day round trip to Marada oasis, a place where the population were at the time suffering from a severe epidemic of malaria. Peter soon also travelled to the more remote group of oases around Jalo.

Peter's initiation into life on the desert fringes was interrupted in October when he received news that his wife and their children were now on their way back from South Africa to Egypt. Once they had reached Alexandria, he asked for leave, and, after a difficult journey by truck and then the train from Tobruk, was reunited with his family on 31 October after their enforced two-year separation. He made the most of the social life in his beloved Alexandria, where the family soon found accommodation and schools, and returned to work in late November. Peter's regular diary entries covered the period of leave but stopped shortly afterwards, in February 1945. Although a subsequent diary may have been lost, it is also possible that, with his family more within reach, he no longer felt the need for the daily companionship that keeping the diary had provided.

Despite being written many years later, the memoir provides a good summary of his experiences in the Agedabia district and throws an interesting light on the local realities of 1944/45. Here, the ever-changing front lines between the Allies and the Axis forces throughout 1941 and 1942 had left many places heavily battle-scarred. Moreover, in the 1940s, which was long before any oil was discovered in Libya, there were simply no roads into the desert, only camel caravan routes and rough tracks whose condition depended on the surrounding terrain and the quantities of blown sand in any one area.

The last of Peter's surviving diary extracts end on a note of irritation and frustration over his lack of further promotion, as several of his British Military Administration colleagues were now overtaking him in seniority. Meeting one who had just been promoted to major he 'found it impossible to congratulate him ... as he spends his time in the bar'. Indeed by this stage, he and his fellow officers were apparently so often either nervous or stressed that the availability of alcohol seems almost to have become a key requisite in maintaining morale.

Although Peter claimed to be 'determined to write to the Brigadier' to make his case for promotion, any such effort was unsuccessful as he was not promoted until more than a year later, long after Duncan Cumming had left Cyrenaica for a more senior posting in Cairo.

## FROM THE DIARY

[Arrival at Agedabia]

### 14 September

*Left Benghazi at 2p.m. for Agedabia, and arrived at 5.30p.m. Shower of rain at Magrun. Road bad between Ghamines and Magrun but otherwise not too bad. Hemmings arrived about 7p.m. going to Tripoli.*

**15 September**

*Very pleasantly fresh at nights here and much pleasanter than Benghazi. Spent the day looking through important files until I could absorb no more. My 8 cwt [truck] being made serviceable for tomorrow's trip to Marada. Called on the Mudir and was much impressed by Collard's methodical organisation. Also called on Saleh Pasha el Aterwich, the Mustashar. Col Hammond the new PMO [Principal Medical Officer] arrived tonight to come with us to Marada. A far better man than his predecessors.*

[Trip to Marada oasis]

**16 September (Saturday)**

*Got up before 7.0a.m. and hoped to get away by 8a.m. but didn't leave till 8.30, with 3 vehicles, 8 cwt, 15 cwt and a Fordson car. Got to Mersa Brega by 10.30 and stopped for ¼ hour and reached Agheila at 11.15. Left Agheila at noon and drove over desert tracks. One soft patch bogged the 15 cwt and while it was being got out we had lunch. Road got progressively worse and about 3p.m. [Major] Collard suggested driving so we stopped and the truck wouldn't start, which delayed us ½ hour. Road frightful at first but then much better. Collard drove pretty hard. Country very dull and typically desert. Passed a salt marsh about 4p.m. Fordson broke down about 5p.m. but only a choked feed. Collard tried to shoot a gazelle but without success – the only one we saw. Reached a point within sight of Marada about 6.30p.m. and camped down. Quite a cool wind. Turned in about 9.30 and slept very well though I woke at 2.30a.m. and again about 6a.m.*

**17 September (Sunday)**

*Very damp and quite a heavy dew. I had no ground sheet or coat to cover my clothes and they were damp. Left at 8.45 and were in Marada by 9.30. Queer shaped hills of clay with flat tops, sticking up out of the salt flats and the earth all broken by escaping gas. Date palms and mud huts and a fort is all that the place consists of. The PMO [Principal Medical Officer] went to hunt for mosquitoes and look at ill people and Collard and I saw the Mudir who looks very ill having had malaria 2 months ago. Found a 15 cwt police truck with a flat tyre there, which had come by itself contrary to instructions. Had lunch and left about 3.0p.m. and drove almost non-stop until 6.30p.m., though Collard wanted to go further. Fired at tins with a service rifle before sunset and looked for the new moon but didn't see it. Lovely sunset. Turned in about 10p.m.*

[End of Ramadan]

## 18 September

*Up at 7.30 but didn't get away till after 9.0a.m., Collard driving the 8 cwt. Saw a lot of bustard and I tried my hand with the rifle at one but missed and stalked another and lost it. Then I thought I saw it and took careful aim and fired, and it was only a piece of paper. The PMO went after a flock with a gun but lost them. Got to Agheila about 11.0a.m. and saw the Mudir again and had tea and left at noon with the Mudir to see reported cases of typhoid but suspected typhus. PMO went with Mudir and we came on. Lunched at Mersa Brega and left at 2p.m., and shortly after put up two bustard right on the road. I went after them and stalked them and fired two shots, which missed and then they disappeared completely – must have flattened down on the ground. Got back at 3.45 and found Mossy here and also Misson and Coles, two other mess members, so we were seven in the mess. PMO arrived about 5p.m. and reported two cases of typhus but not bad. Some doubt as to whether the Eid [end of Ramadan] had begun and we didn't see the new moon but were told it began this morning.*

## 19 September

*Got up later today as it is a holiday. After some work in the office, went to look at wells nearby which need repairs. Plenty of water everywhere round here and it is good water but very hard.*

*Brig was supposed to arrive today but is coming tomorrow … Had tea with the Mudir, Saleh Pasha Aterwich there. Played bridge this evening. Misson and Coles are very poor. Lyall doesn't play.*

## 20 September

*Brig ill and not coming at all as he is going to Cairo for the weekend. … Went for a walk round the town and Collard showed me the warehouses etc. Stopped for coffee with a merchant.*

## 21 September

*Took my first court today and had two cases – one of sodomy. Gave 3 years.*

*Kufra convoy supposed to arrive today but heard it only left Benghazi at 5p.m. Charles Shackleton rang up to say he is off on Saturday. His family left South Africa on 17th. Hope Maidie [Peter's wife] did too. Very cool weather here. Mac [Macintosh] arrived about 10.30p.m. with one vehicle only. Other two in convoy not been seen.*

## 22 September

*Went to Zwetina [Zuwaytinah] with Collard, Macintosh and the Egyptian doctor. Perfect day and a lovely place with a lagoon protected by a reef. A boat*

*full of large fish had just arrived so we bought some and had it for dinner. I
went for a run along the beach.*

### 25 September
*First day in harness here. Had a lot of visitors and busy day. Maj Moir and
officers for GMC [general military court] arrived p.m. Played bridge after
dinner.*

### 26 September
*Court sat at 2.30 and finished at 5p.m. Sentence of 5 yrs for murder in
revenge.*

### 27 September
*Bought a Misurata rug for £7. Walked round the Suq with White in the morn-
ing.*

### 29 September
*Letters from Maidie. She has still not started but hopes to get away soon.
Ghibli [sandstorm] today and very dusty and hot.*

[Trip to Jalo oasis]

### 3 October
*Got away at 9.40a.m. and did 15 miles in the first ¾ hour but had to wait
for 3 tonner so that our speed is 15mph or less … 3 tonner didn't turn up. …
Went back … found Lomax driving it on another track. Was very angry and
read the riot act. He might have missed us altogether and would never know
it. … Got terribly held up by soft sand round Sahabi and all the vehicles got
stuck in turn. 3 tonner had to have attention and held us up and we eventually got to Bir Qwetin at just after 6p.m. and decided to stay the night. 77
miles in 8 hours!!*

### 4 October
*Got away soon after 8.30[a.m.] and track improved almost at once. Flat
hard sand as far as the eye can see, with the kilo posts marking the track.
… Reached a fork in the road at about noon and saw Awjila, and our guides
then said we should have to go back to get to Awjila as there was no track
across. Waited for Lomax and then went back and got to Awjila about
12.45p.m. Saw the Mudir and he took us round the town. Picturesque and
very ancient mosques with 6 or 9 conical domes. All made of mud or mud
bricks but one with stone arches, said to have been built over 400 years ago*

*and with Egyptian workmen. Had lunch in the school and then met the sheikhs and went on to Jalo at 4p.m. arriving about 5p.m. The Mudir away at Jikarra. Saw round the town with PMO and inspected wells and then settled down in quite comfortable quarters but flies are awful.*

### 5 October

*Went to Jikarra and met the Mudir just riding into Jalo on a camel so took him with me. Very soft sand at the entrance to the town so left the truck and walked. … No mud or stone huts but all made of palm leaves. Brought back a prisoner and got back at 2p.m. … Went to the office at 4p.m. and talked to the Mudir and paid all wages etc…*

### 6 October

*Held a court this morning whilst PMO attended the sick. Had two cases and sentenced them both. Met all the sheikhs and talked to them for a bit. Had an early lunch and got away just after 1p.m. Reached Awjila in ¾ hr but Lomax didn't turn up till 2.15[p.m.]. Got away at 2.30 and cut across the desert and reached the track after 18 miles. Got to Qwetin at 5.30p.m. and hoped to go on to Sahabi but Lomax was held up and didn't arrive till 6.30 so we camped there. Cold and damp tonight.*

### 7 October

[After several breakdowns in the desert] *Left the truck and came on with PMO in his vehicle and travelled in comfort. Got in soon after 4p.m.*

### 21 October

*Letter from Maidie arrived at lunchtime posted in Alex on 18th. She is staying in a pension and says the villa is too small but she is taking a flat under Mrs Watt's. They landed on 15th so the journey was quick. Am greatly relieved that they are back. Wrote off asking for leave straight away.*

[Departure for Alexandria]

### 28 October (Saturday)

*Very hot and muggy and rainy looking and thousands of flies. Tried to get away by 9 but didn't get away till 9.40a.m. Slight rain on the way. Had lunch at the officers' club and left for Barce at 2p.m. Very black clouds out at sea and quite heavy rain before Tokra. Got to Barce at 4p.m. and went and saw various people including Thorby and the Brig. Went round to [Major Sholto] Douglas's house at 6.30 and found that my suitcases had not been covered with the ground sheet which I had bought specially and were soaking and the rain had got inside. Fortunately I could dry them in front of Douglas's stove. Dined with the Brig and played bridge afterwards.*

## 29 October (Sunday)

*Mist early and very damp. Went round to HQ just before 9.0a.m. and got away at 9.35a.m. Two buses today as a lot of people are going on leave – some on home leave. Got to Beda [al-Bayda] at 11.30, where [Major] Johnson[1] joined us and left at 12.30. Got to Derna at 2.15. Had to sit in the back of a 3 tonner and it is not too comfortable. Stayed with Collard, [Major] Grisewood[2] was there too. Talked for a bit and then I went for a walk in the harbour, which is silting up with seaweed. Went to the Club at 6.30 till 8.0p.m. Real English beer there. A great treat. Went to bed about 11.0p.m.*

## 30 October

*Up early and ready to start at 8.45 but E-P [Edward Evan Evans-Pritchard] not up yet having been up late last night. I had to call him at just before 9. Got away at 9.40. Road bad but we were a full load and not too uncomfortable. Stopped at Tmini for a few minutes and got to Tobruk just after 2p.m. Stopped for a minute or two at the Club but everything shut so we went up to railhead and after getting everything aboard had a meal at Naafi. Train left at 6.30p.m. Had a few drinks and went to bed about 10p.m.*

## 31 October

*Woke up about 6.30a.m. and found we were still 50 km from Similla where we were due at 5.30. A lot of mist in the night and we went slowly. Got in just before 9.0a.m. and got bkfst. Left at 9.30 and went well till Daba where we stopped for an hour and then we heard that a train ahead had broken down and we would have to wait till 2p.m. Got to Amriya at 5.30 where the train had to be searched by MPs [Military Police] before we were allowed to feed and we had had nothing since bkfst. Meal consisted of a weak stew and bread and weak warm tea. Had to change into the Alex train, which didn't leave till 7.30p.m. Very close and hot. Got to Sidi Gaber at 8p.m. and arrived at 812 Av Farouk at 8.30p.m. Maidie had given me up for the day and was having supper upstairs with Mrs Watt but I couldn't allow that. Children fast asleep.*

---

[1] CAO of Derna.
[2] BMA Controller of Agriculture.

## FROM THE MEMOIR

*Agedabia was a desert district and it included the oases of Jalo, Jaghbub[3] and Marada. Jalo lies about 180 miles due south of Agedabia and it was a two-day journey by a fairly well defined track to get there. It was a walled town and incredibly dirty and never before or since have I seen so many flies as I encountered there. They settled on face and hands in swarms and it was impossible to do any work without having an attendant with a horsehair fly whisk keeping them off. Eating was a problem and the only way of keeping the flies from swarming over the food was to put it in a drawer in a desk in a darkened room, opening the drawer just long enough to take a mouthful and shut it again.*

*The track to Jalo ran over very rough and undulating country for the first 80 miles, which included a patch about ½ a mile of soft yellow powder which it was almost impossible to negotiate without getting stuck at least once. There was a ruined Italian fort at a place called Hassinat, where we invariably spent the first night and after that the going improved and it was generally possible to cover the remaining 100 miles or so between breakfast and lunch. For most of this stretch, the desert is flat and hard and absolutely featureless, but one had to be careful not to drive along tracks made by previous vehicles, which had broken the top crust and exposed soft sand underneath. As long as one drove on virgin desert one could drive as fast as the vehicles would go for quite long stretches but one had to keep one's eyes skinned for dips and depressions and, unless one was navigating by sun compass, had to be careful to keep the main track to right or left in sight, otherwise one could lose it altogether. On my first trip and in one of these flat hard stretches, we noticed some peculiar tracks crossing the main track diagonally, and we stopped to investigate. The tracks were similar to what one might expect a very light tank to make but this was a single track and there was no known vehicle that proceeded on a single track. It was obviously profitless to follow the tracks in the hopes of finding what had made them and we proceeded on our way completely mystified. Several months, and two trips, later, the mystery was solved. It happened to be blowing fairly hard that day but not enough to whip up the sand and reduce visibility which was very good. In that flat featureless landscape, where one never saw a living thing, anything moving caught the eye at once. At first we saw a small black dot away to the right and moving slowly and steadily on a converging course. As we approached, we saw it was an inanimate object being blown along by the wind and, when we got near enough to identify it, it turned out to be an empty 4 gallon petrol 'flimsy', of which there must have*

---

[3] Unlike the other oases mentioned, Jaghbub is located in the remote east of Cyrenaica, near the Egyptian border; it was a key Sanussi centre where non-Muslims were generally forbidden entry.

*been millions discarded by the British Army all over the desert, rolling on its side over and over and leaving in its wake the apparently single tank track, which had so mystified us on our first trip. Hundreds of these petrol tins must have been blown by the wind for hundreds or perhaps thousands of miles to fetch up eventually perhaps in the Northern Sudan against a small desert shrub and form the base of a new sand dune.*

*The oasis of Marada lies 80 miles due south of El Agheila at the base of the Gulf of Sirte, and to get there one drove down the coast road to El Agheila about 70 miles from Agedabia and then turned south over a very rough and rocky track. In a 15 cwt Dodge one could average only 10 miles an hour and when I returned from my first trip to Marada I had worn a large hole in the back of my shorts from rubbing against the back of the seat. The oasis lay at the edge of a very large area of salt beds, from which the Italians had been extracting potassium sulphate before the war, but in spite of this the springs of water of which there were over 100 in the oasis, were absolutely sweet and pure, and I remember being amazed to see one of these springs welling up out of the ground within five yards of the edge of the salt beds. The inhabitants of Marada were an indolent lot and terribly debilitated by malaria, which was rife in the oasis. As malaria was unknown anywhere else in North Africa, troops were not issued with prophylactics, but anyone likely to visit Marada was warned not to spend a night in the place, and we would make camp about five miles out and visit the oasis in daylight. The products of the place were dates and maize and it was very productive of these.*

*It happened that the officer in charge of the Police detachment at Agedabia, an Ulsterman from Londonderry, had been a fishery expert before the war. He was an interesting man and I always took him with me on my desert journeys because his endless stories helped to pass the time on these dull and wearisome trips. On his first visit with me to Marada, he told me that the oasis of Siwa in Egypt had been cleared of malaria by the introduction into the springs there of a small fish which fed on mosquito larvae and he thought that this could be done equally well in Marada. Most of the springs had been dug round to form wells or pools from which the inhabitants drew their water supplies and these were the breeding grounds of the mosquito. As soon therefore as we got back to Agedabia I started the ball rolling and with the help of an enthusiastic PMO a consignment of these fish was produced in a remarkably short space of time and flown to Benghazi. We of course were only notified after their arrival there and, as soon as we heard the news, Major Kinnaird drove straight off to Benghazi, where he found that the fish in a glass tank had been sitting on the airfield for than 24 hours without a change of water. The original number of fish was said to be 400 and he counted 300 dead but under his care the remainder survived. He had to make elaborate plans for the transportation of the fish to Marada and after two or three days he arrived with the fish in 44 gallon drums with one end removed and covered with a muslin top, and almost immediately set off again for El Agheila, where he would spend the night so as to make an early start in the morning on the rough journey to Marada, which he reckoned would take 15 hours at no more than 5 mph. He had to take spare closed tanks of water to replenish the drums which would be slopping over all the way. I arranged to leave Agedabia the following morning and catch him up somewhere near Marada, which I did and I had already made camp when he drove up after dark. Next morning we drove in to Marada and the operation began. It must be explained that the fish were fingerlings of only 1½' to 2' in length, and he had no idea how many had survived and had not been able to see them since he decanted them into the drums two days before, because the only drums he had been able to obtain were so rusty that the water had immediately turned red and was quite opaque. He had prepared a 4 gallon petrol flimsy with the top cut off and the bottom perforated with small holes, and this he used as a scoop to catch the fish in the drums. He decided to put six fish into as many springs as the fish lasted out, and we hoped it might be as many as ten springs, but as it turned out we were able to introduce 6 fish into no less than 30 springs that day, and during the operation not one dead fish was found. This was no small triumph for Major Kinnaird, who deserved a medal for his care and attention to detail. There was probably no other man in the Middle East at the time who could have successfully carried out the operation, and yet I doubt if his name is even known in Cyrenaica, and he certainly did not receive any public recognition. … The fish flourished and before I left it had been possible to transfer their progeny to other springs.*

*It was a curious anachronism that although I was in charge of the District I was only a Captain and one of my subordinate officers was senior to me in rank. I pointed this out to higher authority, mentioning that my predecessor had been a Major and that my assistant, who was a Lieutenant and due for promotion could not be promoted as long as I remained a Captain. I got no reply to this approach but shortly afterwards my assistant was promoted to Captain but there was no promotion for me!*

## FROM THE DIARY

[After returning to Agedabia from his leave in Alexandria]

### 14 December

*Court today. I judged 10 cases before lunch and one after lunch which lasted from 2.45p.m. to 5.45p.m.*

**15 December**

*A bad day. Mudir came and reported that money was missing from the tax receipts. … Summoned the clerks and then asked for Lyall. He asked to see me alone and then said he knew about it and had agreed to make it up himself because it was his fault and he hadn't told me because he didn't want a court of inquiry. The amount involved is £30 and I couldn't believe that he had lost it and it must have been taken by one of the clerks. I said I wouldn't say anything officially if he made it up but I decided to look into the thing myself and found that no check had been made since early October and about 16 Oct the revenue clerk decided to start putting some of the amount into his own pocket. Lyall was busy and didn't check, and receipts bore no resemblance to amounts supposed to be handed in. Spent all afternoon on it and found the amount less than was thought. Col Doyle[4] arrived this evening.*

**17 December (Sunday)**

*Tea party at Omar Mukhtar Club today as it is the Mohammedan New Year.*

**19 December**

*Went off to Zwetina to see about recently enclosed gardens causing trouble. Had tea at Naja [camp] of Sheikh Daw Geawi. Tried to make friends with my horse without result.*

**20 December**

*Horse still very nervous. I got on him but didn't go for a ride and told the groom to see him and he rode round the town to get him used to everything.*

**21 December**

*Went for ride on the horse at 5p.m. and though still a bit nervous he went well. Has a comfortable trot but a very uncomfortable canter. I didn't gallop him because he is unshod and his nails want cutting and one is cracked.*

**25 December**

*Christmas Day! And not a letter or a present from anybody. Had a short carol service in the concert room conducted by CSM Eade to which about 12 men came including we 3 officers. Played soccer afterwards. … Visited the men's mess and gave them a toast and a bottle of beer each and then had our own lunch which was a dull affair. … At 9.30 went round to the men's concert where beer was flowing freely and most of the men were well on.*

---

[4] Commanding Officer of the CDF.

**26 December**

*Mail in at lunch time and only a calendar and a short note from Maidie. I'm thoroughly browned off.*

**27 December**

*Left in 8 cwt [truck] for Benghazi at 9.30 and arrived at 12.15. Handed over confiscated valuables including 200 gold sovereigns and a bag of mail for Syria. Lunched at the Club and then went to Naafi for stores. No whisky or gin. Called on SCAO [Senior Civil Affairs Officer]. Met Vincent Evans who asked me to dinner and then went to 'Saloon Bar' at Torelli.[5] Very good show.*

**28 December**

*Maj Roberts asked me to lunch and I left at 2.45p.m. 8 bottles of beer from my ration stolen in the Mess. Arrived back at Agedabia at 5.45p.m. Got inoculated in Benghazi.*

**29 December**

*Cape Corps concert party arrived just before lunch with Lt Ralston in charge. Ex Sgt Maj of last war and an American South African. Queer card and very amusing. Mail arrived and only one letter from Maidie. Saw the show this evening, which was pretty poor.*

**1 January 1945**

*New Year's Day. A howling west wind blowing and air full of sand. Horrible day. Received notables to tea and sweets at 11.0a.m., and worked in the office. Smart arrived back from Agheila and Kinnaird from Agedabia. Cinema this evening. Quite a good show.*

**4 January**

*Perishing cold and temperature down to 31°. ... Sat in court all morning in my fleece lining and trench coat and tried 3 cases.*

**5 January**

*No letter from Maidie. Lyall promoted Captain wef 25.7.45.*

**6 January**

*ENSA [Entertainments National Service Association] party arrived about 1.30. 15 of them of whom ten are Jews making up an orchestra. ... Had the*

---

[5] A show performed by a travelling ENSA troupe.

*show at 7p.m. and enjoyed it. It was the best all round show I have seen. Sat up till midnight as the manager had a bottle of Scotch.*

### 24 January

*Cols Sillery and White arrived at 5p.m. and decided to stay the night. Lyall went to Benghazi to fetch cash. I rode after lunch. I wanted to talk to Sillery about my promotion but couldn't get him alone. … Determined to write to Brigadier and put my case. The more I think about it the more unfair it seems. Hear that Forman and MacDonald are both Majors. Why should they be and a CAO still remain a Captain, with an assistant [i.e. Lyall] the same rank and a DC [District Commander] as a Major. Am completely browned off.*

### 26 January

*Forman arrived with his crown [i.e. a major's insignia] up. Found it impossible to congratulate him as I think it is a disgrace, as he spends his time in the bar.*

### 27 January

*Sheikh Senussi Mustadi who came with Forman came to see me this morning. He looks younger than he did and is a nice old man.*

### 28 January (Sunday)

*Got up to hear the news at 8.0a.m. Russians still advancing and now less than 100 miles from Berlin. Appalling weather in England and Western Europe and freezing conditions. Wrote a letter to* Illustrated London News *about Arabs' help in 1940 when we appeared to be done for. … Letter from Maidie. Very upset because I accused her of neglecting me as haven't had letters from her twice a week. Played volleyball this afternoon and had Mitarachi in for bridge.*

### 3 February

*Made preparations for the trip to Marada this morning and left 2.50. … Got to Agheila about 5.15p.m. After settling a/cs went for a walk round the town which is an abomination of desolation.*

### 4 February (Sunday)

*About 35 miles from Agheila picked up a black woman who was walking from Agheila to Marada to see her mother. She had left on Friday. She was 15 miles from a well with 45 miles to go and was quite unconcerned. Arrived at Marada at 3.30 and walked round looking at gardens and springs and then climbed the Qara [possibly misspelling of Qasr, or castle] which has an ancient wall round the top and a cave. An Arab showed us a Queen Victoria 1900 penny, which he had picked up here! Had tea with the Mudir and then came home [i.e. to the mess]. Had dinner and then went to a dance. Very dull – only three veiled women with too many clothes on doing a bottom waggle. Stayed about an hour.*

### 5 February

*Dreamed a lot last night but not about the dancing women. ... I had to meet the sheikhs and at about 11.15 we went out in the Jeep to the potash mines and looked round a bit. Huge piles of unprepared potash waiting to be processed but the whole thing has gone to wrack and ruin. Two bubbling wells on the spot. Came back and looked at the aerodrome, which is not as good as it looks from the fort and has a hump in the middle. After lunch went out to Khadra, which is 10 miles west and where all the inhabitants were sent by the Italians in 1942. One very good well there with cold water but dozens of mosquitoes which settled on one everywhere. Got back at 5p.m. and after a mug of tea went down to see the dispensary and then back to the fort. Dinner with the schoolmaster who is brother-in-law of Isra Mahdi the merchant who supplies Marada.*

### 11 February (Sunday)

*The major and I set out in the Jeep for Kasr Haneya but it took us an hour and a half to get there (only 6 miles) owing to three stoppages with water in the petrol. The major cooked lunch and then Eade and a REME [Royal Electrical and Mechanical Engineers] chap with some police came along to explore the place. It is interesting and obviously old and there is a moat all round it cut out of solid rock, and inside at ground level it is all vaulted. It is full of sand and nothing much to be seen but there is supposed to be an underground passage to Agedabia.*

[The daily diary entries stop at this point]

chapter 8

# POST-WAR HIATUS
# AND CONFUSION
CYRENE AND TOBRUK,
JUNE 1945–APRIL 1946

A S THE SECOND WORLD WAR ended with the surrender of
Germany and then Japan in mid-1945, the future of Cyrenaica
and the rest of Libya was hardly a priority in the discussions among the
major powers. Britain had hoped to play a decisive role in determining
the fate of the former Italian colonies in Africa, but clearly there was
no easy consensus on this question in the light of the new realities of
the post-war world, and so Libya became one of the more contentious
of the low-profile issues that had to be postponed for later bargaining.
Looming much larger were the political and economic conditions in
Europe and the future of European possessions like India and those in
South East Asia. Meanwhile, elsewhere in the Middle East, Britain was
facing some uncomfortable new challenges. The escalating conflict between Arabs and Jews in Palestine was rapidly taking centre stage and
threatening to unravel the stitching of Britain's delicate relationship
with the whole Arab world.

Amid all the uncertainty, Britain was weighing up the strategic
advantages of its presence in Cyrenaica. A War Office paper discuss-
ing future planning in 1945 suggested that the existing number of
British Army personnel in the territory could soon be nearly halved
from 29,000 to 15,300, but at the same time the RAF was considering doubling its presence at the different airfields, with its personnel
thought likely to rise from 2,600 to 5,200.[1] The Royal Navy also had an
interest in developing the harbour at Tobruk. But Britain could not be
sure about the future of either Cyrenaica or Tripolitania until a peace
treaty was signed with Italy, an issue on which there was no immediate

---
[1] 'Future Maintenance of Cyrenaica', 28 March 1945, WO 230/196.

progress. For the time being, as the occupying power, the emphasis was simply on Britain's international legal obligation under the Hague Conventions to provide 'care and maintenance' and thus to stop short of establishing permanent institutions.[2]

For the individuals in the British Military Administration in Cyrenaica, reporting as they did to the War Office, the end of international hostilities brought the opportunity for either complete demobilisation or else home leave. The sudden dispersal of many of the BMA's 80 or so members of staff from mid-1945 onwards had consequences for consistency and cohesion in what was in any case a temporary government. The official historian of the period noted that it was 'unfortunately not considered possible to offer reasonably long-term contracts nor to arrange that even a proportion of the officers would be engaged for future employment under the Colonial Office.'[3] To fill the constantly appearing gaps, those available were shifted around from post to post for short periods. And to add to the burden, the BMA was being asked to take over responsibility from both the Royal Navy and the British Army for key services like ports, public works, electricity and firefighting.

At a time when tens of thousands of troops were being shipped back from the Far East through the Suez Canal, the frustrations and delays experienced by Peter Synge and his family in obtaining a passage on a ship to Britain were probably fairly typical, but his memoir provides a revealing insight into the prevailing confusion. His efforts to return again to Cyrenaica were then dogged by bureaucratic inefficiency. All told, this meant that after he took leave in early September 1945 from his latest posting, where he was managing both Barce and Cyrene districts, having expected to be away no longer than two months, Peter was still awaiting a return passage from England over Christmas and well into the New Year.

Peter's memoir reveals that by the time he arrived back in Cyrenaica in January 1946 he found himself all but forgotten. He was at first informed, very perfunctorily, that he was to take over the running of Tobruk, including its harbour with more than 100 sunken ships. It was only after some time that he was able to introduce himself to the new Chief Administrator of the BMA, Brigadier P. B. E. Acland. As soon as

---

[2] The issues surrounding the international negotiations over Libya are explored most fully in S. Kelly, *War and Politics in the Desert: Britain and Libya during the Second World War*, London, 2010, and S. L. Bills, *The Libyan Arena: The United States, Britain and the Council of Foreign Ministers 1945–1948*, Ohio, 1995.

[3] Rennell of Rodd, *British Military Administration of Occupied Territories in Africa during the years 1941–1947*, London, 1948, p457.

Acland heard that Peter had already served three years and was clearly overdue for promotion, he invited him to take up a senior post at head-quarters in Benghazi, marking the start of what would be much the most interesting and challenging (and final) phase of Peter's time in Cyrenaica.

The hasty manner of Peter's initial posting to Tobruk reflects the impact on the BMA of the departure from Cyrenaica of Brigadier Duncan Cumming who, up to September 1945, had paid very close attention to all appointments throughout the country and had run everything with his distinctive personal touch. But Cumming had now taken over in Cairo as Chief Civil Affairs Officer for the Middle East – with responsi-bility for all the occupied enemy territories, including Eritrea, Somalia, Tripolitania and Cyrenaica. This meant that he was deeply involved in diplomatic business most of the time, being called to London on three different occasions for consultations with the government and spend-ing May 1946 in Paris as a member of the UK delegation to the second full meeting of the four-power Council of Foreign Ministers (United States, Britain, France and the Soviet Union).

In Paris, the issues of Libya and Eritrea proved to be sticking points, especially with the Russians, although in October 1946 a clause was accepted in the draft peace treaty with Italy, which provided for Italy's renunciation of sovereignty and for the continuation of the existing British administration for a year after the signing of the treaty (which finally took place in February 1947).[4] This seemed to buy some time for the continuation of the status quo, but there remained huge uncer-tainty about what might follow.[5] Britain may have wanted to maintain its presence through a trusteeship arrangement, but it was far from cer-tain that this would be acceptable to all the Allies or to political opinion on the ground. Speculation was rife in Cairo and other Middle Eastern capitals as different ideas were floated, including the not entirely fanci-ful prospect of Egypt being awarded the trusteeship of Cyrenaica.

To underpin its strong interest in the territory, Britain remained fully invested in its tested ally Sayyid Mohammed Idris, who, for his part, was looking for political benefits from the post-war negotiations and was beginning to draft proposals for the independence of Cyrena-ica – no doubt already well aware that Britain wanted military facilities in return (see Chapter 9). From his base at the Middle East Headquarters

---

[4] Rennell of Rodd, *British Military Administration of Occupied Territories in Africa during the years 1941–1947*, London, 1948, p473 & p536.

[5] For a full account of the negotiations at this stage, see S. L. Bills, *The Libyan Arena: The Unit-ed States, Britain and the Council of Foreign Ministers 1945–1948*, Ohio, 1995, pp37–44.

in Cairo, Cumming was well placed to maintain contact with Idris, who had not yet abandoned his comfortable exile in the city.

There had already been extensive negotiations concerning those houses and farms in Cyrenaica that were to be allocated to Idris personally (primarily the Rommel House in Beda [al-Bayda] and the Borghi Farm at Abiar), as well as discussions about the properties promised to nearly 100 members of his extended family. The process of allocating money and land to the most prominent among the Sanussis had been set in motion before Cumming left Benghazi in 1945 – on 1 January 1945, when Brigadier R. D. H. Arundell had first drafted the outlines and costs of this ambitious settlement scheme. 'There can be no doubt that the Senussi family, who have served us well and have suffered severely at the hands of the Italians, must be allowed to return to their native land,' Arundell had told his bosses in London. 'The problem is how they are to maintain themselves after their return. The family still enjoys such prestige that it would be most damaging to British interests if they were reduced to penury and indignity.'[6]

Arundell had stressed that he considered the problem of the future of the Sanussi family as 'perhaps the most difficult and dangerous problem which the present and future administration of Cyrenaica will have to face.' In his opinion, this justified spending £30,900 on the repair of premises, the purchase of flocks and herds, and the provision of farming implements for Sanussi family members, as well as the continuation of monthly allowances to the heads of the different branches of the family, amounting to £2,700 per annum (excluding payments to Idris himself). To drive home his argument, he added: 'It is considered that the solution now suggested has a very reasonable prospect of success and, if successful, will prove extremely cheap at the price.'[7]

These proposals were beginning to be implemented just at the time Peter Synge started work at BMA headquarters in Benghazi in April 1946, but the official correspondence shows that the BMA almost immediately found it hard to keep track of which Sanussi members qualified for the promised grants and allowances, and to know what to do about those members of the family who took the money but then did nothing to develop the properties they were allocated. The problems associated with accounting for the funds and tracking their use continued to escalate over the following year. The amount of administrative time spent on the issue suggests that the well-being of the

[6] R. D. H Arundell, CCAO, GHQ, to DCA, WO, 1 January 1945, WO 230/194.

[7] R. D. H Arundell, CCAO, GHQ, to DCA, WO, 1 January 1945, WO 230/194.

Sanussis was by now being given absolute priority among the responsibilities of the administration.

Another problem in Benghazi was the administrative vacuum left by Cumming's promotion. The first replacement, Brigadier Acland, who had previously served in both the Sudan Political Service and the Sudan Defence Force, was demobilised suddenly and retired in June 1946 – whereupon his unlikely successor was Brigadier J. W. N. Haugh, a career soldier who had no track record either of service in the Middle East or of civil administration.

Cumming later acknowledged that 'the atmosphere of uncertainty and frustration' over the future status of Cyrenaica 'made the task of administration an awkward one'.[8] The BMA had not only lost its previously strong leadership on the ground, but also appeared now, under Haugh, to lack a clear sense of mission. Over this period, British official government policy seemed to have become more strictly limited to 'care and maintenance' under War Office management.[9] With staffing at a low level and no funds for repair and development, the BMA was hard-pressed to perform its normal duties and singularly ill-equipped to reassure the people of Cyrenaica about the future. These glaring shortcomings would not be addressed until more than a year later, and only after a sharp escalation of the stresses and uncertainties on the ground.

## FROM THE MEMOIR

*In May 1945 I was lucky enough to get a few days leave in Alexandria and shortly after my return I was posted back to the Jebel. Barce had ceased to be an administrative district as all the big estates in the area and the Barce Plain were being farmed by the Agricultural Department … so now I found myself in charge of [both] Cyrene and Barce Districts and I obtained permission to live in Graziani's villa in Cyrene and bring my family up from Egypt. The villa was small but delightfully situated overlooking the Temple of Apollo to one side and from the terrace one looked down over the steeply falling escarpment to the blue Mediterranean.*

---

[8] D. C. Cumming, 'British Stewardship of the Italian Colonies: An Account Rendered', *International Affairs*, Vol XXIX, 1953, p18.

[9] Cumming's retrospective account noted: 'The foundation of our administrative policy was the Hague Convention, which had apparently been drafted with European rather than colonial conditions in mind. … The Hague Convention, and the limitation it puts on the occupying Power to legislate only to meet military necessity, had to be read to mean that good government was also a necessity during a prolonged occupation.' D. C. Cumming, 'British Stewardship of the Italian Colonies: An Account Rendered', *International Affairs*, Vol XXIX, 1953, p13.

*Although I think my wife was not the first British wife to live in Cyrenaica, certainly my two boys were the first British children ever to live there, as before the war Cyrenaica was a closed country to all foreigners, and in 1945 mine were the only ones near at hand. So even if they gain no other distinction in life they can claim that one. During their stay we made frequent visits to Apollonia, where we bathed in the clear waters of the little harbour. Apollonia had once been an important seaport but most of it had disappeared into the sea and the only ruins of any importance as far as I remember were the remains of a Byzantine church.*

*With the war in Europe over, schemes for sending officers and men home on leave were put into operation, and the words "Python", "Lilop" and "Liap" were bandied about. Python was the scheme whereby those who had been abroad for more than four years were to be posted home. Lilop which meant "leave in lieu of Python" speaks for itself, and Liap was "leave in addition to Python" and was 28 days home leave for those who could not be posted home that year. I was eligible for none of these but as the result of my leave in May another baby was on the way and I was allowed 28 days "compassionate Liap" to accompany the family home and we left Cyrenaica on 2 September for Alexandria to collect our belongings from the bungalow which we were still renting, but during the dusty railway journey from Tobruk the younger boy Anthony developed violent conjunctivitis in both eyes. Fortunately there was a naval eye specialist at the Naval Hospital at San Stefano to whom we took him and within a week he had recovered and we proceeded to the married families' transit camp at Ismailia to wait for a ship. There we found that we had just missed a ship and that all shipping had been diverted to the Far East to bring home released prisoners of war from Singapore, Malaya and Japan, and nobody could say when we should get a ship. At first we had commodious accommodation in a permanent building but as the camp filled up we had to be moved into a Nissen hut meant for a married couple and it was none too roomy for the four of us.*

*Eventually on 31 October, we entrained for Port Said and embarked on the* Rangitata *of the New Zealand Shipping Co and sailed the following day. This ship was a refrigerator ship built to carry frozen meat and about 40 passengers, but the holds had been converted into dormitories and the cabins had had extra bunks fitted, and on this trip she carried 500 passengers. There was complete segregation and the male officers were berthed in 16 berth dormitories in the holds, while wives and families were put into four-berth cabins, which had originally been single-berth cabins. Some of the officers had got married during their overseas service and the wives were of all nationalities. ... Although the public rooms were absurdly inadequate for the enormous number of passengers and the cabin accommodation was cramped, the superb food which was served compensated us for everything else, and we who had spent seven weeks eating cold beef, dehydrated potatoes and dried peas appreciated it all the more.*

*We passed the coast of Cyrenaica on 2 November, which was the date by which I should normally have arrived back there, allowing for a month travelling. We had a calm and uneventful voyage and arrived home on 11 November, having last seen England six years ago. We spent about ten days with my parents ... and then went over to Ireland to stay with my wife's parents. ... It was wonderful to be home again though life was still very grim with food and clothes rationing and very little in the shops. In Ireland things were easier and life there seemed unchanged.*

*On 11 December I reported back to the Transit Camp at Southampton at the end of my leave but to my surprise I was told that there was no ship sailing and none expected. After two days there I asked if I could go back to Godalming [in Surrey, where Peter's parents lived], which was only two hours away by train and was told I could as long as I could be summoned by telephone if a passage turned up. ... I spent Christmas in England for the first time since 1923.*

*I reported back to Southampton on 27 December and was told the same old story of no vacancies on any ship sailing for the Middle East. ... On 2 January when I went to the Company office and was told "no passage" for the umpteenth time, I said: "Look here. This is fantastic. I was given 28 days leave commencing on 2 September and I have been already four months away from my station. I want a warrant to the War Office." So I got my railway warrant and went to the War Office and eventually saw an officer who had to do with postings, and told him my story. He verified my statement with somebody in Q movements and I told him that I wanted an air passage, so he said he would see what he could do and I was to go back to Camp and wait.*

*Eventually, after another 10 days waiting I was told to report to Hurn, and on 14 January I flew in an RAF Dakota with aluminium benches running along the sides and rifle racks as headrests. We all donned flying suits and I remember my feet nearly froze in spite of being encased in fur-lined boots, and we eventually landed at El Adem. There I was met by an officer who informed me that I had been appointed to relieve him as Civil Affairs Officer, Tobruk, and as the Navy had just evacuated the port I should be Harbour Master, Tobruk! What a grand sounding title for someone who knew nothing about signalling or berthing or anything else to do with ships, except the ability to sail a small boat. The next day, I was shown over the harbour installations and it was apparent that the Navy had removed everything that could be of use to them. There was the signal station, which contained a chart of the harbour and nothing else. No flags of any sort and not even a signal halyard.*

*The stores were empty except for an opened tin or two of paint. Afloat there were two pontoons, which belong to the Ministry of War Transport and were to be removed as soon as the winter storms were over: one rusting and pitted lighter and two steel lifeboats, one of which had an engine which had just been rendered useless by the Arab mechanic in charge, who had run it with the water cock turned off, and it had seized up.*

*Tobruk had not changed much since I had passed a night there just two years ago. It was still a dead town but a few houses and offices had been made habitable for the few military personnel who lived there. It was the HQ of a Zone and commanded by a Lieutenant Colonel. I lived in a mess with the Zone Commander and his staff. There was not a pane of glass in any windows in the town and the windows of the habitable buildings were filled with that opaque substitute called "windowlite" which was simply tacked on to the window frames so that one could not open a window. One night soon after my arrival there was a very severe storm and the 'windowlite' made loud bangs with every fierce gust of wind.*

*The next morning I went down to the harbour to inspect the pontoons and make sure that they were secure and had come to no harm from the gale, which was an easterly one and had raised quite a heavy swell in the harbour, which is open to the east. The pontoons were secure but the old lighter had broken adrift and had beached itself on the western shore of the harbour, on a flat sandy beach. I felt that I ought to secure it with an anchor but there was not anchor not chain nor a spare warp or rope to be found and I was forced to leave it where it was. However, not many days later another gale sprang up from the north-west and blew all night. When in the morning I surveyed the harbour from the mess balcony the lighter had vanished and I felt fairly sure that it had hit one of the many sunken wrecks in the harbour and would never be seen again but ... eventually found it riding quite comfortably in a little indentation amongst the rocks and apparently none the worse for its adventures.* [But later it sank anyway.]

*I had three vehicles attached to me in Tobruk. One was a 15 cwt truck, one a 3 tonner and the third an ambulance which was fairly constantly in demand for taking Arabs who had blown themselves up in minefields or by tampering with ammunition (both of which still littered the desert) to Derna hospital which was 100 miles away. One day ... I took the ambulance along the quays to the furthest point where the last of the railway sidings ended in a heap of rubble and here was the only place I could park the vehicle and turn it round. ... It took me perhaps 10 minutes to inspect the pontoons and I returned to the vehicle and was just about to climb into the cab when I saw to my amazement a closed railway wagon hurtling along the siding towards me. It only took me a second to realise that the up-ended sleepers would not stop the wagon but they might derail it, so I yelled to my driver and ran to the cover of a warehouse to watch the crash. The wagon was not derailed but its speed was slowed down a little and as its wheels ploughed into the rubble its buffers caught the body of the ambulance fair and square and demolished it like a house of cards, the whole ambulance was pushed sideways down the slope of the ground, but the wagon stopped without touching the chassis of the vehicle. … Presently a locomotive manned by Indians arrived on the scene and towed away the wagon and not long afterwards the ambulance was driven away by me none the worse except that it now had no body and was useless as an ambulance.*

*It transpired that the railway wagon was standing on level ground out-side the RASC [Royal Army Service Corps] Supply Depot three miles away from the harbour when the wind caught it and it began to move. Before any-one could reach the hand brake it had gathered speed and became a runaway. It crossed the main road twice without hitting anything and entered the har-bour area where the line branched into four or more sidings. … By a strange trick of fate the points were all set for it to hit my innocent ambulance parked at the end of siding for 10 minutes. … I was not surcharged. It was presum-ably treated as a war casualty.*

*At the end of February, I received a telegram (sent off on the 16th but posted from Benghazi by a stupid officer who could have easily telephoned it) announcing the birth of Richard on the 15th, from Ireland, but as he was not expected much before the end of the month, I had not been anxious.*

*During the first three weeks of my double assignment as Civil Affairs Officer and Harbourmaster, I did not dare to leave the place because I received several signals a day from FOLEM (Flag Officers Levant and Eastern Medi-terranean) to VAM (Vice Admiral Malta) copied to Harbourmaster Tobruk, notifying the departure from Port Said of various small Naval craft which might have to put into Tobruk for one reason or another. A study of the chart of the harbour showed that it was littered with wrecks and there seemed to be no clear passage between them and there was certainly no buoyed passage. I had no idea what I was expected to do in the event of a ship coming in but I felt I ought to be there if only to catch and make fast a mooring rope. However, as no ship of any sort was even seen passing the port, let alone entering it, I decided that it was time I got acquainted with the rest of my District and as the flow of signals had almost dried up it seemed safe to assume that noth-ing was ever likely to enter the port. Accordingly, one morning I set off for Bardia, a small port 100 miles east of Tobruk, which was famous in 1940/41 as the place were 150,000 Italians troops under Marshal Bagdolio had sur-rendered to General Wavell. It was a small garrison town situated on top of a cliff some 50 feet above the sea and the harbour was a creek, which could only accommodate one or two small coastal vessels, or a submarine or two. It was a disappointingly small town dominated by fairly extensive but ruined barracks, but the Arabs had returned to live there and there were a few pitiful little shops selling odds and ends and it had a population of not more than 200 Arabs. I stayed there an hour or two and listened to complaints by the Mayor and a few of the prominent traders and promised to do what I could to increase the amenities of the place and then returned, and on my way home I called in at Gambut, a pitiful huddle of huts made chiefly of beaten out petrol tins, and got back to Tobruk after dark. As I came down the escarpment to the south of the harbour I noticed the lights of several vessels in the harbour, which seemed a bit unusual but as the need for a drink was uppermost in my mind I went straight to the mess and, as I entered, I was greeted with a shout of "Hello Harbourmaster! Have you seen your harbour?" I replied that I had noticed a lot of lights then I was told that a flotilla of no less than nine landing craft had come in during the afternoon and had calmly and completely negotiated the wrecks and tied themselves up to the quays and had not required my services.*

*Next morning, I called on the Commander and apologised for my absence but he was not at all concerned and explained that he knew the harbour and had called in for fuel, which was being supplied by the RASC. In the office, I looked through the signals which had come in but there was no mention of this particular flotilla, and as the Navy was obviously capable of coming and going as they wished without any help from me I ceased to bother any more about the harbour.*

*Some time later, a small Naval survey ship called in and I took the opportunity of going afloat in one of their motor boats and taking a look at the wrecks and the passages between them and was able to see for myself that the wrecks were not nearly as densely packed as they appeared on the chart, and I became a happier man. In April, a consignment of flat-bottomed sailing boats arrived by road from Alexandria, supplied by Army Welfare for the use of officers and men. These were light assault boats built for paddling across canals and they had been cleverly fitted with centreboards, thwarts and masts and supplied with a foresail and Bermuda rig mainsail. I had great fun rigging these boats, and giving lectures on the rudiments of sailing and lessons in sailing to anyone who wanted to learn. Thereafter I had no difficulty in employing my spare time and got quite a thrill from sailing across the well decks of several ships, which were lying upright on the bottom with their hulls submerged but their superstructures standing above the water.*

*Tobruk was a backwater and I seemed to have been forgotten. A new Chief Administrator [Brigadier P. B. E. Acland] had been appointed since I had gone on leave and I had never met him. When, therefore, I heard that he was visiting Derna, I got permission to go down to Derna to meet him. I pointed out that my five months' absence was not my fault and that I had served in five out of the six Districts in Cyrenaica and knew the country pretty well. While I had been away, young chaps who had been Sergeants when I first came to Benghazi had been commissioned and promoted to Captain and here was I, at the age of 41, still a Captain. He listened sympathetically and went away and, after less than a month, I was posted to Benghazi as Political Secretary with the rank of Major.*

*I moved to Benghazi at the end of April and lived in the Senior Officers Mess, in a building which had once been the Banco d'Italia and later Navy House. There was a vast improvement in the place since I had first been there and it was beginning to look more like the capital city of the country.*[10]

---

[10] Many houses and shops must have been repaired by this time, although it is hard to find documentary evidence that any work had yet started on the major buildings or the massively bomb-damaged harbour. It was only in September 1946 that Cumming succeeded in convincing the British Foreign Office that 'the possibility of approving certain additional expenditure on public works ... (including reconditioning the port of Benghazi) should be examined.' Conclusions of discussion on the future of the Italian Colonies with Foreign Secretary and British officials, Paris, 6 September 1946, WO 230/214.

# chapter 9

# THE BMA HITS TROUBLED TIMES
## BENGHAZI, APRIL 1946–APRIL 1947

THROUGHOUT HIS LAST 18 months in Cyrenaica, Major Peter Synge's role in the British Military Administration was at a very senior level. And so it is both a surprise and a puzzle – especially given the detail that his diary and memoir provide about his earlier experiences – that the part of his memoir covering the 1946–47 period makes little mention of the key events that occurred in Benghazi during these months, or the ongoing changes in British policy concerning the territory or, indeed, of his very close involvement in all these developments.

In mentioning his day-to-day and high-level responsibilities so minimally, it could be that Peter felt that some issues were still too sensitive to discuss in detail – even in the 1970s, when writing his memoir. But a comparison of his account with the extensive reports in War Office and Foreign Office documents suggests that his reticence is much more likely to be explained by his complex feelings about the way in which his time in Benghazi came to an end in October 1947, when he was moved to another senior posting in Eritrea. It seems most probable that he chose to write less about his work and more about his family life and leisure activities (such as playing tennis and organising sailing races in Benghazi harbour, in his role as Commodore of the Officers' Sailing Club) because his removal, following a disagreement with Duncan Cumming, had left him feeling badly treated. And ultimately, although he clearly felt that he deserved more recognition for the work he did in Cyrenaica, he probably thought that his intended readers (his descendants) would not be overly interested in the details.

The extensive correspondence and reports stored in the British archives help to fill in the key elements of Cyrenaica's evolution in

1946–47 that are entirely missing from Peter's own account. What emerges clearly is that he was unnecessarily modest about his own role in helping to keep the administration running through this difficult phase. The evidence in the archives reveals that he was not only heavily involved in managing the subsidies to and the settlement of Sanussi family members (see Chapter 10), but also in the selection and training of Cyrenaicans to take over senior administrative posts. In the increasingly sensitive political environment of the time, these were tasks that made him vulnerable to criticism from the Sanussi camp, and yet despite this, it turns out that very shortly before his departure he played a significant role in the final effort to convince a reluctant Sayyid Mohammed Idris to return to Cyrenaica permanently (see Chapter 11).

The overall reality in Cyrenaica at this time was that whenever the BMA was tested, it was found to be vulnerable to criticism from political figures and activists in the newly combative local media. Unwittingly, the administration itself now became one of several political centres in play in Benghazi, although its freedom of action was heavily limited by decisions being taken over its head in Cairo and London. As it came under pressure from different sections of the population, the BMA itself may well have been at risk of splitting into different factions.

In the labyrinthine post-war negotiations on the future of Cyrenaica and at a time of high expectations and uncertainty about how the situation would develop, two individuals still held the key – as they had from the beginning – namely Duncan Cumming and Sayyid Mohammed Idris. The newly promoted Major General Cumming was successful in persuading his superiors to keep betting on Idris, who for his part was driving an increasingly hard bargain. Their complex negotiations, held in secret, only reached significant conclusions at the end of September 1947.[1]

As of April 1946, Peter Synge's substantive appointment in the BMA was as Political Secretary and he also served as Acting Chief Secretary for several months in both 1946 and 1947, the second most senior post in the administration and one that gave him the temporary rank of lieutenant colonel. All this time, he was deputising for the incoming Chief Secretary, whom he refers to only as 'an experienced administrator', without giving his name. The records reveal this to be Eric De

---

[1] S. L. Bills, *The Libyan Arena: The United States, Britain and the Council of Foreign Ministers 1945–1948*, Ohio, 1995, pp74 and 80–1.

Candole, who was not only the first civilian to hold the post but also went on to become the principal figurehead in the next era in Britain's relations with Cyrenaica, from late 1947 onwards.

Essentially a military regime backed by an occupying force, the BMA was easy to portray as insensitive to local feeling, but what made things much more difficult for its reputation was that a crude insensitivity was on display in the form of the Chief Administrator appointed in June 1946 – Brigadier J. W. N. Haugh. Peter's memoir describes him as 'completely unsuited to his new post', and as 'a regular soldier, who had not the slightest idea of administrating an Arab country'. By contrast with Cumming and his short-term successor P. B. E. Acland, Haugh's limitations were obvious. 'He could speak no Arabic and did not begin to understand how the mind of the Arab worked and had had no experience of dealing with civilians of any country,' Peter wrote. 'I had great difficulty in getting him to take the slightest interest in the populace or their welfare. ... It was my misfortune to have to accompany him whenever he had to attend any function involving the civil population and act as interpreter, but he had nothing to say to the Arabs which made any sense to them.'

The bitterness in these words suggests a feeling that Haugh's lack of imagination had cast a shadow over Peter's own career in the BMA. From all the available evidence, it is clear that Haugh's time in office reflected the mechanical rules and norms of the War Office in their most basic form. This could hardly have been more out of tune with the more creative management style of Cumming and his little team of trusted 'experts', who had prided themselves on their sensitivity to Arab opinion. By the time that Cumming and his new coterie in Cairo had managed to establish a new rationale for the British presence in Cyrenaica in late 1947, it was Peter Synge's fate to be seen as part of Haugh's administration, which was by then widely regarded as out of touch and having outstayed its welcome (see Chapters 10 and 11).

European occupation of Arab countries was only marginally more acceptable to local opinion at that time than it would be now, and the risks of allowing the occupation of Cyrenaica to drift indefinitely had been well understood by some senior officials as soon as the European war ended. In a top secret memorandum to Britain's British Middle East Defence Committee in July 1945, Brigadier R. D. H. Arundell had warned: 'If Cyrenaica is to become a strategic base it is obviously necessary that the constitutional and diplomatic aspects of the problem should be satisfactorily solved in advance. Provided the people of Cyrenaica get the sort of regime they want, under British guidance and control, the presence of British troops would be welcomed.' Arundell also emphasised that 'the continuance of a temporary administration for a moment longer than can be avoided is most undesirable. Political uncertainty keeps the population unsettled.'[2]

## NEGOTIATING THE POLITICAL FUTURE

The most prominent urban notable in Cyrenaica at this time was Omar Pasha Mansur al-Kekhia, who had held political office under Ottoman rule before 1911. On his return from exile in 1945, he set about arguing strongly for immediate independence under Sayyid Mohammed Idris. Others agreed with this, but held different views about whether or not Cyrenaica should tie itself to Egypt or unite with Tripolitania in an independent Libya. To keep up with such debates inside the territory, the BMA relied mainly on officials in the Benghazi Municipal Council, such as Ali el Fellag, Yusuf Lenghi and Abu al-Qasim al-Sanussi (the Sanussi family member within the administration), but their continued support for the BMA could not be relied on. Meanwhile, the younger activists in the Omar Mukhtar Clubs (which by now were fully established and active in all the main towns) wanted independence by any means possible and felt no special loyalty to the Sanussi cause.

As international negotiations dragged on over Libya and the other former Italian colonies, British policy sometimes irked the other three powers. At one stage in the negotiations of the Council of Foreign Ministers in 1946, Britain argued for immediate independence for the whole of Libya, but the French and Russians suspected a plot to establish influence behind the scenes and pushed instead for United Nations trusteeship, which Britain did not favour.[3] In London, in June 1946, British Foreign Secretary, Ernest Bevin, stressed to his officials that it was 'essential for us to retain strategic facilities in Cyrenaica' and recommended 'various administrative measures immediately in order to convince the inhabitants of our active interest in their well-being and in their progress towards self-government'. He suggested

---

[2] R. D. H Arundell, CCAO, to the British Middle East Defence Committee, 10 July 1945, FO 1015/81.

[3] E. A. V. De Candole, *The Life and Times of King Idris of Libya*, published privately 1990, pp77–8.

that the appointment of an official council to support Idris would satisfy the Americans' concern for self-government, even if the French would be alarmed about the precedent this might set for Morocco or Tunisia.[4] Plans for limited self-government under Idris received Bevin's support at a further meeting in September.[5]

Duncan Cumming's responsibilities as Chief Civil Affairs Officer now covered all the former Italian colonies, but he spared no effort in pushing Britain's cause in Cyrenaica. In September 1946, he defined the challenges he faced to a Foreign Office colleague. 'The Libyans are peculiarly outspoken people' and 'very suspicious of the intentions of Europeans,' he wrote. 'With Russia, France, Italy and the Arab states exerting pressure in various directions the problem is much more difficult and it will be a scramble to reach our aims.' And rather ominously he added: 'Given a first rate staff [in Benghazi] we could probably keep the internal situation in hand; with my present staff it will be remarkable if we avoid trouble.'[6]

Cumming's foremost priority was to keep Idris onside and so two fluent Arabic speakers were assigned to liaise closely with him. Employed by a Cairo-based 'Civil Affairs Agency' that was responsible to the Foreign Office in London, the intermediaries were Jose Campbell Penney, who was on loan from the Sudan Political Service as a political adviser, and Cecil Greatorex, who had been Peter's colleague in Benghazi in 1943. Their confidential discussions with Idris were reported only to Cumming and to the Foreign Office, while most of the details were withheld from the BMA (from which Cumming, in any case, clearly expected very little at this point).

In July 1946, Idris asked his private secretary, Omar Sheneib, to prepare for the British government a list of observations and proposals about the future. This expressed sharp criticism of the BMA and of its failure either to prepare for the independence of the territory or to repair the war damage on the ground. It also called for the appointment of a 'constitutional government' and for Arabs to take up senior administrative posts. This was the opening salvo in a negotiating process that was to reach its climax the following year.[7]

---

[4] Minutes of Foreign Office meeting concerning Cyrenaica and Tripolitania, June 1946, FO 1015/987.

[5] Conclusions of discussion on the future of the Italian colonies, Paris, 6 September 1947, WO 230/214.

[6] D. Cumming, CCAO, to Scott-Fox, FO, September 1946, WO 230/214.

[7] Translations of documents entitled 'My Observations' and 'My Suggestions', Idris to D. C. Cumming, 24 July 1946, WO 230/214.

Cumming's commentary on these proposals described Sheneib as 'an ignorant, hot-headed, agitator' and argued that his denunciations of British policy deliberately ignored reality. Writing to the Foreign Office, Cumming defended the BMA's achievements in training Arabs to accept more administrative responsibility and in undertaking public works to repair some of the war damage. Significantly, he repeated a recommendation – first put forward in 1945 – that Idris be accorded the title of amir and be given a formal British decoration for his services to the war effort, but he added: 'The Sayed should be told we will continue to press for a settlement leading to the independence of Cyrenaica provided he will promise us the military facilities we require.'[8] This neatly summarises the game plan that Cumming was confident would win through in the end.

Idris then made two brief visits to Cyrenaica in July and August, hoping to harness nationalist feeling behind his demands for an autonomous constitutional government. After the first visit, when he called for 'the full freedom and independence of the country, for which our people participated in the war and contributed valuable services for the benefit of their allies', his subsequent hasty return to Cairo was interpreted as a protest against Britain, and so he went to Benghazi a second time, where a huge gathering in August was addressed by Omar Pasha Mansur al-Kekhia, who declared: 'All the small countries that had collaborated with Britain have realised their aspirations except Barqa [Cyrenaica] which is anxiously awaiting and hoping.'[9] Idris urged patience, but this time announced his approval of the formation of a National Front (al-Jabha al-Wataniyya) supposedly representing all elements in the country, which would work towards achieving the country's freedom and independence.

This activity set off a kind of political process, which Britain had to find ways to accommodate. On 30 November 1946, the al-Jabha al-Wataniyya made a full declaration of policy addressed to the British authorities, demanding the recognition of the Sanussi amirate under Idris and permission to form a national government to administer the country in preparation for national independence.[10] For their part, the Omar Mukhtar Clubs were by this time 'indifferent to older leaders', according to the Libyan historian Majid Khadduri, and issued political statements and indulged in criticising the Jabha.[11]

---

[8] Commentary by D. C. Cumming, undated, FO 1015/91.
[9] M. Khadduri, *Modern Libya: A Study in Political Development*, Baltimore, 1963, pp59–61.
[10] M. Khadduri, *Modern Libya: A Study in Political Development*, Baltimore, 1963, pp61–2.
[11] M. Khadduri, *Modern Libya: A Study in Political Development*, Baltimore, 1963, p64.

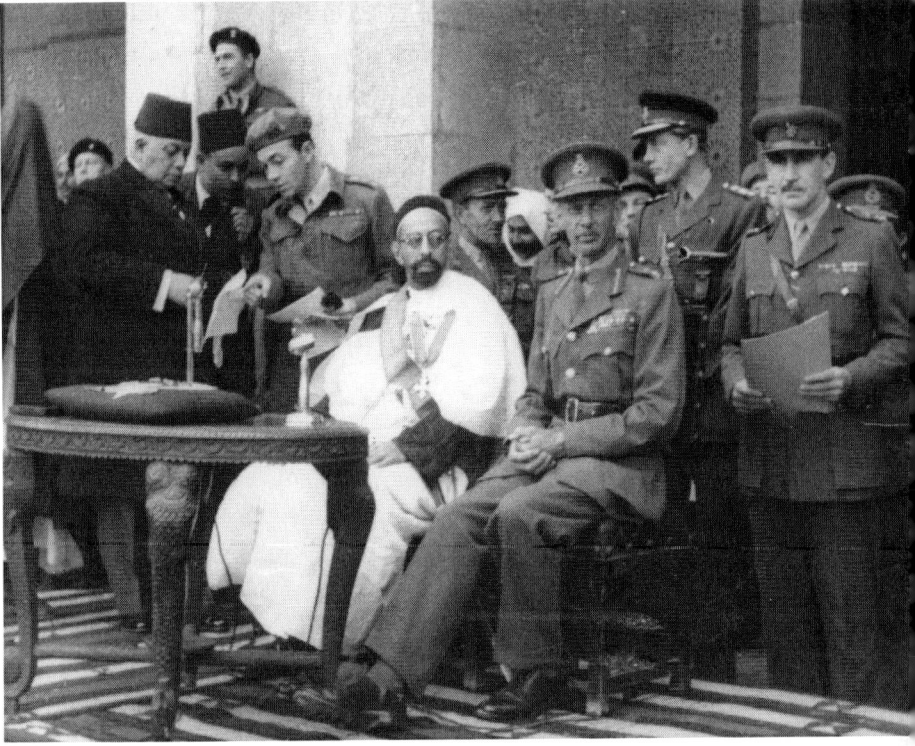

Figure 21. *Sayyid Idris in Benghazi for the award of the KBE, January 1947, with General Sir Miles Dempsey* (seated) *and Brigadier Duncan Cumming* (holding folder). Peter Synge Collection

## THE DEALINGS BEHIND THE KBE

In January 1947, in an event choreographed from Cairo rather than Benghazi, the British establishment invited Idris to Benghazi to bestow on him the honorific title of amir and make him a Knight Commander of the Order of the British Empire (KBE), all in clear preparation for an eventual assumption of power under British tutelage.[12] The British commander in the Middle East, General Miles Dempsey, was there for the ceremony, which took place in the still bomb-damaged palace of the former Italian governor, Rodolfo Graziani, in the company of all the

---

[12] E. A. V. De Candole, *The Life and Times of King Idris of Libya*, published privately 1990, pp78–9.

159

best-known local personalities and the senior officers of the BMA, Peter Synge included (as his photo of the event testifies).

Coinciding with this event, the War Office in London sent a working party to study and report on the administration of both Cyrenaica and Tripolitania, in the hope of defining a strategy satisfactory to the other powers. The working party issued its report in January 1947, which recommended a three-stage process for Cyrenaica: (i) continuing the military administration for a short period only; (ii) establishing an Arab state under British trusteeship, with financial assistance for at least ten years; (iii) establishing a fully independent state, during which Cyrenaica could possibly be unified with Tripolitania, backed by a treaty of alliance with a major power. It was at the same time recommended that Idris should take up permanent residence in Cyrenaica.[13] These British proposals still depended on the agreement of the other powers and on the support of the people of both territories. In Tripolitania, there was a clear reluctance in some quarters to accept the authority of Idris and the Sanussis, and direct negotiations between Cyrenaican political leaders and their Tripolitanian counterparts broke down when the latter refused to lend their support to Idris.[14]

Idris was by now raising the stakes, as shown by his tactics concerning the KBE ceremony, when he had literally refused to board the train out of Cairo for the investiture until he received a substantial amount of money. A sum of more than £2,000 was paid, and when Cumming was later rebuked by his superiors at the War Office for giving this without proper authorisation, he vigorously defended his action as dictated by 'important political considerations'.[15]

Although some had hoped that Idris would stay on in Benghazi after the investiture, he went straight back to Cairo and was adamant that he would not take up residence in Cyrenaica until substantial progress had been made in meeting his demands for a constitutional government, and until he received more favours, including a car suitable to his status and the settlement of his debts in Cairo (which, he claimed, totalled at least £8,000).[16]

---

[13] A. Pelt, *Libyan Independence and the United Nations: A Case of Planned Decolonization*, New Haven and London, 1970, p45, and E. A. V. De Candole, The Life and Times of King Idris of Libya, published privately 1990, p82.

[14] The differences between Tripolitania and Cyrenaica are fully explored in the pages of Adrian Pelt's *Libyan Independence and the United Nations: A Case of Planned Decolonization*, New Haven and London, 1970.

[15] Correspondence between CCAO and Deputy Under Secretary, WO, 15 & 18 February 1947, WO 230/214.

[16] D. C. Cumming to J.W.N. Haugh, 28 January 1947, WO 230/214.

*In temple ruins Cyrene . 1947*

*In Tobruk  1946*

*Principal Mosque Benghazi*

*The new Services Sailing Club . Benghazi R.C Cathedral in background*

*The Commodore swigging champagne after winning a race. Benghazi 1947*

Figure 22. *Page from Peter Synge's photograph album covering 1946-47.*
Peter Synge Collection.

Figure 23. *Two family photos: Peter Synge's wife and three sons at Cyrene* (above) *and Peter with his youngest, Richard Synge, 1947* (right). Peter Synge Collection.

Far from expressing surprise at any of these demands, Cumming took a philosophical line on this style of bargaining, as a telegram to his superiors at the time made clear: 'Position of the Amir is dominant and we cannot afford to alienate him but sooner or later we may have to tell him that Britain will not support him indefinitely if she ceases to be interested in Cyrenaica or if he fails to give our policy his support.'[17] Throughout 1947, Cumming became increasingly effective in convincing sceptical officials in London that he could eventually bring off the return of Idris.

Duncan Cumming's requests to London for better-qualified officers in the BMA began to bear fruit in February 1947, when Eric De Candole was appointed Chief Secretary. Like others before him, De Candole, the son of an Anglican bishop and nicknamed 'Deacon', was a member of the elite Sudan Political Service and had very recently served as Deputy Governor of Sudan's Northern Province. The archives indicate that De Candole brought a sharp political insight to the challenges being posed by the rising opposition to military rule and sought above all to manage things to the benefit of Idris and the Jabha.

Contrasting assessments are contained in the secret Monthly Political Reports signed off by either De Candole or Peter Synge over the course of the following months. Analysing the political opinions being expressed by members of the Omar Mukhtar Clubs, De Candole drew a distinction between the 'extremists' and the 'moderate progressives'. The former, he wrote, 'look to the Arab League for their salvation and support a policy of amalgamation with Tripoli under a republican form of government', while the latter 'favour a democratic form of government under the Senussi Amirate as the binding factor, in union with Tripoli'. De Candole felt that 'the key to the situation lies with the Amir himself', who commanded 'the respect of the moderate progressives'.[18]

The reports compiled by Peter, by contrast, tended at this time to denounce all the adherents of the Omar Mukhtar Clubs, among whom were many employees of the BMA itself. Reporting in April 1947 that a senior employee, Mustapha Ben Amer, had set up a new weekly newspaper *El Watan*, which had published a poem by Ahmed Rafiq al-Mehdawi openly critical of Idris, the sheikhs and the British, Peter noted that Ben Amer 'has now been warned to behave himself'. Possible countermeasures against the Omar Mukhtar Clubs were noted with approval:

---

[17] Telegram, CCAO to DCA, 15 February 1947, WO 230/214.
[18] BMA Monthly Political Report no 15, E. A. V. De Candole, 31 March 1947, WO 230/202.

'A movement is afoot by the Jabha to close these clubs and reorganise them, as their present activities are an insult to the national hero and martyr for whom they are named.'[19]

By mid-1947, British policy in the international negotiations over Libya had begun to reflect the interests of Mohammed Idris and the Sanussi network. In his own researches in the archives, historian Scott Bills found that 'British policy was driven not only by strategic considerations but also by the fact that the Sanusi held strong sway in Cyrenaica. London would have to come to terms with Sayyid Idris. The Sanusi shaped British policy in a subtle but distinct way, representing people to be accorded more than titular respect.'[20]

---

[19] BMA Monthly Political Report no 16, P. M. Synge, 29 April 47, WO 230/202.
[20] S. L. Bills, *The Libyan Arena: The United States, Britain and the Council of Foreign Ministers 1945–1948*, Ohio, 1995, p107.

# chapter 10

# THE AMIR AND HIS RELATIONS
## BENGHAZI, MAY–JULY 1947

ALL THE WHILE THAT Sayyid Mohammed Idris continued to stay away over the summer months of 1947, the people of Benghazi became noticeably more disillusioned with British rule. Idris may have been fully acknowledged as Cyrenaica's amir but it was not clear how, if or when he might actually rule. Even the al-Jabha al-Wataniyya (National Front), which consisted largely of conservatives strongly loyal to Idris, began to turn against the BMA and accuse it of failing to hand over the reins of power. At the end of May, Eric De Candole wrote: 'It becomes increasingly apparent that, dominated by their implicit faith in the Amir, the mass of the people of this Territory will take no step or give no opinion in his absence. Until that is achieved no real cooperation will be forthcoming.'[1] Here again, De Candole was underlining Duncan Cumming's commitment to Idris as the best guarantee of Britain achieving its aims in Cyrenaica.

Throughout this period, local dissatisfaction came close to defiance of the British as represented by the BMA but, in Cairo, Idris was still playing a game of cat and mouse in the hopes of extracting more concessions. His main concern was to achieve internationally recognised power, status and authority, but he was nevertheless happy to consider financial inducements to accommodate British interests. He was not averse to using members of his staff to voice a wide range of conflicting opinions, sometimes in response to the ebb and flow of different strands of Arab nationalism at the time, but more often in the hope of increasing both the stakes and the inducements offered. He did not appear to want money for himself, but rather viewed it as a means to underpin his influence and to extend his patronage.

---

[1] BMA Monthly Political Report no 17, E. A. V. De Candole, 31 May 1947, WO 230/202.

At the prompting of Cecil Greatorex, in May 1947 Idris wrote to Cumming that he wanted a government that he would appoint himself, along with 'the abolition of the military regime and all that goes with it and its replacement by a civil regime'.[2] Idris was at this stage attempting to show that he meant business by threatening to refuse all cooperation, causing Cumming to write to his superiors: 'Things have changed a good deal since the matter last went to the Cabinet. On the one hand British prestige has declined in these parts and agitation against us is at a premium. On the other I understand that our strategic interests in Cyrenaica have increased. Of course the wheel may turn again if Egypt and the Arab League are snubbed by UNO over Palestine and the Anglo-Egyptian Treaty. But on the whole it appears that the prospects of a favourable outcome to our present policy in Libya have declined. Although opinion in Cyrenaica itself is still favourable, the Amir is a hard bargainer who may leave the arena altogether if we put much pressure on him.'[3] Reading between the lines, one can see Cumming being as persuasive as possible in making the case for sustained and substantial support for Idris.

By June 1947, there was no easing of the anti-British feeling and Cumming was highlighting the signs of a new radicalism: 'Even in Cyrenaica the situation is less favourable. A United Libya movement has been organised. ... Our policy in Libya has become an easy target for both Libyan nationalists and the anti-Imperialist campaign of the Arab League,' he wrote to the War Office. He pointed out that Idris was determined to increase his price and was demanding that Britain foot the bill of his official household expenses to the order of £23,800 a year. Cryptically describing the prospect of Sanussi rule as 'a form of Arab medievalism tempered by British advice', Cumming said there was no longer a prospect of Cyrenaica developing in the same 'orderly and modest' way that had been seen in Transjordan and so 'something more advanced in its initial stages, and more expensive, must now be contemplated.'[4] At the end of June, Cumming was again flagging the risks of failure, and even suggested that Idris was 'looking for an excuse to retire from the arena because his close association with Great Britain involves more odium than he can bear.'[5]

When Idris took himself off to Lebanon at the height of the summer, ostensibly for health reasons but principally to register his

---

[2] Translation of letter from Idris to D. C. Cumming, May 1947, FO 1015/91.
[3] CCAO to DCA, 4 May 1947, WO 230/215.
[4] CCAO to DCA, 24 June 1947, WO 230/215.
[5] Telegram, CCAO to DCA, 30 June 1947, WO 230/215.

Figure 24. *Sayyid Idris at the time of his January 1947 visit to Benghazi, after which Britain acknowledged his title as amir of Cyrenaica.* Peter Synge Collection.

disappointment with Britain, Cumming shifted the focus to speeding up the return to Cyrenaica of the large extended Sanussi family, most of whom had been living in exile in Egypt and other neighbouring countries since the 1920s. More than 100 of Idris's cousins had been identified as ready to return. Some had already done so, but others were now looking to get their share of the inducements on offer before the promised resettlement money dried up.

In June, De Candole reported that a new Sanussi Agricultural Settlement Scheme had been drawn up 'on the same lines as the new Barce Plain and Hill Farms Schemes with the object of establishing the principal members of the Senussi family firmly in the Territory'. Costing an estimated £12,000, the new scheme would include seven farms with a total area of 1,012 hectares, with the administration supplying machinery, plant and technical supervision.[6]

There had been fitful progress in returning some of the main Sanussi heads of family since the costly proposals put forward by Brigadier R.

---

[6] BMA Monthly Political Report no 18, E. A. V. De Candole, 1 July 1947, WO 230/202.

D. H. Arundell had been approved the previous year (see Chapter 8). Senior BMA officials – and since mid-1946, Peter Synge had been one of those most involved – were keeping track of which of the Sanussis were qualified for the promised resettlement grants and allowances. BMA officials also had to monitor those who got into financial difficulties or failed to develop the properties they were allocated. As the voluminous office correspondence testifies, this became an extremely time-consuming exercise.

Some of the challenges of the Sanussi settlement issue had been outlined earlier by Oxford Professor Hamilton Gibb (whose article about Idris's 1944 visit in the *Picture Post* had so outraged Norman Anderson – see Chapter 6). In a background paper for the Foreign Office in March 1944, Gibb wrote: 'One of the main complications of a Senussi principality is the large number of descendants of the founder of the house, Sidi Muhammed ben Ali el Senussi, all of whom will expect to be provided for by grants of land, pensions and the like, and who, if they are not satisfied, will intrigue against the ruling Amir and the protecting power. It is clearly undesirable to impose a new landed aristocracy upon the country, and effective measures will have to be taken from the outset to control the cadet branches of the Senussi house. But for the Amir himself some considerable source of revenue will have to be found, if only to meet the demands made upon him by Arab traditions of hospitality.'[7]

One of the first of the senior Sanussis to move to Cyrenaica, Mohamed Safi al-Din had taken a farm at Cremonini in 1945 and by September that year was already in financial difficulties. When he had asked for a new loan, the administration had told him he should have taken an active interest in the farm and said it did not want to set a precedent by lending him more.[8] By 1947, the same Safi al-Din was being considered a political liability because of the links he had developed with the Egyptian government and his attempts to oust the Amir's brother, Mohamed al-Rida, from the presidency of the Jabha.[9] Nevertheless, his prominent standing in the Sanussi hierarchy meant that he had to have his share of any new benefits.

Once approval came through in January 1946 for the grants and regular payment of allowances to the six heads of the families, the BMA began sending frequent requests to Cairo for the release of money. At first it was Norman Anderson, who defined the nature and purpose of

---

[7] Paper on 'Problems of Cyrenaica' by H. A. R. Gibb, 25 March 1944, FO 371/41511.
[8] BMA to GHQ, 13 September 1945, WO 230/194.
[9] BMA Monthly Political Report no 18, E. A. V. De Candole, 1 July 1947, WO 230/202.

each payment and tried to clarify the confusion about the number of sons each of the heads of the families actually had. Later it was Cecil Greatorex, who took note of cases of over-expenditure on the ongoing improvements to Idris's estate at Abiar, his house at al-Bayda and another that had belonged to Rodolfo Graziani, situated beside the sacred waters of Lethe, just outside Benghazi.

In May 1946, Greatorex wrote: 'I would point out that there is still a large amount of repairs to be carried out on the houses for the remaining members of the Senussi family and I do feel that the Sayed's requests for repairs to his property should either be brought to an end or he should be told that his amount has been well overspent and that the remaining members would suffer in consequence.' That same month in Benghazi, the short-term Acting Chief Administrator, Colonel Stanley Parker, was also raising his concerns: 'I consider that the sum of £10,000 allocated for settling members of the family other than Sayed Mohammed Idris will not ... suffice for the needs it was intended to meet. But I find it impossible now to estimate the probable deficiency. ... Other members of the family are only now beginning to tour the country with a view to selecting eligible properties.'[10]

By June 1946, the newly promoted Major Peter Synge (signing 'for Chief Secretary') was joining in the expressions of concern, writing to Greatorex that the whole business of monthly and rehabilitation grants 'is getting too involved and needs clarifying'. Similar letters and memoranda flew back and forth with ever-increasing frequency over the following year. A sensitive problem arose in October over the management of a big former Italian farm known as Cerasola, where Sayyid Saddik al-Rida, another cousin of Idris, was in dispute with his business partner, Mohamed Budajaja [Budagagia]. Signing this time as Chief Secretary, Peter suggested that Idris be informed of the dispute 'which has caused a certain amount of unpleasantness in Barce'.[11]

With the return of more Sanussi family members, there were further dilemmas for the BMA in the early months of 1947. In March, Peter (reverting to the formula 'for Chief Secretary') wrote mentioning the recent return to Benghazi of Sayyid Sanussi Mohammed al-Abid, who was asking for financial assistance, and the possibility that more, including Sayyid Ahmed Ben Idris, Sayyid Jamal al-Din and others, 'may return in the near future to avail themselves of the grants provided by a generous government'. He reported that Sayyid Ahmed Ben Idris had

---

[10] C. Greatorex and S.Parker to CAB, GHQ, May 1946, WO 230/194.
[11] Miscellaneous correspondence, WO 230/194.

'stolen his elder brother's birthright and an awkward situation therefore arises'. Peter asked what should be done about this grant and if the provision of rehabilitation grants of £1,000 should be made to Sayyid Sanussi [Mohammed] al-Abid and Sayyid Jamal al-Din, and if a further £1,000 from the sum available to the Chief Administrator should be offered to each of them for repairs to their houses. He also requested guidance as to what they should be told in the meantime.[12]

## AN ARGUMENT ABOUT PEACHES

Recalling many years later how things escalated over the return of the Sanussis, Peter's otherwise terse record of this period in his memoir makes one of its most interesting revelations, which is worth quoting in full:

'On the appointment of a new Chief Secretary, I reverted to Major and to my old post of Political Secretary, and early in 1947 it was decided in Cairo that the various members of the Senussi family, in exile there, should return to Cyrenaica, but first they were to inspect the various possible places where they might settle, and it was my job to take them round. Of course, they chose the best of the Italian farms, which had been taken over by the Agricultural Department and were being efficiently run. They all had mature peach orchards and vineyards, as well as well-kept farmlands and a reasonably good house, and the best of them were chosen by the Senussi family.'

'It was obvious, though, that they knew nothing about farming, and were not interested in it, and merely wanted to live in comfort with their wives and draw a pension from the government,' Peter added. 'In due course, when the Chief Civil Affairs Officer, Maj. Gen. Sir Duncan Cumming ... came to Benghazi to hear the results of their visit, I told him that they had chosen this place and that, but that in my opinion it would be a shame to hand them over to people who 'simply wanted to sit under the peach trees and suck peaches all day long'. At that, Gen. Cumming got very angry and said: 'Synge, you are obviously not the right man for the job.' Consequently, a few months later, I was posted to Eritrea, which was a terrible blow to me, as I was very

---

[12] Miscellaneous correspondence, WO 230/194.

happy in Cyrenaica. I approached Brig. Haugh, but he took the view that a military posting was an order to be obeyed without question and refused to interfere.'

Reading this story, it would appear that Peter had come to the view that the whole Sanussi settlement scheme was misconceived but, by openly expressing his doubts about it, he was in effect challenging a fundamental policy to which first Arundell and then Cumming had been fully committed for the past three years. Now Cumming was urgently pushing it as a priority, in the hopes that it might help get Idris to move to Cyrenaica in the near future and so cement the political alliance that Cumming and his bosses had been nurturing.

Peter's statement that the return of the Sanussis 'was decided in Cairo' suggests that he was not fully acquainted with the rationale behind the decisions he was being asked to implement. Unlike De Candole, he was probably unaware of the bigger issues affecting British strategic thinking and planning for the eastern Mediterranean. To Peter, what mattered more was the potential misallocation both of valuable farmland and financial resources, and he expressed his disapproval accordingly.

Although Peter regretted having to leave, he must have been partly gratified by an apparent vindication of his stance before he moved on. As the archives reveal, he had not been alone in expressing concerns, with Parker, Greatorex and others raising the same issues for much of the preceding year. In June, new Chief Secretary Eric De Candole managed to persuade Cumming to investigate potential 'mismanagement' in the use of the grants for the Sanussis with the result that, in August, Cumming took the files relating to the case with him to London for discussions with the War Office. In July, De Candole referred to the weaknesses in 'the scheme as originally framed and administered' and proposed a modified version. On the specifics, he wrote: 'The grant of £10,000 for rehabilitation has proved inadequate. … The major part of it has already been exhausted on repairs to the Amir's residence and four other houses for the families. … The new scheme is therefore based on a carefully considered plan to complete the rehabilitation of the families concerned by establishing them on a sound bases as farmers. … It will be necessary therefore to appoint an officer to take charge.'

De Candole listed the seven Sanussi notables to be included in the new scheme as Sayyid Safi al-Din Mohamed Sherif (already identified as troublesome), Sayyid Saddik Mohamed al-Rida, Sayyid Mohamed al-Rida al-Mahdi and sons, Sayyid Ibrahim Ahmed Sherif, Sayyid Shams al-Din Ali, Sayyid Ahmed Ben Idris Mohamed al-Abid and Sayyid Izz al-Din Hilal. The first two of these were already occupying farms 'not yet in efficient operation' but which 'could be got running on sound lines', namely Sayyid Safi al-Din Mohamed Sherif at Brunetti and Cremonini and Sayyid Saddik Mohamed al-Rida at Cerasola. The other five did not yet have farms and it was proposed to lay out properties for them in the Marzotti valley just south of Barce, an area suited to 'mixed farming of the type most suited to these people'.[13]

Detailed agricultural and financial reports were then commissioned from the experts available to the BMA, with a view to identifying any mismanagement and recommending new measures, but no blame was apportioned for funds already misspent. It seems doubtful that any knuckles were rapped, other than those of Peter Synge for daring to question the fundamentals of what Professor Gibb had previously warned could be seen as 'the imposition of a new landed aristocracy'.

There may have been other factors that influenced the decision to redeploy Peter, especially the fact that he was identified with the poorly performing Chief Administrator Haugh. Whatever the case, he had not become part of Cumming's inner circle and could not compete with more experienced Arabist professionals. There was a clear distinction between the elite administrators (selected from Oxford and Cambridge and trained as Arabists) and those from other backgrounds, who had simply offered their services for the duration of the war and had, mostly unquestioningly, followed orders according to changing circumstances.

With three months left to serve in Benghazi, Peter was still given plenty to keep him busy. Benghazi and Derna had by this time become the leading hotbeds of debate about the future, often with the direct participation of the more politically active and outspoken Cyrenaican Arabs in the administration, who happened also to some of the best educated people in the territory. As Political Secretary, it was Peter's job to keep track of the ongoing debates and he would have had a good idea of what was being discussed in the Omar Mukhtar Clubs, not least because many of the leading BMA employees were themselves active within them. Among some of the intelligentsia, discussion was beginning to favour a political solution under the aegis of the Arab League.

Duncan Cumming and senior British officials in Cairo and London were only too well aware of the strong Egyptian influence in the Arab League and so, in the circumstances, they wanted to keep Cyrenaica out

---

[13] Further correspondence in WO 230/194.

of the Egyptian orbit as far as they possibly could. The long, troubled Anglo–Egyptian relationship was itself once again in crisis and if Britain were ever forced to give up its military facilities in Egypt, those in Cyrenaica could provide a very valuable alternative.[14] All in all, the pressure was mounting on Cumming – as much from far beyond Cyrenaica's shores as from its political activists in Benghazi and Derna – to deliver a conclusive deal with Idris. This had been his goal for the past five years and he was now more determined than ever not to let any opportunity for a result slip from his grasp.

---

[14] Foreign Secretary Ernest Bevin told senior US officials in September 1947: 'In case we withdraw from Suez, we must have some base to fall back upon. We consider Cyrenaica as that base.' See W. R. Louis, *The British Empire in the Middle East, 1945–1951*, Oxford, 1984, p260.

# chapter 11

## QUIET DEPARTURES, AND A TRIUMPHANT ENTRANCE
### BENGHAZI,
### JULY–NOVEMBER 1947

I
N CYRENAICA, where Ramadan was observed with great dedication, most citizens obeyed the rules and strictures of the Sanussiyya, with the result that a long month of daylight fasting could make people irritable, especially when it occurred in the hottest of the summer months. This was certainly true of 1947, when Ramadan started in mid-July, just as the more politically minded citizens were eagerly awaiting signs of political change in the territory, or at least of the long promised return of its amir-in-waiting, Sayyid Mohammed Idris. And the local situation was heavily influenced by the ongoing international negotiations over the future of the former Italian colonies ahead of a planned visit by a Four-power Commission of Investigation (from the United States, Britain, France and the Soviet Union).[1]

A joint meeting of conservatives and progressives held on 9 August, 'Sanussi Day',[2] registered a protest against both the continued stay of the British Military Administration and the delay in handing over power to the amir. In the weeks after this, there was yet more public discontent as the different political factions stepped up campaigns in favour of associating with either Egypt or Tripolitania. Peter Synge, who signed the BMA's Monthly Political Report for the month of August, reported that there were 'disquieting symptoms of a hardening opposition to the continuation of military government and a swing of feeling away from Great Britain.'[3]

---

[1] 'The Chiefs of Staff feared armed rebellion against their thinly manned BMAs. The spectre of new Palestines was regularly invoked.' S. L. Bills, *The Libyan Arena: The United State, Britain and the Council of Foreign Ministers 1945–1948*, Ohio, 1995, p82.

[2] The seventh anniversary of the British–Sanussi agreement signed in 1940.

[3] BMA Monthly Political Report no 20, P. M. Synge, 2 September 1947, WO 230/202.

While most people in Benghazi were being kept in the dark on progress, Sayyid Mohammed Idris was indeed being convinced to return. But he was taking his time about it and, having already tested the British determination to conclude a deal (and its willingness to go along with the increased demands of the Sanussi family), he now began to dictate his own final terms.

In a confidential report to Duncan Cumming on a meeting with Idris in Alexandria on 27 July, Cecil Greatorex listed the amir's specific demands, first among which was the removal of the Chief Administrator (Brigadier J.W.N. Haugh) and other officers 'already known to you as having been somewhat tactless in their dealings with the population'. In this context, Greatorex made specific reference to two individuals, namely Sholto Douglas, who had, in fact, already left, and a certain Spencer Cooke; if there were others, they were not named.[4]

Visiting London at the same time, Cumming discussed Idris's latest demands at a meeting of Foreign Office and War Office officials, for which the official minutes read as follows:

'The removal from Cyrenaica of one or two British officials "who are inexperienced in handling of Arabs and their affairs or are unsympathetic to himself [Idris] and the Senussi family"': General Cumming explained that the principal official concerned was the Chief Administrator himself who, although a competent administrator during a period when a policy of "care and maintenance" was being implemented, knew no Arabic and had insufficient experience of the details of civil administration to function successfully during a period of transition when a more liberal policy was in the course of adoption. ... It was agreed, therefore, that this condition would be accepted in practice.'[5]

This official judgement on Haugh was uncannily echoed, some 30 years later, by Peter in his memoir (see Chapter 9).

Among the other issues where a deal with Idris now seemed close were the appointment of an administrative council (with equal numbers of British and Arab members) and the immediate repair of Graziani's palace in Benghazi to serve as the seat of government (at an estimated cost of £3,500). There was a further step forward in September, when Greatorex sent formal proposals for the 'Civil List' to be paid

---

[4] C. Greatorex to D. C. Cumming, 8 August 1947, FO 1015/91.
[5] Minutes of meeting at Foreign Office, 24 July 1947, WO 230/216.

to Idris for the performance of his functions as amir and for the running of his household in Benghazi. Noting for the benefit of his superiors in London that 'local political opinion in Cyrenaica is becoming increasingly unsettled by anti-BMA propaganda and by the uncertainties of the future.' Greatorex argued that 'the Amir's presence alone can restore its stability' and that 'certain inducements are not only justifiable but necessary'.

In total, the proposal amounted to £1,000 a month for Idris and £655 a month for his staff and for contingencies, altogether a little less than Idris had first asked for.[6] However, a very special inducement, and one that Idris had specifically demanded six months previously, was the presentation on 11 September of a prestigious vehicle, a Humber Pullman, to serve as his official limousine.[7]

Such was the secrecy over the negotiations in these delicate final stages that Jose Campbell Penney sent out a special memorandum warning against 'any premature disclosures' that would be 'extremely embarrassing to [Idris] and to us, particularly in view of the criticism which Great Britain, and her projected "stooge monarch", have recently come in for in the Egyptian press.'[8] Even the BMA was itself being kept out of the loop and had to ask Cairo to keep it more fully informed.[9]

## IDRIS AGREES

Even at the very end of September, when Idris at last signalled to Cumming that he was ready to return, the news was still being kept from Benghazi, where the mood remained both fractious and heated. Eric De Candole noted that the rift between the Sanussi loyalists and the intelligentsia who rallied around the Omar Mukhtar Clubs had broken out into 'open manifestations of factional hostility' against the National Front. Slogans such as 'Down with the Jabha' and 'The Jabha is the Supporter of Colonisation' were painted on various streets and walls. In one instance, a refuse bin containing dead rats and a dead cat was painted with the words 'This is the Sanussi Family'.[10]

Ali [el] Fellag, Secretary of the Benghazi Municipal Council, was thought to be the chief instigator of the political activities of the Omar

---

[6] Proposed Civil List for HE Amir Idris, C. Greatorex, CAA, to GHQ, 10 September 1947, FO 1015/91.
[7] C. Greatorex to D. C. Cumming, 12 September 1947, FO 1015/91.
[8] J.C. Penney, CAA, to CAB, 9 September 1947, WO 230/215.
[9] S. Parker, CAB, to E. A. V. De Candole, BMA, 25 September 1947, WO 230/215.
[10] BMA Monthly Political Report no 21, E. A. V. De Candole, 1 October 1947, WO 230/202.

Mukhtar Clubs (estimated by the BMA to have 500 members in Beng-hazi and 300 in Derna), which at the time were aligning themselves with demands for association with Egypt. And even such a senior figure in the central administration as Mahmud Makhluf of the BMA's Public Information Office lent his name to these demands.[11]

Peter's report on the proceedings of a supposedly secret Omar Mukhtar meeting in August played a key role in convincing Idris to hurry back to take charge of a political situation that risked spinning out of his grasp. From Cairo, Penney wrote to London that the report 'helped him [Idris] to make up his mind' because 'he realises generally that local political opinion requires his urgent personal direction.'[12] The meeting in question had been held at Ras al-Hilal, near Derna, and Peter wrote that it had decided to build up a strong movement to demand an Egyptian trusteeship from the international commission that was due to visit the territory in the coming months. 'The movement includes the Omar Mukhtar Clubs and Youth League and the majority of the employees of the Administration,' said the report. 'Both Sayed Safi el Din el Senussi and the Grand Qadi are believed to be in sympathy with it. At present it has a large potential following in the towns but little among the tribes. It may gain some ground in Derna district, where signs of a desire for rapprochement with Egypt have been for some time evident and where grain scarcity has recently caused some discontent.'[13] The August report provides evidence that Peter, even at this late stage, was now becoming rather more politically astute, as was fitting in his role of Political Secretary; he was also receiving assistance from a new team of officers who had arrived to support De Candole, among them Major Gervase P. ('Jeff') Cassels, who would shortly take over as Political Secretary himself.

With the reshuffle at the top of the BMA beginning to take effect, De Candole was becoming increasingly assertive, at first imposing a ban on the *El Watan* newspaper and subsequently taking a political line that deliberately downplayed the activities of the Omar Mukhtar Clubs. Perhaps to drive the point home, he chose to distance himself from Peter's version of the events of August. In a message to Cumming he acknowledged 'increased dissatisfaction with the continuance of the present regime', but kept the focus on the views of the amir's sup-porters in the Jabha, who were continuing to insist that Idris should

---

[11] BMA Monthly Political Report no 20, P. M. Synge, 2 September 1947, WO 230/202.
[12] J.C. Penney, CAA, to Scott-Fox, FO, 12 September 1947, WO 230/215.
[13] BMA Monthly Political Report no 20, P. M. Synge, 2 September 1947, WO 230/202.

return as soon as possible and as head of state.[14] In his subsequent report for September, De Candole described the 'recent pro-Egyptian tendency' as 'a somewhat tactical move designed to put pressure on the Administration rather than a genuine desire for subordination to Egypt.'[15]

By early October, the negotiated change of regime had started to get underway in earnest. Brigadier Haugh relinquished his post on 9 October to become District Commander in Tripolitania, an entirely military rather than administrative appointment, while De Candole took over as Acting Chief Administrator in his place. With Haugh now out of the way, Idris was expected to arrive to complete the symbolic transition to an administration that could present itself as civilian rather than military in nature. But the amir, who so often extracted perverse satisfaction from keeping everyone waiting, once again managed to find reasons for a final delay. On 19 October, after Idris had already been promised £8,000 for the settlement of his Egyptian debts, Cumming went to see him to wish him bon voyage, fully expecting Idris to leave within the next few days, but he now demanded £2,500 as an advance on the promised £8,000.[16] On 25 October, Idris sent ahead his private secretary, Omar Sheneib, but Idris himself did not finally leave Cairo until 11 November.

During this transition, the focus was on choosing Cyrenaicans who could serve both in the ruling council and in the new administration itself. This involved formalising the salary structure, identifying good candidates and presenting names for consideration by Idris and his advisers. Peter Synge's final item of correspondence in the files, written on 11 October, was a strong defence of the abilities of Ali Jerbi, who had been deemed unsuitable by Idris but was 'considered to be the ablest Libyan official in the department, and to the best of our knowledge ... not actively associated with the recent Omar Mukhtar movement.' Peter added that the amir 'may have been misled as to Jerbi's sentiments'.[17] His letter achieved its purpose because De Candole's correspondence some months later made the following observation: 'The Amir ... has come round to a more liberal attitude towards individual intelligentsia whom he formerly denounced as traitors, such as Ali Jerbi.'[18] Departing

---

[14] Top secret telegram, E. A. V. De Candole to D. C. Cumming, 13 September 1947, FO 1015/987.

[15] BMA Monthly Political Report no 21, E. A. V. De Candole, 1 October 1947, WO 230/202.

[16] Top secret telegram, CinC, MEF, to WO, 19 October 1947, FO 1015/91.

[17] P. M. Synge, Acting Chief Secretary, to CAA, 11 October 1947, WO 230/215.

[18] E. A. V. De Candole to D. C. Cumming, 7 January 1948, WO 230/215.

with at least some credit for having helped the BMA to fulfil its aims and to train up qualified Cyrenaicans, Peter and his family left for Eritrea very shortly after this.[19] It was only a matter of weeks before Idris arrived to take up permanent residence.

## GRAND CEREMONIALS IN BENGHAZI

Idris finally set off from Cairo by road on 11 November, although he was then held up en route at Mersa Matruh as the Egyptian government used delaying tactics in issuing export licences for his substantial quantity of baggage. This was interpreted by Cumming as a last-minute attempt by the Egyptian Ministry of Foreign Affairs to persuade Idris to issue a statement committing him to 'a promise to sacrifice all for the complete independence of Libya and the unity of Cyrenaica, Tripolitania and the Fezzan.' If true, this was presumably a ploy to enhance Egypt's case for trusteeship with the anticipated international commission.[20] Eventually, however, the convoy crossed the border between Egypt and Libya on 15 November and proceeded over the following days through Tobruk, Derna and Barce to Benghazi, where Idris arrived on 21 November.

Describing the official welcoming parade held on 24 November, the new Acting Chief Secretary, Major Jeff Cassels, reported that 'the warmth of the welcome along the route and in the capital showed that his personal influence remains as strong as ever, and that Senussi loyalty

---

[19] The memoir describes the family's departure from Benghazi in October 1947 as being almost as traumatic as the one they had experienced in 1945. 'We packed up all our belongings and prepared to leave. The plan was that Maidie and the two boys [Anthony, aged 6, and Richard, 1½ – the eldest, Patrick, aged 11, was by now at boarding school in Ireland] should sail to Malta in an awful old Corvette named the *Empire Peacemaker*, but known as 'the Sickmaker', and catch a liner which would call at Massawa, while I flew to Asmara, but things did not go according to plan, and when the *Peacemaker* arrived she lay off outside the harbour all day, and no orders to embark were given until late afternoon. Then we embarked on a tug, which towed a barge carrying our belongings. Although it had been calm all morning, the wind had got up and the sea was quite rough and when we got alongside, the tug was lifting on every wave and I judged it too dangerous to try to pass the children across, while Maidie and the other women were scared stiff, so I went aboard myself and asked to see the Captain, who was angry at being kept waiting all day, but agreed that it was too dangerous. Meanwhile, our belongings had been hoisted aboard so they had to be unloaded back on to the barge and eventually we got back ashore and had to go and stay at the Officers' Club. The following day I flew to Ismailia and, a few days later, Maidie and the boys embarked on a Prince Line ship for Port Said, from where they came by train to Ismailia and we stayed again in the Transit Camp, where we had stayed so long in 1945. There I got malaria and went to hospital for a week, but before Maidie's ship arrived I was able to fly to Asmara and arrived there in November.'
[20] CinC, MEF, to WO, 12 November 47, FO 1015/91.

is still the dominating force in Cyrenaican politics.'[21] Idris was met outside Benghazi by Acting Chief Administrator Eric De Candole and the District Commander, Brigadier R. C. Cruddas, and was driven to Graziani's palace 'through cheering crowds, escorted by mounted police'.

In a display of British imperial pageantry, a salute of 19 guns was fired from *HMS Cardigan Bay*[22], whereupon Idris inspected a guard of honour composed of contingents from the [Royal] Navy, the King's Dragoon Guards and the Cyrenaica Defence Force. While Jeff Cassels observed that 'the crowds were most enthusiastic', he also noted that the Omar Mukhtar faction had stationed people at strategic points to lead cheers both for independence and for the Arab League. The report added that Idris was concerned to reconcile factional strife by 'boosting the Jabha and ignoring the political existence of the Omar Mukhtar party'.

In his speeches, Idris made a strong point of defending the role of Britain, which he said supported the independence of both Cyrenaica and Tripolitania in international conferences. He also made the point that Britain had already left India and had decided to leave Palestine and evacuate Egypt, while helping Syria and Lebanon to attain their independence, 'and we wish, therefore, to be friends with her. She has previously kept her promise to the Senussis in every conference that was held in the past.'[23]

In the few short weeks between the quiet departure of Haugh and the triumphant arrival of Idris, the two-year hiatus that had prevailed in Cyrenaica since 1945 finally came to an end. A new era beckoned, even if the final outcome could not be predicted. In an altogether experimental manner, the temporary British administration that had prevailed in Cyrenaica since Peter Synge's arrival in January 1943 was about to become a de facto system of indirect rule that would enable Idris to take executive powers. The wider functions of the BMA had by now become overwhelmingly skewed towards the single political aim of settling and establishing Idris and his extended family, which was seen as essential to ensuring a close, long-term alliance.

It was not just the Egyptian press that was describing the new system as a 'stooge monarchy'. Even the chief architect of the transition,

---

[21] BMA Monthly Political Report no 23, G. P. Cassels, 3 December 1947, WO 230/202.
[22] It is worth noting that in imperial India, such salutes were calibrated according to the relative ranks of the local princes, maharajas or nawabs. The most prominent five of these rulers were regularly granted 21-gun salutes, while a further five received 19-gun salutes and others, of lower rank, received 17, 15 or less.
[23] BMA Monthly Political Report no 23, G. P. Cassels, 3 December 1947, WO 230/202.

Duncan Cumming, had admitted to being aware that he was introducing 'a form of Arab medievalism tempered by British advice' (see Chapter 10). However, Cyrenaica seemed to offer new promise at a time when the harsh post-war realities were forcing Britain to renegotiate its relationships everywhere else in the Middle East.[24] As Cumming revealed to De Candole in January 1948, 'it is certain that HMG [His Majesty's Government] will remain in Cyrenaica at almost any cost.'[25]

---

[24] 'Between March 1946 and January 1948, the British Government attempted treaty renegotiation everywhere [in the Middle East]. And everywhere it failed except in Transjordan – the one country so small and poor that even the impoverished British exchequer could offer something worth having.' E. Monroe, *Britain's Moment in the Middle East, 1914–1971*, London, 1981, p156.

[25] Secret telegram, D. C. Cumming to E. A. V. De Candole, 15 January 1948, FO 1015/987.

# chapter 12

## AN EVOLVING NEW
## ORDER IN BENGHAZI
### CYRENAICA, 1947–51

B Y THE END OF 1947, although Benghazi still showed many of the scars of wartime bombing, a major effort had been made to repair and furnish Graziani's shattered palace so that it could become the symbolic centre of a new government for Cyrenaica. Renamed the Manar Palace, it was intended that Sayyid Mohammed Idris should reside there, but soon after his arrival in November, he made it clear that he preferred the peace and quiet of the villa that had been kept ready at Fuweihat [al-Fuwayha], beside Lethe's Grotto.[1] This was in line with

Figure 25. *Al Manar Palace, 1947.* Cassels Collection.

---

[1] E. A. V. De Candole, *The Life and Times of King Idris of Libya*, published privately, 1990, p85.

Figure 26. *Benghazi, Municipal Square and Central Mosque, 1947.* Cassels Collection.

Idris's lifelong habits of ascetism, but it also showed that from the out-set as a new ruler he preferred to manage the affairs of state as far away as possible from public view.

Benghazi's rise as the capital of independent Cyrenaica after Idris's return is vividly recorded in the memoir and photographs left by Peter Synge's immediate successor as Political Secretary, Jeff Cassels, who between 1947 and 1950 was one of a select group that worked closely with local politicians and administrators to manage the political trans-formations that took place under the general direction of Eric De Can-dole and Idris.[2]

De Candole quickly became a close and trusted confidant of the amir (and future king) and took over as Chief Administrator of Cyre-naica in the second half of 1948. His title soon changed again to Resi-dent (a colonial era term meaning the most senior British government representative), as a semi-autonomous Cyrenaica came to be merged into an independent Libya through the auspices of the United Nations General Assembly. It was a time of rapid change and intensive local politics against the uncertain backdrop of the international delibera-tions over the future of Libya.

---

[2] Cassels had been recruited by the Colonial Office to work in Nigeria in 1938. In 1939 he joined the Royal West African Frontier Force and served in Kenya, Ethiopia and Egypt, mostly in administrative work relating to the former Italian colonies.

Figure 27. *Benghazi, Roman Catholic Cathedral and the Secretariat (formerly and subsequently the Berenice Hotel), 1947.* Cassels Collection.

Figure 28. *Benghazi, the AKC Cinema and Navy House, 1947.* Cassels Collection.

From the time Idris arrived, in November 1947, Cyrenaica was put on the road to what the Foreign Office at the time hoped would be 'an Arab state under British trusteeship'. Of the options being considered by the four-power Council of Foreign Ministers[3], the one most favoured by Britain was what Cassels described as 'a British protectorate over Cyrenaica where they could run a happy little show rather on the lines of Transjordan after World War I'.[4]

With the return of Idris having helped them to regain the political initiative, the new British administrators set about establishing a working partnership with Cyrenaican civil servants and politicians. Over the next two years, the management and rules of the War Office came to be replaced by supervision from the Foreign Office and, in the course of 1949, the British Military Administration was transformed into a civilian administration under the nominal leadership of Idris.[5]

## IDRIS SETTLES IN

The evolution into a civilian administration only came about after a rather uncertain, almost nervous, beginning, while De Candole was still trying to find ways for Idris to assume a measure of de facto power. At first, Idris was simply 'handling local politicians and advising on the most suitable Cyrenaicans to fill higher posts in the administration'.[6] On 7 January 1948, De Candole reported to Duncan Cumming in Cairo his favourable impressions of Idris's 'qualities of judgement, perception and firmness', noting that 'both in official and personal matters he is an adept at driving a hard bargain, probably learned in his dealings with the Italians over 20 years ago.' On the negative side, however, De Candole pointed out that Idris 'finds it difficult to say "no" and is too easy-going with the importunate', and that he was surrounded by 'disreputable adventurers who exercise a malign influence over him'.[7]

By 15 January, Idris was already deeply absorbed in the international negotiations about the future, but he had not yet made a firm promise to stay on in Benghazi. Remembering how things had turned out at the time of the KBE investiture the previous January,

---

[3] The Council consisted of Britain, France, the USA and the Soviet Union.
[4] Cassels memoir, p3.
[5] Cassels memoir, p3.
[6] E. A. V. De Candole, *The Life and Times of King Idris of Libya*, published privately, 1990, p86.
[7] E. A. V. De Candole to D. C. Cumming, 7 January 1948, WO 230/215.

and fearing that Idris would again find reasons to leave, Cumming sent De Candole a secret telegram urging him 'to play for time if necessary' and stressing the arguments he should use. 'Our task will be to convince Amir that he must accept British trusteeship and a subsidiary agreement similar to former agreement with Transjordan which will give us full strategic facilities,' he said. 'If necessary, inform Amir that details are being worked out as a result of my visit to London. If sending Greatorex here, would help he should proceed at once, but Amir should in NO circumstances be permitted to leave Cyrenaica at this juncture.'[8]

The pressure clearly worked. It also helped that Idris was preoccupied by the upcoming visit of the special Commission of Investigation being sent by the four-power Council of Foreign Ministers to look at the constitutional future of the whole of Libya. The leading politicians in the Jabha agreed to form a National Congress (al-Mutamar al-Watani). Idris's brother, Mohamed al-Rida, was elected to lead an executive committee to draw up a programme for the future of Cyrenaica.

By the time the Commission arrived in Cyrenaica, for a stay of three weeks in April 1948, the National Congress was ready to present comprehensive proposals for independence.[9] The Congress told the Commission that its main demand was for Cyrenaican independence and a constitutional government under Idris, ahead of any union with Tripolitania. Idris himself told the Commission that he agreed with this and that he desired to cooperate with Britain on the basis of an alliance. It was a good display of self-confidence, but the Commission, when it presented its report some months later, was not persuaded that Libya as a whole was ready for independence. And with the Soviet Union increasingly determined to frustrate the strategic interests of both Britain and the USA, the high-level diplomacy still produced no consensus concerning the future of the two main parts of the country. When the four powers met in September 1948 and once again failed to find a solution, the issue was referred to the UN General Assembly. As Saul Kelly noted, the British and US governments now began to realise that 'they stood a better chance of securing their strategic aims from the UN than from the Council of Foreign Ministers, where the Soviets could exercise an effective veto.'[10]

---

[8] Secret telegram, D. C. Cumming to E. A. V. De Candole, 15 January 1948, FO 1015/987.

[9] M. Khadduri, *Modern Libya: A Study in Political Development*, Baltimore, 1963, p70.

[10] S. Kelly, *War and Politics in the Desert: Britain and Libya during the Second World War*, London, 2010, p234.

Different aspects of the complex international diplomacy over the future of the Italian colonies have been explored thoroughly by the historians Scott Bills, Saul Kelly and William Roger Louis. Taking into account the differing and changing perspectives of each of the four powers over the issue throughout 1948 and 1949, their research clearly demonstrates that the prospect of British trusteeship of Cyrenaica became one of only very few ideas on which both British and American policymakers managed to agree consistently.[11]

'Let there be no mistake that the dominant motive [for Britain] was the establishing of a strategic base in Cyrenaica,' declares Louis. In their effort to secure this critical alternative to the facilities in Egypt, Bevin and the Labour government in London were 'prepared to pay a high price, perhaps by bartering the other former Italian colonies ..., perhaps by accommodating the Italians and the French as well as the Americans, or perhaps by constructing a vast national edifice based on Cyrenaica that would extend over Tripolitania and the Fezzan. All of these possibilities were studied by the Labour empire builders with an exuberant calculation worthy of their Victorian predecessors. It was the last that proved to be the most attractive. ... Here was a state that was to be subsidized largely by the Americans, held together by the Senussi, and controlled indirectly by the British.'[12]

Foreign Secretary Ernest Bevin was initially prepared to see Tripolitania placed under Italian trusteeship, although this was later substituted with the idea of returning Somalia to Italy – in compensation for its loss of influence in Libya and in a bid to maintain collective European influence in Africa, even while Britain hung on to its own dominance in the eastern Mediterranean.

With Cyrenaica now intended as the major peacetime base in the Middle East, the decision to redeploy 8,000 British troops from Palestine to Cyrenaica during the summer of 1948 forced the British Government to sanction the building of suitable accommodation and to speed up the preparation for self-rule.[13] The increasing uncertainties in the wider Middle East in 1948 brought a new dimension to De Candole's task in

[11] S. L. Bills, *The Libyan Arena: The United States, Britain and the Council of Foreign Ministers 1945–1948*, Ohio, 1995; S. Kelly, *Cold War in the Desert: Britain, the United States and the Italian Colonies, 1945–52*, Basingstoke, 2000; W. R. Louis, 'Libyan Independence, 1951: The Creation of a Client State', in *Decolonization and African Independence*, eds. P. Gifford and W. R. Louis, New Haven and London, 1988.
[12] W. R. Louis, 'Libyan Independence, 1951: The Creation of a Client State', in *Decolonization and African Independence*, eds. P. Gifford and W. R. Louis, New Haven and London, 1988.
[13] S. Kelly, *Cold War in the Desert: Britain, the United States and the Italian Colonies, 1945–52*, Basingstoke, 2000, p94.

Cyrenaica when his house in Benghazi was attacked by a street mob. This incident was blamed on the Omar Mukhtar Club as their response to the escalating Arab-Jewish war in Palestine and, soon afterwards, the Club was declared 'subversive'.[14]

'Under the modus operandi we established, I concentrated on administrative matters and left political questions entirely to [Idris],' De Candole later claimed.[15] This sounds unlikely to be the whole story. Kelly's book *Cold War in the Desert* reveals that by early 1949 Idris was advising the Foreign Office that the best way to clamp down on the growing discontent in Cyrenaica at the delay in reaching a decision on the future would be for him to proclaim independence, form a government and propose a treaty with Britain. In response, Bevin readily agreed with this, writing that the best plan would in fact be to encourage Idris 'to proclaim himself and put himself in a position in which he could conclude a treaty'.[16] In the territory itself, Jeff Cassels's recollection was that Britain was responding to 'the relentless pressure of political events' by granting the Libyans in Cyrenaica 'a measure of local autonomy'.[17]

## INDEPENDENCE, PHASE ONE

On 1 June 1949, Idris proceeded to make a unilateral proclamation of independence for Cyrenaica. It was an event that clearly had the tacit approval of the Foreign Office, although it could not be formally recognised as such. Certainly, the British press was well enough briefed to report on it as an entirely favourable development.[18] For his part, Eric De Candole declared that Britain agreed to the formation of a Cyrenaican government with responsibility for internal affairs, and also recognised the amir as its head.[19] During the accompanying ceremony at the Manar Palace, the only dissenting voices came from Omar Mukhtar Club supporters, who felt that unity with Tripolitania should have come first and shouted: 'Down with sham independence.'[20]

---

[14] E. A. V. De Candole, *The Life and Times of King Idris of Libya*, published privately, 1990, p89.
[15] E. A. V. De Candole, *The Life and Times of King Idris of Libya*, published privately, 1990, p94.
[16] S. Kelly, *Cold War in the Desert: Britain, the United States and the Italian Colonies, 1945–52*, Basingstoke, 2000, p117.
[17] Cassels memoir, p2.
[18] 'A Cyrenaican government will now be formed with full authority over internal affairs.' *The Manchester Guardian*, 3 June 1949.
[19] *Cyrenaica Observer*, Benghazi, 5 June 1949.
[20] M. Khadduri, *Modern Libya: A Study in Political Development*, Baltimore, 1963, p72.

Figure 29. *Amir Mohammed Idris takes the salute outside Al Manar Palace after returning from his visit to Britain, September 1949.* Cassels Collection.

All in all, the summer months of 1949 turned out to be the high point in Cyrenaica's special status in British eyes. Within weeks of the independence announcement, the Chief of Imperial General Staff, Field Marshal Sir William Slim, arrived in Benghazi for talks with Idris, who made the trip from his summer retreat in al-Bayda to offer him tea at the Manar Palace, and a series of symbolic naval visits began. The aircraft carrier *HMS Ocean* led the first of what would become regular calls by ships of the Mediterranean fleet.[21]

As a mark of his acceptance within the fold, Idris then went on to make a formal state visit to Britain in July 1949. For a man who so valued his privacy and paid such attention to small details, this was a major undertaking. Because of his fear of air travel, the expedition was helpfully undertaken by a British warship from Tripoli to Marseille, and thereafter by train and ferry as appropriate. The organisers made sure to include a visit to Oxford, where Idris met Professor Hamilton Gibb and must also have been greeted by Professor Edward Evan Evans-Pritchard, though this is not recorded. Evans-Pritchard's painstaking research into the Sanussis did so much to justify Idris's claim to rule Cyrenaica, and

---

[21] *Cyrenaica Observer*, Benghazi, 12 June 1949.

190

his book *The Sanusi of Cyrenaica* happened to be published in 1949. And as he couldn't favour just one Oxbridge university, Idris also took the train to Cambridge, where he was no doubt pleased to catch up again with his former close helper and adviser, Norman Anderson, now newly appointed Professor of Islamic Law.[22]

Probably the most significant aspect of Idris's visit only became apparent much later. Behind the scenes the British government was preparing to accept, albeit reluctantly, the inevitability of pan-Libyan independence under the auspices of the UN. This was definitely not Britain's preferred option because it meant expanding the horizon far beyond Cyrenaica and incorporating the less certain complexities of Tripolitania, but it was by now becoming the only solution on which all the parties concerned could agree. 'We are coming to the conclusion that the solution for Libya must be independence,' Bevin wrote in July.[23] Louis regards this as 'one of the most decisive moments in actually bringing

Figure 30. *A contingent of the Cyrenaica Defence Force in the September 1949 ceremony.* Cassels Collection.

---

[22] E. A. V. De Candole, *The Life and Times of King Idris of Libya,* published privately, 1990, p104.
[23] Quoted by W. R. Louis in 'Libyan Independence, 1951: The Creation of a Client State' in *Decolonization and African Independence: The Transfers of Power, 1960–1980,* New Haven and London, p162.

about the birth of the Libyan state' and concludes that, for Bevin and his advisers, 'the task now was to make sure that Libya would become a British client-state.'[24]

Following detailed negotiations in London, the Foreign Office allowed De Candole to issue a 'transitional powers' proclamation on 16 September 1949; this empowered the amir to enact the Cyrenaican constitution and defined the powers of the government and the Chief Administrator (De Candole), now to be known as the British Resident. This meant that De Candole could legislate by decree on foreign affairs, defence and matters relating to Italian property, while British advisers for legal and financial matters were to be appointed by the amir with the approval of the Resident.[25] The internal half of the administration was to be placed in the hands of a Cyrenaican Prime Minister, with departmental ministers for the interior, justice, health, agriculture, public works and communications.

Although De Candole regarded Idris as 'a born leader whose dignified bearing set him apart', the amir at first found it hard to choose those who should run his new country, and those who managed to exercise power around him often aroused great opposition and/or jealousy. Such was the case with the first substantive Prime Minister of Cyrenaica, Omar Pasha Mansur el Kekhia, whom De Candole described as 'an irascible and headstrong old gentleman, trained in the Ottoman methods of forty years earlier, and incapable of adapting himself to British standards or Arab aspirations. He began to reorganise the administration according to his old-fashioned ideas, and his methods, which were a mixture of Turkish procedures of a somewhat medieval character and Italian reliance on secret police and informers, brought him into collision with British staff and Arab personalities alike.'[26]

In March 1950, to widespread relief, the National Congress persuaded Mansur el Kekhia to resign and Idris replaced him with Mohammed al-Saqizli, whereupon a much more obviously British-friendly administration began to take shape. One of the photos in Jeff Cassels's album shows Saqizli surrounded by some of his key ministers: Suadallah bin Saud (health), Hussein Mazer (the interior), Abdulqadir el Allam (agriculture) and Ali Jerbi (the former senior civil servant who was now

---

[24] Quoted by William Roger Louis in 'Libyan Independence, 1951: The Creation of a Client State', in *Decolonization and African Independence: The Transfers of Power, 1960–1980*, New Haven and London, p170.

[25] M. Khadduri, *Modern Libya: A Study in Political Development*, Baltimore, 1963, p74.

[26] E. A. V. De Candole, *The Life and Times of King Idris of Libya*, published privately, 1990, p109.

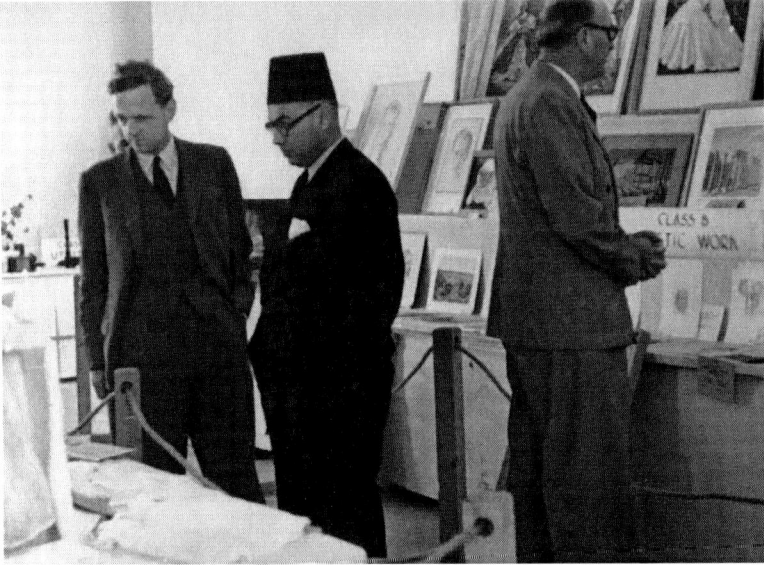

Figure 31. *Jeff Cassels with Ali Jerbi (Minister of Works and Communications) and D. Clark (Financial Advisor), 1950.* Cassels Collection.

Figure 32. *Those identified are* (left) *D. Clark (Financial Advisor) and* (right) *Brigadier Wood (Department of Public Works) with Works and Communications Minister Ali Jerbi, 1950.* Cassels Collection.

Figure 33. *Cyrenaica's Government Ministers in 1950,* (left to right) *Health Minister Saadallah bin Saud, Lt. Col Moberley, Interior Minister Hussein Mazeq, Prime Minister Mohammed Saqizly, Agriculture Minister Abdulqadir El Allam, Works and Communications Minister Ali Jerbi.* Cassels Collection.

Figure 34. *Health Minister Saadallah bin Saud and Interior Minister Hussein Mazeq, 1950.* Cassels Collection.

Minister of Works and Communications and, in addition, was serving on the UN Council for Libya). Cassels said he got on well with those in office at this time and that he felt 'considerable sympathy with their desire to be free from all imperial yokes, whether Italian, British or any other', adding that in return they showed him respect for his abilities and, more importantly, trusted him.[27]

This was indeed a time of remarkably close Anglo–Cyrenaican cooperation. Cassels's former title of Political Secretary changed to Chief Inspector of the Interior, reporting to the Minister of the Interior.[28] Hardly had he settled into this post when, in the spring of 1950, he also became Supervisor of Elections, with responsibility for organising elections in June to an entirely new House of Representatives, as he later recalled:

'This was a daunting prospect as no elections of a Parliamentary kind had ever been held in Cyrenaica before and the whole electoral machinery had to be built up from scratch. However, all went well, I received full support from the Ministers concerned, the electoral arrangements worked smoothly, and by 6 June 1950 an elected Cyrenaican Assembly consisting of representatives from all parts of the territory had been lawfully constituted.'[29]

Although the registered electorate was of limited size, with 60,000 registered voters, all of them male, there was a high turnout in the towns of 78 per cent in Benghazi, 92 per cent in al-Marj and 89 per cent in Derna. Even in the main tribal electoral districts around Benghazi and the Jebel region, the turnout reached 66 per cent, although it was much lower in other rural or desert areas.[30]

In a report to his minister, Cassels praised the work of the police in guarding the registers and ballot boxes and in handling the large crowds that thronged the polling stations, ensuring that there were 'no major incidents'. He also made a point of naming the Cyrenaicans who had played a constructive role in managing the elections, notably his deputy supervisors (Mutasarifs), Ali Jauda, Hussein Taher and Busef Yasin.[31]

---

[27] Cassels memoir, p6.
[28] Cassels memoir, p5.
[29] Cassels memoir, p5.
[30] G. P. Cassels, Supervisor of Elections, letter to Minister of Interior, 13 June 1950. (Cassels's papers.)
[31] G. P. Cassels, Supervisor of Elections, letter to Minister of Interior, 13 June 1950. (Cassels's papers.)

Figure 35. *Those identified are Mahmud Quertin (wearing fez) and Jeff and Mary Cassels, at a reception given by Egyptian Consul-General in Paradise Restaurant, Benghazi, April 1951.* Cassels Collection.

After the success of these elections, Cassels was offered the post of Head of the Cabinet Secretariat in Cyrenaica but, taking into account what he felt to be the volatility of Middle Eastern politics[32], he decided to return to his original service in Nigeria. He left Benghazi in April 1951, not knowing that he would be lured back to Libya much sooner than he had expected, as recounted in Chapter 13.

Britain's special relationship with Cyrenaica posed a major challenge for the UN Commissioner, Adrian Pelt, who had been appointed by the General Assembly in December 1949, with the ambitious brief to achieve full independence for the whole of Libya before 1 January 1952. For its part, Britain was already tantalisingly close to recognising Cyrenaican independence in return for a treaty that provided it with the guarantee of military facilities for the foreseeable future. On Pelt's first visit to Benghazi in early 1950, the treaty was mentioned by Idris (rather than by De Candole, who only admitted it once Pelt challenged him) and he realised that such a treaty 'would have planted a bomb under the United Nations plan for Libya' by provoking strong

---

[32] Cassels memoir, p6.

Figure 36. *Those identified are (each wearing a fez and facing the camera) Bashir Effendi Mughrabi and Interior Minister Hussein Mazeq, at the Egyptian reception of April 1951.* Cassels Collection.

Figure 37. *From left to right the Grand Qadi, the Greek Patriarch and Sheikh Mustafa Saqizly, at the Egyptian reception of April 1951.* Cassels Collection.

protests in Tripolitania. Reacting quickly, Pelt succeeded in persuading Idris to delay the signing at least until the UN agenda was further advanced. His subsequent discussions with the Foreign Office in London were much more complex than this, but ultimately highly significant in that they brought a new perspective to the future of both Cyrenaica and Libya.[33]

Pelt's arrival on the scene also happened to come in the wake of a renewal of the previously stalled efforts to find a mutually acceptable form of unity between Cyrenaica and Tripolitania, an outcome that British policy had previously dismissed as unlikely.[34] Pelt's later account dates the origins of this improvement in relations between the political forces in both territories to the two visits that Idris made to Tripoli in July and August 1949, on his way to and from his state visit to Britain, whereupon even the radical Congress Party of Beshir Saadawi in Tripoli dropped its previous opposition to possible Sanussi leadership of a united and independent Libya.[35]

## ANGLO–CYRENAICAN RELATIONS IN RETROSPECT

After World War I, British imperial rule in the Middle East came to be organised on the basis of creating kingdoms and what historian David Cannadine describes as 'a large new dominion based on a romantic, admiring, escapist view of Arab social structure'; this soon became so widespread across the region that, during World War II 'kingship and rural hierarchy remained the essential basis of British perception of the Middle East.' Although already on the brink of vanishing altogether, the British sphere in the region was for a brief time thereafter 'more extended (and more royal) than ever before', says Cannadine. 'Here was the final extension of the Churchillian enterprise begun in Cairo in 1921.'[36]

---

[33] A. Pelt, *Libyan Independence and the United Nations: A Case of Planned Decolonization*, New Haven and London, 1970, pp166–172. A more detached account of the diplomacy over this period is provided by S. Kelly, *Cold War in the Desert: Britain, the United States and the Italian Colonies, 1945–52*, Basingstoke, 2000, pp132–143.

[34] In May 1949, the British and Italian foreign ministers, Ernest Bevin and Count Sforza, had proposed an arrangement that would provide British trusteeship over Cyrenaica, Italian trusteeship over Tripolitania (from 1951) and French trusteeship over the Fezzan – each to run for ten years. The news not only provoked riots in Tripoli, but was vehemently condemned by the Omar Mukhtar Club in Benghazi. A. Pelt, *Libyan Independence and the United Nations: A Case of Planned Decolonization*, New Haven and London, 1970, pp48 and 79.

[35] A. Pelt, *Libyan Independence and the United Nations: A Case of Planned Decolonization*, New Haven and London, 1970, p53.

[36] D. Cannadine, *Ornamentalism: How the British Saw their Empire*, London, 2001, pp77–8.

The provisional creation of the Kingdom of Cyrenaica fitted neatly within this pattern, not least because it followed so closely in the wake of Transjordan's evolution from amirate to independent kingdom in 1946 (once the British mandate in that country had expired). Although Cyrenaica never did become a trusteeship as the Foreign Office had intended, it had its brief moment of glory in the imperial sphere as a quasi-protectorate and amirate between 1949 and 1951, in the process becoming the foundation stone of the new Kingdom of Libya, the unexpected outcome that seemed to favour Idris and the British alike.

Those who played short-term roles in managing parts of the administrative process in Cyrenaica, such as Peter Synge and Jeff Cassels, were not in any sense directing policy or much concerned with explaining the changes in emphasis along the way, except where these changes immediately affected them and what they saw as their duty. But the records they kept do provide us with key elements to understanding the evolving story.

What started as the ad hoc management of a shattered territory in wartime conditions, including basic administration and law and order, became a test case for British policy in the post-war period. However, from the very beginning, the omens had been remarkably positive for the development of a strong mutual relationship. After the collapse of the Italian presence, Britain was not seen as a colonial oppressor, but rather as a powerful ally of the Cyrenaicans and other Libyans, and an ally that could put a definitive end to the unpopular Italian regime. Before the war, tens of thousands of Italian colonists had been settled in the most productive agricultural areas, Italians had been favoured over Libyans in the provision of infrastructure and basic services, and those who resisted Italian rule had been brutally punished. Simply by being ready to start again on a clean slate, the British automatically gained significant credit.

After their arrival in December 1942, the British administrators had a free rein to set the agenda, decide on methods and choose their local allies. In all of this they were largely pragmatic. At the strategic level, they followed the 'Arabist' ideological bias pursued in other parts of the Middle East, as in their favouring of the Sanussiyya and the senior tribal sheikhs, but in day-to-day matters, the relationship with ordinary Libyans was conducted at a much more mundane but essential level: the British negotiated with the Cyrenaicans over the price to be paid for their barley, eggs or meat, decided which tribes had the right to bring their livestock to certain water wells, and delivered clear judgements in innumerable court proceedings. Throughout the war years at least, it seems that such matters were mostly managed with fairness and in good conscience, and certainly without stirring any significant cause for popular opposition.

The groundwork laid by Duncan Cumming and his initial coterie of colleagues – notably Ralph Hone, Norman Anderson, Hugh Foot, J. F. P. Maclaren, E. E. Evans-Pritchard, Bill Bailey and D. H. Weir – set the tone for the way the relationship developed after the war. Looking back later, Duncan Cumming attributed what he saw as his ultimate success in Cyrenaica to three factors: (i) 'the people liked our methods'; (ii) 'at the beginning of our occupation we had a fair number of experienced Arabic speaking officials' and (iii) 'Idris himself never lost confidence in us'. [37]

By the end of the war, 'a fairly good staff had been collected,' Cumming also recalled, 'but most of it disappeared when demobilisation began, and thereafter changes were rapid.' But he added: 'I cannot speak too highly of the work done by many who would never have experienced work of this kind in normal circumstances. We had our failures, but my recollection is one of admiration.' For his own part, Cumming admitted being able to use almost dictatorial powers (as Peter had learnt to his cost): 'Under the pressure of events, and in the absence of the vested interests of permanent officials, it was possible to perform administrative acrobatics which would normally be considered impossible.'[38]

The other side of the coin is that the available local administrative capacity among the Cyrenaicans (consisting mostly of *mudirs* in the rural districts and administrative and clerical officials at district headquarters) was quietly increasing, even if only by default, so that a transition to a more autonomous system of government had at least begun by the time Idris returned on a permanent basis in November 1947. There is a good example of this in the way the career of Ali Jerbi progressed over the years. Under the Italians he had served as a *mudir* and as an administrator of Arab affairs, but he was quick to assist the British during their successive occupations, first as Mayor of Derna in 1943.[39] After 1944, the BMA gave Jerbi responsibility for education and

[37] D. C. Cumming, 'British Stewardship of the Italian Colonies: An Account Rendered', *International Affairs*, Vol XXIX, 1953, p18.

[38] D. C. Cumming, 'British Stewardship of the Italian Colonies: An Account Rendered', *International Affairs*, Vol XXIX, 1953, pp20–1.

[39] Ali Jerbi met the travel writer Freya Stark in Cairo in 1943 and she quoted him as saying: 'I hope that all will be well. I hope they (the Allies) will not think that because we are backward, and have had no opportunity, we are not fit to keep our own land. We have everything

then general development. His overall competence, affable personality and fluency in several languages made him a strong candidate for the senior positions he then took on: Minister of Works and Communications in Cyrenaica and, in 1951, Foreign Minister in the provisional government of Libya.[40]

A less prominent example of those who worked closely with the British was the Sanussi loyalist Hussein Taher, a *mudir* under Italian rule, who risked his life assisting the British commando raid on Rommel in November 1941 (see Chapter 5) and became a widely respected *mudir* of al-Bayda and surrounding districts under the BMA for the rest of the war. He was later a deputy supervisor of the Cyrenaican elections of 1950, when his work received high praise from Jeff Cassels. Others serving the administration in the main towns of Benghazi and Derna were not necessarily at all loyal to the Sanussis. In the turbulent year of 1947, the BMA could not prevent one of its own senior Public Information Officers, Mahmud Makhluf, from supporting political demands for association with Egypt, as Peter noted in his last official report (see Chapter 11). However, this illustrates how the British did at least allow a greater measure of freedom of association and expression than became the norm in the years that followed.

In 1947, Cassels was among a new intake of administrators supporting Eric De Candole with a reasonably good level of professional training and some previous experience in the region. After 1949, he seems to have been one of only a handful working for the internal half of the administration under Cyrenaican management. Apart from those in the armed forces, most British officials in Cyrenaica were there to handle De Candole's continuing responsibilities for foreign affairs, defence and legal and financial matters. Any that stayed after 1952 were designated as advisers, mostly on short-term contracts.

In the years that followed, British influence in Libya survived and flourished somewhat longer than was destined to be the case in Egypt, Iraq or even Sudan (from where so many of its temporary administrators had been seconded during the early days of the BMA). From tentative beginnings in the midst of war through to the 1960s, the relationship became and remained remarkably strong in

---

to learn; but we *will* learn; our heart is in it. Give us our chance, give us protection, give us twenty years, and we will have learnt to govern ourselves as well as other Arab nations have learnt it.' F. Stark, *East is West*, London, 1945, p82.

[40] A. Pelt, *Libyan Independence and the United Nations: A Case of Planned Decolonization*, New Haven and London, 1970, p205.

a country where a paradoxical combination of imperial and post-imperial priorities and concerns happened to coincide, overlap and coalesce. However, what it could not guard against was the rise of bitter opposition to this close relationship from not only Arab nationalists across the Middle East, but also an increasing number of young Libyans.

# chapter 13

# FEDERAL ELECTIONS
## LIBYA, 1951–52

I N NOVEMBER 1949, after a succession of different proposals had fallen foul of Cold War rivalries, the United Nations General Assembly finally agreed that Libya should be given its freedom as an independent sovereign state 'as soon as possible and in any case not later than 1 January 1952'.[1] This decision kicked off a rushed transition process under the personal management of Dutch diplomat Adrian Pelt, who was given the title of UN Commissioner for Libya, working with a specially constituted Council for Libya (with nominated delegates from six countries: Egypt, France, Italy, Pakistan, the UK and the United States, and four Libyan representatives).

Perhaps most significantly, Pelt set in motion the mechanisms for appointing a National Constituent Assembly of Libya (NCAL), with 20 members each from Cyrenaica, Tripolitania and the Fezzan.[2] This established, for the first time, a vital forum for full negotiations between the different political groups across Libya. One of the first decisions of the Assembly was the establishment of a federal monarchy under Idris, who was duly proclaimed King of Libya in December 1950, a whole year before the final declaration of its UN-recognised independence.[3] Although this was inconsistent with the original political hopes and ideals of many in Tripoli, the Tripolitanians were kept in line with the promise of independence in the near future and were given top posts in the provisional government that

---

[1] H. S. Villard, *Libya: the New Arab Kingdom of North Africa*, Ithaca, NY, 1956, p32.

[2] For the full story of the two-year transition to independence, see A. Pelt, *Libyan Independence and the United Nations: A Case of Planned Decolonization*, New Haven and London, 1970.

[3] M. Khadduri, *Modern Libya: A Study in Political Development*, Baltimore, 1963, pp180ff.

was appointed in March 1951, under Mahmud al-Muntasser as Prime Minister.[4]

The two years allocated for the transition was by Pelt's own admission 'too short a time; a little longer would have been better, provided it had been prescribed at the outset.' But Pelt also felt that the whole process, which ended with Idris's declaration of independence for Libya on 24 December 1951, achieved a remarkable level of cooperation between the administering powers (Britain and France), the UN mission, the Council for Libya and the Libyan people themselves (as represented by the NCAL, the provisional government and the king).[5]

One of the most difficult issues to be dealt with was the holding of federal elections in the immediate aftermath of independence. These were expected to confirm the legitimacy of the transition, to determine the political character of the government and to reflect the level of popular support for King Idris and his political allies. It was in order to conduct these elections that Jeff Cassels was persuaded to return to Libya within weeks of having left Benghazi in April 1951.

The following extracts are drawn directly from the account of events that Cassels wrote some 35 years later (entitled 'The Libyan Federal Elections 1951/52: A personal account' and dated 6 March 1987). It not only makes a complete story in itself but also provides a very clear picture of the policy priorities of the British and the Libyans alike.

## FROM JEFF CASSELS'S MEMOIR

*Three powers, Britain, France and the USA, were anxious to retain military or air force bases in the new Libya after independence and had, for some time, been negotiating with the Amir with the expectation that he, and he alone, would be empowered to approve such arrangements. The new constitution, as drafted by the NCAL, had originally contained a provision authorising the future King, on his own sole authority, to declare war and conclude peace and enter into treaties with foreign states. However, at some stage in 1951, the powers concerned were shocked to learn that the NCAL had put forward an amendment reading: 'The King shall declare war and conclude peace and*

---

[4] The two Cyrenaicans in this provisional government were Ali Jerbi at Foreign Affairs and Omar Sheneib at Defence. A. Pelt, *Libyan Independence and the United Nations: A Case of Planned Decolonization*, New Haven and London, 1970, p734.

[5] A. Pelt, *Libyan Independence and the United Nations: A Case of Planned Decolonization*, New Haven and London, 1970, pp876–8.

enter into treaties with foreign states <u>which he ratifies after the approval of Parliament.</u> [Cassels's underlining]

In this way the question of elections and, arising out of them, the flavour and attitudes of the new Parliament-to-be, had suddenly become, for HMG and the other governments concerned, matters of considerable importance.

And so it was that in about June 1951, while spending our leave with my mother in Wiltshire, a phone call came through from the Foreign Office requesting my presence in London urgently. ... On arrival in Whitehall I was ushered into the presence of the Director of the Political Department, Roger Allen (later Sir Roger Allen, KCMG, British Ambassador to Iraq and other countries). ... What he said was broadly this. Libya would become fully independent within a few months. ... One of the first tasks of the new Government after independence would be to pass an Electoral Law and hold elections and they would need advice and help in undertaking this. ... In his view I was the right man for the Libyan job. I knew the country, I got on with the Libyans, I spoke the language (sic)[6] and, most important of all, I had not long ago successfully run an election in Cyrenaica. ... It would be impossible, especially at short notice, to find anyone else with so much relevant experience and he felt that, in the public interest, I must put aside my objections about Libya and accept the situation.

He went on to elaborate briefly. For reasons of which he was sure I was aware, it was important that the new Libyan Parliament should consist mainly of people who were, to say the least, not ill-disposed towards Britain. On this point there was currently concern in the Foreign Office about the activities in Tripolitania of the Tripolitanian National Congress, led by the Libyan demagogue Beshir Saadawi. These people, who were basically xenophobic and opposed to having foreign, particularly western, installations and influence in the new Libya, were currently actively engaged, with the backing of King [Farouk's] government in Egypt, in building up support for themselves; and reports were now coming in that their activities were having considerable impact upon the local population. By contrast the Prime Minister and the other Ministers-designate, who were all nominees of the Amir, and in a moderate way pro-western, belonged to no party and so far had done no campaigning at all. This imbalance could not be allowed to continue.

What Roger Allen seemed to be suggesting was that my task, along with that of any other British or Libyan colleagues who might be involved, would be not only to hold elections but to ensure that they yielded a favourable result – favourable, that is, to the Prime Minister and a pro-western Libyan government.

---

[6] As becomes clear later in this account, Cassels was modest about his proficiency in Arabic.

*Listening to this produced mixed feelings. The moral aspects did not worry me unduly; this was the era of the "cold war" and a spot of political skulduggery did not seem out of place. ... Yet there would be formidable problems, administrative as well as political. And what if the political gamble failed and the whole thing ended in disaster? It was not a pleasant thought.*

*Thereafter I was taken aside by one of Roger Allen's aides to settle a few final details and it was at this point that the question of election money was raised. It had apparently been decided that a sum of money should be set aside for the Libyan Prime Minister to use in his election campaign and I was asked for my views as to how this should best be handled. Would I be prepared to handle it myself? I asked how much was involved and was given the answer, which set alarm bells ringing in my head. Visions floated into my mind of the Prime Minister's campaign failing and endless enquiries from the Foreign Office as to what had happened to the money, with myself as the obvious scapegoat. Besides, if even a hint got around that I was handling political money, the whole elections might become discredited. I replied firmly that I could have nothing to do with this.*

## BACK TO LIBYA

*A week or so after this briefing I found myself on a BOAC flight bound for Libya. I was alone: my wife and the two boys were to follow a few days later. (Ironically the aircraft's route was first stop Tripoli, then on to Kano and Lagos. It was the same plane as I would have taken had we been travelling by air to Nigeria.)*

*The next day was spent in moving into my new office in the main Government building and calling upon the people with whom I would be working. These were divided between the British Residency (which was still, in theory, responsible for Tripolitania's external affairs) and the Government Secretariat (which housed the federal Prime Minister's office and other Ministries).*

*My first contact was with Charles Gault, Counsellor in the Residency, a permanent member of the Foreign Service and the main link between the British Administration in Tripoli and the Foreign Office. A key man in fact. And I was concerned lest he should be the same kind of stuffy and pompous FO Counsellor as we had once suffered from in Cyrenaica, a man named Lambert. I need not have worried; Charles was the opposite of this – most able, totally unstuffy and good-humoured. I felt instinctively that, if the going in Libya got tough, here was a man who would not let us down.*

*After a brief introductory chat he handed me a classified file containing the recent correspondence with London about the Libyan situation and the coming elections and told me to read it. Which I did then and there in his presence. When I had finished, he looked me in the face and said that, as he*

206

*read the correspondence, it was my job to run the elections and obtain a satisfactory result: and added "using any means short of murder".*

*These words may have been spoken partly in jest. But jesting or not, they gave me comfort. The fact is that, ever since my briefing with Roger Allen in the foreign office, I had been beset with doubts. Had those things about the elections really been said to me? Did Governments actually behave in this way? It was reassuring now to receive confirmation from such an eminently sane and reliable source – underlined, may I add, by what I myself had just read in the classified file – that the Foreign Office briefing had indeed taken place. It had not been a dream.*

*I also met in the Residency Cecil Greatorex, whom I had known briefly when working at GHQ in Egypt: and I had met him again in London while on leave. He was now on the British Resident's staff in Tripoli. Having lived many years in Egypt he was fluent in Arabic and well versed in Arab affairs and throughout my time in Tripoli was to prove a valuable contact as well as a friend [with] whom I could let my hair down.*

*My next port of call was the Government Secretariat to see Lord Oxford (the Earl of Oxford and Asquith), British Adviser to the Prime Minister-designate of the provincial federal Government. Like myself, he was a member of the British Colonial Service seconded to Libya, but we had not met previously.*

*He was an able, scholarly man, but probably – or so it seemed to me – more suited to a well-ordered British Colonial Administration than to the hurly-burly of Arab politics. After the usual courtesies he told me that the constitution was still being drafted by the [National] Constituent Assembly (NCAL), there was still a long way to go, and neither the Prime Minister nor anyone else yet knew when the elections would be held. And from the way he said this I got the impression, rightly or wrongly, that he himself would be only too happy if they were never held. In a word I felt that he did not care much for me or my mission.*

*To be fair to Lord Oxford, his position was not an enviable one. As a good Administrator – and he was a first class Administrator – it was obvious that Libya's prime need at that time was for a period of stability to see the country through to independence and beyond. And here was this interloper from London with a mandate to organise, of all unsettling things, parliamentary elections: and apparently not to be too squeamish about how this was to be achieved. From his point of view my appearance on the scene at this juncture must have seemed an unmitigated disaster. Small wonder that, initially at any rate, he regarded me with a certain distaste.*

*However, I would like straightaway to record that, as time went by and [the] elections became inescapable, his attitude changed markedly. On the personal side he continued to maintain a certain distance, for which I would be the last to blame him. But on the official level he was generous in offering assistance and advice whenever this was asked for. I shall always remember him with respect and gratitude.*

*A day or two later I was summoned to meet the top man himself – Mahmud Bey Muntasser, Prime Minister-designate of the provisional federal Government. Our paths had crossed once previously when, in 1948, he had visited Benghazi; in a chance meeting then I had taken an instant liking to him.*

*By profession a businessman, with no previous knowledge of politics but endowed with a high degree of common sense and energy, he was one of the few native-born men in the country who seemed in nearly all respects to fulfil the requirements of high office; and it had come as no surprise when the Amir had so appointed him. He was also one of nature's gentlemen – cultured, friendly and a pleasure to do business with. Whether he was tough enough, only time would tell.*

*He spoke no English – or if he did, I never heard him speak it – and all my conversations with him were in Arabic. This put quite a strain on me as I could not afford any misunderstandings with such an important personality. However, I was actually able to overcome the difficulty by preparing myself for meetings with him in advance (though, as this narrative will later indicate, preparation was not always possible!).*

*After welcoming me back to Libya, he spoke of the local situation. As I knew, the UN had set a time limit for independence by 1 January 1952. But they had not fixed any deadlines for either the holding of elections or the convocation of Parliament: these dates would be decided locally by the National Constituent Assembly (NCAL) in consultation with the provincial Government, i.e. himself and the other Ministers, and could not in any event take place before the proclamation of the constitution. The NCAL were working on the constitution. But there were still many difficulties to be overcome and it was premature at this stage to reach any decision about the elections. Meanwhile, however, there was preparatory work that could usefully be done, such as meeting the District Commissioners and drafting an Electoral Law.*

*Asked about Beshir Saadawi and the Congress Party, he said it was true they were having some success in building up support in Tripolitania, particularly in the towns. But they had not so far had much success in the rural areas: and he felt that, once the Ministers, with the Amir's support had got into their stride, support would build up strongly in favour of the Government. However, he was not unaware of the dangers and was watching the situation carefully.*

*He added, without prompting on my part, that I would always have direct access to him if I encountered any problems.*

*This discussion left me with mixed feelings. On the minus side nobody in the Government seemed in any hurry to hold elections which, though I recognised there were genuine obstacles in the way, was depressing for me personally. Nor did there seem much inclination on the Government's part to move on the political front and it looked as though the Congress Party would be left to have it all their own way for a while yet. On the plus side, the Prime Minister had seemed confident that the Government would be able to counter the Congress Party threat in the long term. He had given me the green light to start initial preparations for elections. Most important of all, he had been welcoming and I seemed to have established a good working relationship with him.*

*On balance I reckoned that, though things had not gone quite as I would have wished, the plusses outweighed the minuses. And with that, for the time being, I would have to be content.*

## THE ELECTORAL LAW

*The drafting of the Electoral Law presented no problem for, although I had no experience of legal draftsmanship, I had already decided to adopt as a basis the Electoral Law which we had used successfully in Cyrenaica in 1950, but suitably amended to take account of any problems we had encountered during the Cyrenaica experience. Its main provisions, as they finally emerged, were:*

(a) *Every male Libyan over 21 years of age, unless a lunatic, bankrupt or in prison, was entitled to vote. In other words it would be a direct, as distinct from an Electoral College, election.*

(b) *Only voters of the age of 30 years and above would be eligible to stand for election to the Parliament (or House of Representatives, as it was officially to be called).*

(c) *Where an election was uncontested, the unopposed candidate would be automatically elected.*

(d) *For the purpose of elections, each of the three regions of Libya (Provinces, as they were now to be called) would be divided into Urban Electoral Districts and Rural Electoral Districts. In the rural areas the voting procedure would be simpler than in the towns and better suited to the needs of illiterate people.*

(e) *Both Urban and Rural Electoral Districts would be sub-divided into constituencies of approximately 20,000 inhabitants each. Every constituency would be represented in Parliament by a single Deputy.*

*From the political point of view, perhaps the most important provision was (d) above – the different voting systems in Urban and Rural Districts. In the Urban areas, which were a small minority (for the whole of Libya only 9 seats out of 55), one would find the full panoply of Western-style democracy – a secret ballot with voting papers, ballot boxes and so on. By contrast the provisions relating to Rural Districts (46 out of 55) required no more than that the Registering Officer, in the presence of a small Committee, would write in the register the name of the candidate for whom the elector wished to vote. In other words, in every five out of six of the Electoral Districts of Libya the voter was relying upon the good faith of the Registering Officer and his Committee to ensure that his vote was properly recorded.*

*An almost equally important provision from the political viewpoint related to the appointment of electoral staff. Here the Law laid down that responsibility for appointment of the Supervisor-General of Elections, the three Provincial Supervisors, the Registering Officers and Returning Officers in both Urban and Rural Electoral Districts, as well as the Committees to decide objections, lay with the federal Minister of Justice: and the Supervisor-General in his turn was the man empowered to appoint persons to assist Registering Officers and Returning Officers in the discharge of their duties. In other words all of the electoral staff were Government appointees and the great majority of them were themselves Government officials. A real "old boys' network"!*

*There were of course sound practical reasons for this state of affairs. In the case of the voting system in the Rural Districts, it was basically to cope with the problem of illiteracy: how else could the votes of tribesmen who could not read nor write be recorded? As to the appointment of electoral officials there simply were not sufficient numbers of educated people outside the Government service to provide a practical alternative. Moreover there were economic reasons: the cost of employing an army of non-governmental staff, even had they been available, would have been prohibitive. Libya was at that time a poor country.*

*It was also a factor of some importance that similar provisions had been embodied in the Electoral Law used in the Cyrenaican elections of 1950 and no one had seriously complained about them then. On the contrary, apart from one or two minor abuses, the election there had been hailed as an unqualified success by Government and opposition alike. This was, I felt sure, an argument that would appeal to the Constituent Assembly (NCAL), who would be the final arbiters.*

*Nevertheless I was well aware that the Law, as drafted, contained imperfections and could easily be abused: and that, if the Government chose to manipulate the system to achieve their own ends, there would be little I could do to prevent them. In any case, would I want to prevent them? Bearing in mind my brief from the Foreign Office, perhaps a little manipulation from such a source, or even a lot of manipulation would be no bad thing. (The reader will, I hope, note that I am trying to be honest.)*

*Be that as it may, it came as no surprise when I learned that the Congress Party was deeply suspicious of the Government's intentions. Indeed their leader Beshir Saadawi had already in mid-1951 requested the Egyptian Government to ask the UN General Assembly to delay the proclamation of Libyan independence in order that this might be acquired "in accordance with the wishes of the people". When the request was rejected, the Congress launched a campaign for free elections under UN supervision. This too failed: the UN Commission[7] found itself unable to support the request. This left the last word with the NCAL, the arbiters on the constitution. But they too found Saadawi's reasoning unacceptable and came down firmly on the side of a local Libyan solution based on the 1950 Cyrenaican experience. And so it was that, in this form, the Law eventually obtained the seal of official approval.*

*This is not to say that I didn't have some bad moments during the passage of the draft Bill through its various stages, particularly vis-a-vis the UN Commission.[8] Mr Pelt himself, a Netherlander, seemed a decent and fair-minded sort of man, and I had no reason to think that his recommendations would be anything other than sensible and constructive. However, one of two of the Commission's members, particularly the Egyptian and Pakistani representatives, were reported to be deeply antagonistic to the British: and at one stage I heard that they had written formally to the Commissioner challenging, amongst other things, the proposed arrangements for preventing ballot-rigging and demanding that these be changed. This move was countered by the remaining members of the Commission who recorded their "utmost confidence that the Libyan Government would, by due process of law, take any action it might deem desirable … in order to ensure free elections in Libya." Thus the challenge (which, if successful, might have caused a lengthy delay in the passage of the draft Law) came to nought.*

*By contrast my contacts with the NCAL were heart-warming. The Chairman of their Working Group on Elections was Khalil Qallal, a liberal-minded Cyrenaican, for whose intelligence and common sense I had profound respect. And the Principal Secretary of the Assembly was Suleiman Jerbi, an old friend from Cyrenaican days who was one of the brighter young stars in the new Libyan firmament. Our discussions were pragmatic and totally above board – a time schedule for implementation of the Law, problems relating to*

---

[7] In his references to 'the Commission', Cassels means the Council for Libya, which advised the UN Commissioner, Adrian Pelt, and contained representatives from the governments of Egypt and Pakistan.

[8] See previous footnote.

*constituencies, "normal residence" and that sort of thing. But the most strik-ing aspect was the sensible, down-to-earth manner in which these subjects were tackled. There was a real will to face up to problems and overcome them. It seemed to me that this augured well for the future of the new Libya. But how many men such as these were there?*

*In essentials the Electoral Law, when it finally emerged on to the Statute Book, remained much the same as in the original draft put forward by me to the Prime Minister.[9] There were amendments on points of details. But the substance remained basically unchanged…*

*Once the electoral process had been set in motion, events succeeded one another in quick, almost bewildering, succession – with promulgation of both the Constitution and the Electoral Law taking place before Independence (though with polling and counting of votes subsequent to it). This accelera-tion was heartening for me after the apparent lack of enthusiasm for elec-tions which I had sensed on my arrival in Libya. The main stimulus for action came, it would appear, from the attempts of Beshir Saadawi and the Opposition to get their proclamation of independence delayed and a new set of elections held under UN supervision. This move proved self-defeating and brought about a realisation amongst Ministers and members of the NCAL alike, especially the waverers, that elections must be held as soon as possible. To quote Mr. Pelt, the UN Commissioner: "The preparation and adoption of an Electoral Law would have to be taken immediately after the proclamation of the Constitution. For if the elections were delayed, the independence plan would lose a great deal of its force."*

## CHANGES AT THE TOP

*The declaration of Independence on 24.12.51 meant of course that the posts of British Residents in Tripolitania and Cyrenaica ceased to exist and the two incumbents, Travers Blackley in Tripoli[10] and Eric De Candole in Benghazi, disappeared from the Libyan scene. British representation in the new Kingdom was taken over by a Minister (in later months upgraded to Ambassador) in charge of a Legation (later Embassy). A similar hand-over by the French took place in the Fezzan.*

*The new British Minister was Sir Alec Kirkbride, KCMG, CVO, OBE, MC, who for thirty years had served as Adviser and friend of King Abdullah*

---

[9] 'In its technical aspects, the law bore the unmistakable mark of its English draftsman,' com-mented Adrian Pelt, *Libyan Independence and the United Nations: A Case of Planned Decoloniza-tion*, New Haven and London, 1970, p661.

[10] Travers Blackley had been DCCAO and Chief Administrator in Tripolitania since 1943; he had previously worked in the Sudan Political Service since 1922 and in Ethiopia in 1941–42. A. Pelt, *Libyan Independence and the United Nations: A Case of Planned Decolonization*, New Haven and London, 1970, p126.

*of Jordan. He was, needless to say, a most impressive man, an Arabist of the highest order and, I suppose, one the greatest living authorities on Middle Eastern affairs. So far as I personally was concerned, he was outgoing and friendly, and without any trace of condescension.*

*Perhaps the most curious part of our relationship was that, while he talked a great deal, and most interestingly, about his experiences in Jordan and elsewhere, he never once spoke to me about my work in Libya. I took this as a compliment. He seemed to be saying: "Here is a chap who knows what he is doing. Best to leave him alone and let him get on with it." He may also have been influenced by the knowledge that my brief from the Foreign Office, on which he was obviously well informed, did not exactly smell of roses!*

*Though I had been sad to see Travers Blackley go – and Eric De Candole also – I could not help feeling that Sir Alec, with his great reputation and skill in handling Middle Eastern people, was the right man to represent Britain in Libya in the prevailing circumstances.*

*Towards the end of October 1951 the Prime Minister summoned me and introduced me to the man whom he had decided to appoint as the federal Supervisor-General of Elections – a post which he would combine with that of Provincial Supervisor for Tripolitania – as soon as the Electoral Law was promulgated.*

*This turned out to be a delightful elderly Sheikh, Mahmud Al Miselati, who in normal life was a school teacher and learned in the ways of the Koran. Not surprisingly he had no idea how to organise a modern election, or indeed how to run any large-scale administrative operation. But he did have definite ideas as to who should, and would, win the election. One of his favourite expressions was "miyye fil miyye" (one hundred per cent), representing the margin by which, in his opinion, the Prime Minister must achieve electoral success. When I ventured to suggest that this was being a bit greedy and that perhaps 95% or even 90% would do, he shook his head sadly: nothing less than miyye fil miyye would suffice. Like me, he was a bit of a pirate and I became very fond of him.*

## THE PRIME MINISTER'S ELECTION CAMPAIGN IN TRIPOLITANIA

*Meanwhile, Beshir Saadawi and the Congress Party, plentifully supplied with money from Egypt, continued to build up support for their cause in Tripolitania, particularly in the towns. This was hardly surprising bearing in mind that initially they had met with little opposition from the Government. As* The Times *put it: "The Government's information services for their part are limited in staff and funds, while the Prime Minister and the provisional Government have contrived, quixotically it would seem, to remain above party politics." Indeed, by mid-December 1951 this Congress build-up had reached such proportions that certain British expatriates in the Libyan Government had become extremely agitated about the possibility of a Saadawi victory at the polls: and even the Foreign Office were now becoming increasingly alarmed. I personally did not share their view and on 3.1.52 reported to Charles Gault as follows:*

> *My own views on this subject are known to you. If, prior to the dec-laration of independence, a straight vote had been taken amongst the people of Tripolitania over the issue Muntasser v. Saadawi, I have lit-tle doubt that Saadawi would have obtained a majority. But on 19 February it will not be a straight vote between Prime Ministers or even between parties. The electorate will be choosing between personalities from their own districts who have lived among them all their lives. If (and this is an important "if") the Government show discretion and wisdom in their selection of candidates, the combination of these cir-cumstances and the greatly improved position of the Government as a whole should, in my opinion, secure them the necessary majority. We are of course doing our utmost to ensure that the candidates they select are the best men available: but it is a subject about which the Libyans know a great deal more than we do, and we must in the main rely upon them to make their own decisions.*
>
> *When I last visited the Legation, I gained the impression, from various letters that I was shown, that the Foreign Office are greatly alarmed about the elections and the possibility of an unfavourable result. I trust that you will let them know that, while nothing is certain, the outlook is not quite as black as they seem to think. If the Gov-ernment now, with so many cards in their hands, cannot obtain their majority, they are not likely ever to do so.*

*Be that as it may, I was greatly relieved when on an afternoon in late Decem-ber 1951, just before independence, I was called to the Prime Minister's office to meet the man who would be running the Government's political campaign. This was Fadl bin Zikri who at that time, if my memory serves me correctly, held the post of Minister of Interior in the Tripolitanian Provincial Admin-istration and was destined, a few days later, to take over as the new Wali (Governor) of Tripolitania. He was an impressive man, oozing authority. A real go-getter. It seemed to me that his personal strength, combined with the enormous influence which his new post (and indeed his old post also) would give him, made him an ideal choice as the Prime Minister's political manager. Surely now at last the Government's campaign would get under way.*

*In this we were not disappointed. True, the Congress Party contin-ued to dominate the towns. But by mid-January 1952 my friend, the*

*Supervisor-General of Elections, was assuring me that Fadl bin Zikri's endeavours to swing the tribal sheikhs into line behind the Government were achieving notable success. And since the tribal constituencies vastly outnumbered the urban constituencies, the prospects for the Government began to look promising.*

*During all this time I had been able to get around the main centres of Tripolitania – Tripoli City itself, Homs, Misurata, Gharian, etc. – and met the Mutasarifs (District Commissioners) and their British Advisers. Where possible I took my family: and sometimes the Supervisor-General of Elections came too. These trips were useful in ironing out countless administrative problems and also in keeping abreast of the political situation. And needless to say, in a country with a long tradition of hospitality, we were everywhere received with courtesy and friendliness.*

## POLLING DAY

*Polling day on 19 February 1952 came as something of an anti-climax. The electoral officials (Provincial Supervisors, Returning Officers, Registering Officers, Presiding Officers, Committees, counting staff, et al) had all received their marching orders. And so far as I was concerned, there was nothing to do but to utter a prayer and wait.*

*My plan was that, as soon as polling got properly under way, the Supervisor-General and I would tour some of the main polling stations in and around Tripoli to get the feel of things – taking care not to stay too far from Headquarters in case any problems arose requiring our attention there. Being in theory only an Advisor, I had hoped not to get involved with journalists, either local or foreign, and had arranged, or so I thought, for press enquiries to be handled by the Government's PIO [Principal Information Officer].*

*However, the best laid schemes. … Just as the Supervisor-General and I were setting out, in walked an Englishman announcing himself as Frank Giles, correspondent of the* The Times *in Rome, who had been assigned the task of covering the elections in Libya. He had heard we would be visiting polling stations and would like to come with us. I could not but agree. A minute or two later we were joined by another British journalist. … And so, together, the four of us made a tour of about half a dozen polling stations, some urban, some rural. All seemed to be quiet and I got the impression that our journalistic friends were impressed both with the organisation and the orderly way in which people were voting. And certainly, in the polling stations that we visited, there was no evidence of improper practices or intimidation.*

*To begin with I felt a bit wary of Frank Giles. It was not that I was unversed in the art of dealing with the press, but a* Times *Special Correspondent was clearly something out of the ordinary and one needed to keep a*

215

*check on one's tongue. However, this feeling of reserve soon thawed. He was a stimulating companion – extremely well-informed, with a sharp eye for what was going on around him, and as I came to know later, a brilliant and per- ceptive writer of press articles. He asked lots of questions and had obviously heard from his own sources, amongst them some of the more "windy" British sources within the Government, of the threat posed by the Congress Party to the Muntasser Administration in Tripolitania. I did my best to put the situ- ation in perspective, emphasising that, in Middle East politics, personalities often counted for more than parties: and stressing also the sheer size and importance of the rural vote. He seemed receptive. But I think we both felt there was not much point in debating the matter since, within less than 48 hours, the result of the election would be available for all to see.*

*When we got back to the office later in the day we learned that in Misu- rata, a town east of Tripoli City, there had been some trouble in which one Arab had been killed and one British Police Officer slightly wounded: and that one or two other incidents, but with no casualties, had been reported from other places in Tripolitania. However, by and large, the day had passed off reasonably quietly.*

*In a despatch to* The Times *of 19.2.52 Frank Giles reported: "In spite of trouble in some places, polling day in Libya's first general election seems to have passed off successfully. ... At the polling booths visited, both in country and town, this morning by your Correspondent there was no sign whatever that it was not a free expression of opinion, although opportunities for abuse are inherent in the electoral arrangements. There may be more trouble tomor- row ... but for the moment the orderliness and comparative tranquillity of polling do credit to the world's newest state."*

## GERRY MANDER AND THE BALLOT BOXES

*Late that evening I received, a phone message that the Prime Minister wanted to see me urgently in the District Commissioner's office (Muhafazah) in Trip- oli City. On arrival I found the Prime Minister, the Wali and other Libyan members of the Prime Minister's "election committee" – four or five in all, no British except myself – seated around a large table. All looked grim faced and tense and I wondered what had gone wrong.*

*The Prime Minister wasted no time in enlightening me. Reports from reli- able people who had kept watch in the polling station indicated that, in Tripoli City, the Congress Party had scored a resounding victory: it seemed they had swept the board and won all five seats. The Government had hoped to win at least one or two, but the Congress intimidation had kept many Government sup- porters away from the polling booths (sic). The Prime Minister and his advisers felt that the situation called for extreme measures and they looked to me for help in rectifying the voting balance. This would involve going round to selected police stations during the night, opening the ballot boxes and doing whatever else was necessary to secure a result more favourable to the Government.*

*I could hardly believe my ears. Was this real or was I dreaming? Prime Ministers in a real world did not suggest that people should creep around polling stations in the middle of the night rigging ballot boxes. Yet a minute ago I had heard a Prime Minister suggesting that. Quite apart from moral considerations, the ballot boxes were sealed. Could one now open them without leaving evidence of tampering? I had no idea. What made it worse was that I had to some extent brought this situation on myself.*

*To explain what I mean I shall have to go back to the time when I was drafting the Electoral Law. As mentioned earlier, this draft was based in the main on the law which we had used in the 1950 Cyrenaican elections. But in the light of experience or for other reasons I had introduced certain changes. And one of these related to the voting system in the urban districts.*

*Under the earlier Cyrenaican systems the voter, before putting his voting paper into the ballot box, was required to mark it with a cross against the name or symbol of the candidate for whom he wished to vote. This would have made it difficult afterwards to fiddle the result since it would have involved, first sorting all the papers in each ballot box to determine the balance of pro- and ant- Government votes: destroying the requisite number of "antis": and then substituting in their place "pro" voting papers, especially if a large number of boxes had to be dealt with. Moreover, if the result was later challenged in the courts, evidence of malpractice might well have surfaced owing to the false markings.*

*When considering the best system for the federal law – and the reader will remember this was fairly early on in the electoral process when the Foreign Office's warning of the consequences of a possible electoral disaster were still fresh in my ears – I had hit upon the bright idea, which I had read about somewhere, of a system whereby ballot papers were not marked by the voters. Instead, in every polling station there would be a number of ballot boxes equal to the number of candidates: and the name and symbol of one candidate, and one only, was prominently displayed on each ballot box. The voter cast his vote by the simple method of dropping his paper, unmarked, into the ballot box of the candidate he favoured.*

*I had put forward this idea to the Prime Minster as a possible alternative to the Cyrenaican system (without giving any reasons): and he had accepted it with alacrity (also without giving any reasons). So I had incorporated it into the draft of the federal law.*

*This new system would of course make life much easier for the would-be fiddler – whom I shall refer to in future as Gerry Mander, or Gerry for short.*

*All that our friend Gerry would have to do would be to place the ballot boxes of government and opposition candidates side by side, open them, lift out armfuls of the unmarked ballot papers from the opposition boxes and stuff them into the government boxes. And assuming that he could re-seal the ballot boxes without leaving tell-tale traces, it would be difficult for a challenger to prove later that anything untoward had occurred.*

*It had all seemed very neat at the time. What I had not reckoned with was how absurd the whole idea could become in a real life situation. Still less had I envisaged that I myself would be asked to conduct such an operation. I was well and truly hoist with my own petard!*

*Taking a deep breath and stumbling nervously to find appropriate Arabic words – fortunately my vocabulary in relation to all aspects of electioneering had by this time become fairly extensive – I said my piece. There were, I argued, two points to consider.*

*First, the course which the Prime Minister was suggesting seemed to me fraught with danger: it would be impossible to carry out an operation of this kind without people getting to know about it. The Congress Party spies were probably already watching the police stations against such an eventuality. And even if they weren't, we would almost certainly be seen in the Police Station by policemen or others with Congress sympathies who, at that time of night, would immediately guess what we were up to. By the morning the story would be all over the city. And this would be followed by reports in the Opposition press and possibly a court action to get the whole election declared invalid.*

*Second, while it was disappointing that the Congress had done so well in Tripoli City, this was by no means a disaster. A majority for Congress in the City did not mean a majority in Libya as a whole. On the contrary in Tripolitania alone, where the total number of parliamentary seats was 35, it seemed unlikely that Congress would win more than ten or twelve. And if one took into account the strong backing for the Government which was expected in Cyrenaica and the Fezzan, there seemed every prospect that, in the final reckoning, the Government, not the Congress Party, would win the elections and would do so with a big majority. In the circumstances I could not see the need for such a risky operation in Tripoli City as was now being discussed.*

*Despite the bumbling Arabic, my words seemed to have some effect and I could feel the tension almost visibly lessening. There were even a few encouraging nods around the table and, when I had finished, no one made any attempt to put forward counter arguments. The Prime Minster himself looked more relaxed and even smiled. And after a few words with his advisers, he announced that my advice was accepted and his suggestion would be dropped. The change of attitude took place so swiftly that I got the impression his heart had not been in the plan from the beginning and he had only gone along with it because of pressure from some of his advisers – notably, I would imagine, from Fadl bin Zikri, the Wali, though this is only guesswork. After a few pleasantries the meeting broke up and, feeling vastly relieved, I took myself home to a stiff whisky and finally to bed. It had been an eventful day.*

*However, this episode left a deep impression on me. It is true that the story had a happy ending, the plan for rigging the ballot boxes had been nipped in the bud and no political damage had been done. But what of the damage to my self-esteem? Had I really sunk so low that the Libyans actually believed I would rig the results for them in this way? And would I have done it if I thought we could have got away with it? Was this the same Jeff Cassels who, less than two years previously, had run the Cyrenaican elections with scrupulous fairness and gained a reputation amongst the Libyans, or so I was informed by a senior Cyrenaican, for absolute integrity? What a charlatan I had now become.*

*The incident also presented me with a dilemma. To whom, if anyone, amongst my seniors on the British side should I report it? Obviously the fewer people who knew about it, the better: a story like this might travel fast. Moreover, the fact that Lord Oxford, although technically a member of the Prime Minister's 'election committee', had not been invited to our nocturnal meeting, seemed an indication that the Prime Minister (rightly) had a higher opinion of his moral sense than he had of mine and did not want him involved in, or even to know about, dirty tricks of this kind. This left Charles Gault. But while Charles, who was a robust character, might have derived some enjoyment from the story, he might also have felt it his duty to include it in one of his reports to the Foreign Office; and I could just imagine the shiver of apprehension that would run down the spines of that august body if they got to know about it. … In any case, why publicise my shame when there was no real need? I decided to keep quiet and say nothing.*

## GERRY MANDER AND THE RURAL REGISTERS

*A few days later I received another shock. Under the terms of the Electoral Law, the registrars of elections in both Urban and Rural Electoral Districts had to be completed by a certain date. There was then a period allowed for perusal of the registers by the public and a further period for the hearing of objections by special local committees – after which each Registering Officer had to certify his register as being, to the best of his knowledge and belief, a true and correct Register of Electors. The Registers were then considered to be finalised.*

*In addition I had, for my own satisfaction and as a purely administrative measure, obtained from the Registering Officers – this was after finalisation of the Registers but before any voting took place – details of the number of people registered in each constituency. The idea was, of course that, when the time came, we in the Secretariat would be able to compare these figures with the number of people who actually voted.*

*The voting figures, when they became available, revealed some surprising results. In about half a dozen of the Rural Districts the electorate had grown inordinately after the date the registers were supposed to have closed. Moreover it was not just a question of the electoral roll having been enlarged, but in these Districts more people had actually voted than were, according to our records, on the roll. Thus in one District 106% of the electorate had voted, in another 120%, in another 134%, and so on. Even to my unmathematical mind, this seemed a remarkable achievement!*

*There might have been a straightforward explanation for this state of affairs. It must be remembered that these were all tribal areas where nearly all the voters and many of the junior Government officials acting as Registering Officers were Bedouin, or semi-Bedouin: and such people, especially the voters, were unlikely to appreciate the finer points of a comparatively sophisticated, European-style election. Closing down the electoral registers several days or hours before the elections – what an absurd idea! A Bedu was entitled to vote on polling day like anyone else, whether he had been previously registered or not – and who was the Registering Officer, probably a fellow Bedu, to deny him that right? Strictly speaking this was illegal, but it would have been understandable.*

*The only flaw in this theory is that it would have involved considerable numbers of tribesmen flocking in to vote after the registers had closed. And in such a situation surely someone, somewhere, would have raised objections. As it was, we received no complaints on this score.*

*A less charitable explanation would be that the Registering Officers, either on their own initiative or under pressure from on high, had at some stage of the proceedings added to the rolls scores of fictitious names in such a way as to produce the right result for their favoured candidates. It must be remembered that, in the Rural Electoral Districts where a majority of the voters were illiterate, no ballot boxes or voting papers were involved. The Registering Officers, who were all Government officials, simply asked each voter in turn for whom he wished to vote and recorded that choice in the register; and such entry was deemed to be a duly recorded vote.*

*A system of this kind was, of course, open to all kinds of abuse and I reflected ruefully that I had known this all along and had done little to provide extra safeguards. Once again my sins had caught up with me.*

*What to do? If it had been the Cyrenaican elections two years earlier when I had been Supervisor of Elections and everything had been above board, I would immediately have instituted an enquiry and, if necessary, called for fresh elections in the offending districts. But that was Cyrenaica in 1950 and this was a wider Libya in 1952 where the circumstances had changed completely. As the Americans would say, it was a different ball-game. I had a word with my friend, the Supervisor-General of Elections, but he simply smiled and shook his head. Anything as distasteful as an enquiry had obviously never entered his head. And there was no point in talking to the Prime Minister who had his hands full with other more urgent matters: in any case it was obvious what his answer would have been. Once again I decided to turn a blind eye.*

*One more word about these rural results. From such enquiries as I was able to make without stirring up mud, it appeared that in only two of the half dozen or so constituencies mentioned above was it a case of candidate A of the Government party against B of the Congress. In the remainder it was more a question of two local sheikhs with no known political affiliations (though they might have been influenced by one or other of the political leaders) battling it out for the kudos of being a Member of Parliament. This diminution of the political element eased my conscience slightly. But only slightly. The fact is I did not really know the hows and whys of this murky business and as a matter of policy, made no attempt to find out.*

*To round off this chapter, I had better sorrowfully record that, as a precaution against nosey-parkers, it seemed wise to alter our HQ list of registered voters to reflect a more credible situation. Thus, with regards to constituencies where more people had voted than were reported to be registered, I substituted higher figures for the numbers of registered voters so that a reasonable margin prevailed between the registration and the voting figures. I did not feel at all happy about this. But, having once embarked on a cover-up, there seemed no option but to see it through.*

### GERRY MANDER AND THE SLUSH FUND

*And then there was the question of the money which I mentioned earlier in this narrative. Gerry Mander up to tricks again, I fear. The idea of a secret 'slush fund' was not, I gather, a new one. Indeed I have reason to believe that the money weapon had been used by HMG as part of its armoury in setting up some of the Arab Kingdoms in the Middle East in the aftermath of World War I (though whether, prior to Libya, it had been used specifically in the context of an election, I do not know).*

*That a slush fund was being used in Libya, I did know; and I assume though I never saw anything in the files about this, that the object was two-fold. To enable the Government party to defray legitimate expenses. Secondly, and not so legitimate, to give the Prime Minister and his senior aides political leverage in the conduct of their electoral campaign, e.g. settling differences between rival supporters, soothing wounded feelings and generally to induce voters to support Government candidates.*

*According to what I was told in the Foreign Office, the amount involved was sterling £30,000. By today's standards this is peanuts but by the standards of 1951/52 it was a substantial sum of money and provided a clear indication, if any were needed, of the concern, even apprehension, with which HMG awaited the outcome of the elections. Morally, the use of this fund was, I suppose, indefensible and also illegal and I was glad that from the outset I had personally declined to have anything to do with it. In this at least I had shown good sense.*

*However, the reader ought not to be too hasty in passing judgment. The Government party were not the only ones to receive financial backing from an external source: the Congress Party were also receiving outside help. In their case the benefactions came from King Farouk's government in Egypt and, according to reliable sources – and there is no doubt that our sources of information at that time were good – the sum involved was in the region of sterling £140,000. The British were not the only ones involved in this affair with dirty hands.*

*Moreover, when one considers the millions of dollars the Americans must have poured, both legally and illegally, into places like Central America, Chile and Vietnam, and the Russians into Afghanistan, to bolster up regimes of their choice, the modest sum spent by HMG in Libya pales into insignificance.*

*How much difference this money made to the outcome of the elections in Libya, it is difficult to say. My feeling is that, though without it the contest might have been closer, the overall result would have been the same, fund or no fund. However, there can be little doubt that, by the nature of Middle Eastern politics, the managers of the Prime Minister's campaign found the money of considerable help in smoothing out local quarrels and keeping the tribesmen and others happy; and that it gave added scope to the likes of our friend Gerry Mander, or their Arab equivalents, to use their talents to advantage. For this reason the existence of a slush fund was a factor which no chronicler of the events of this era could fail to mention.*

## THE ELECTION RESULTS

*Although the day after polling day (20 February 1952) was the date designated for the counting of votes in both urban and rural districts throughout Libya, the final results were not to become available for another fortnight. This was because, in two constituencies of Tripolitania (Castel Benito and Tajura), fresh elections had to be held in consequence of the destruction by rioters of election registers on polling day and other infringements of voting regulations. The final results were published on 6 March 1952.*

*These revealed that, in Tripolitania, 70% of the electorate had voted, and in Cyrenaica 64%. In the Fezzan only two of the five seats were contested but, in these, 89% had voted. In Tripolitania one quarter of the candidates lost their deposits.*

*The main political results were as follows. In Tripolitania, independent candidates known or thought to support the Government secured 28 seats as against the Congress Party figure of 7. The corresponding figures in Cyrenaica were 13 pro-Government as against 2 Opposition. In the Fezzan all 5 elected candidates were pro-Government. In a word, the Government had secured a very substantial working majority in the Parliament – 46 against 9. This was not quite the "miyye fil miyye" which my friend, the Supervisor General of Elections, had been praying for but nevertheless, from the Government's point of view, highly satisfactory.*

*It was obvious that the people back home would be pleased. And sure enough, on 29.2.52, the British Minister in Tripoli received the following message from the Rt. Hon. Anthony Eden, Secretary of State for Foreign Affairs: "The outcome of the elections in Libya is gratifying, and I shall be glad if, provided you see no objection, you will take the opportunity of telling Mahmud Bey (the Prime Minister) that I am glad the first national elections have gone well, thanks to his wisdom and determination."*

*The Foreign Office also received a message from Travers Blackley, the former British Resident in Tripolitania: "Delighted to see in* Times *that Mahmud has got in with safe majority. He seems to have done very much better than any of us expected and it looks as though he timed his election effort right. I imagine that no small credit should go to Cassels."*

*I still find this last sentence slightly embarrassing. The fact is that, though I had been involved in the political side of things in a number of ways, e.g. drafting the Prime Minister's Manifesto, preparing the Electoral Law with a strong bias in favour of the Government, covering up irregularities in regard to rural voting, etc., my main concern had been with the administrative arrangements for the election which kept my hands full. The political aspects had been handled by a small hand of officials close to the Prime Minister – notable amongst them the Wali of Tripolitania, Fadl bin Zikri, whose contribution to the Prime Minister's election effort had been absolutely crucial. Without this man's enormous influence and powers of persuasion, who knows what the result might have been. Let credit be given where credit is due.*

## THE AFTERMATH

*In the two days after counting day (20 and 21 February) the situation in Tripolitania, which on polling day had been reasonably quiet, deteriorated; and*

*Police reports indicated that the agitation was part of a general plan on the part of the Congress Party to make trouble. Three Arabs were killed when the Police opened fire on a crowd at Castel Benito village near the airport. At Sirte, 250 miles east of Tripoli, a police station was surrounded. There were curfews in the towns of Misurata and Homs. In Tripoli City, where it rained heavily, there was a certain tension but, on the first of the two evenings [20 February] the city remained quiet.*

*The following day after further disturbances a curfew was imposed in Tripoli City. The* Times *reported: "Trouble in the Tripoli area began in a village on the outskirts, where supporters of the Congress Party apparently decided that the defeat of their candidate at the polls was unfair. They moved into the city, and by noon were shouting and throwing stones at the police who had formed a double cordon round the Government offices. It was a ragged purposeless crowd, composed partly of tribesmen, partly of excited boys. After a while the police moved in to break up the crowd, firing and using tear gas. Not far away there was another affray in which shots were fired by the police and members of the crowd."*

*Curfews were imposed in several areas and, in general, my impression was that the police had the situation well under control. But in this I may have been mistaken for, later, one heard that the Government had been worried about their ability to keep the situation in the Province as a whole under control and had even applied to the British Minister, Sir Alec Kirkbride, for the use of British troops to support the police in maintaining law and order. This request was rejected by Sir Alec – presumably on the basis that such an intervention would have created an unfavourable impression abroad so soon after independence. Fortunately, as events turned out, the Police succeeded in keeping on top of the situation without help from outside.*

*The final toll of casualties in Tripolitania between 19 and 22 February 1952, as later reported by the British Legation to the Foreign Office, was 17 killed and 210 persons injured (though it was thought, in fact, there may have been more). Amongst the injured were 7 policemen. In addition over 300 arrests were made.*

*While walking down the corridors of the Government building during the disturbances, I bumped into Christopher Tower, whom I had known in earlier days in Cyrenaica ... on the staff of King Idris. He greeted me with: "Ah, here's the man at the bottom of all this trouble!" It was of course said as a joke. But his voice had an edge to it which made me realise that, however unfair the comment, I was not exactly the most popular Englishman in Libya at that moment.*

*The Government's reaction to the disturbances, when it came, was swift and decisive. In the small hours of 22 February, Libyan police arrested Beshir*

*Saadawi, leader of the Congress Party, together with his brother, nephew and immediate followers. They were taken to Castel Benito airport and put on an aircraft en route to Egypt. (Beshir Bay, although born a Tripolitanian, held a Saudi Arabian passport and his brother and nephew had Lebanese passports; their deportation therefore presented no problems.) The Secretary of the Congress Party, who was a Tunisian, was similarly deported to Tunisia. The headquarters of the Congress Party was raided during the night and a number of papers taken away by the police.*

The Times *reported: "This decisive action had been taken by the Libyan Government because of Beshir Bey's threats, openly declared before last Tuesday's general election, to refute with violence if necessary the verdict of the polls. Disturbances in the last few days have, in the Government's opinion, been the carrying into effect of these threats. Rather than continue to meet force with force as they have been doing … the Government decided to cut at the roots of the trouble."*

*This action had an immediate calming effect throughout the whole of Tripolitania and the rioting ceased almost overnight. The Legation were able to report to the Foreign Office: "Bashir's removal has caused literally no stir at all, except to bring most of the Opposition round to seek to come to terms with the Government. It seems that enough incriminating evidence will have been found to justify the expulsion fully. The documents are still being examined but a second raid on Beshir's house produced several revolvers and automatic pistols, one of which the police say they can prove was used to fire shots at three of the Tripolitanian Ministers when sitting in a cafe in the town last year. The assailant escaped."*

## THE TREATIES

*The Libyan Parliament met for the first time on 25 March 1952 in Benghazi, three months after the Royal Proclamation of Independence.*

*On 29 July 1953 a Treaty of friendship and alliance between Libya and the United Kingdom was signed, giving the latter air and land-base facilities in return for which, for the following five years, the United Kingdom was to pay £1,000,000 per annum to Libyan development organisations, and £2,750,000 to the Libyan budget. This was ratified by the Libyan Parliament on 7 December 1953. On 9 September 1954 an agreement was concluded between Libya and the USA giving the US the right to occupy certain areas in Libya for military purposes, in particular the airbase at Wheelus Field. As a quid pro quo, the US would supply aid. The agreement was ratified by the Libyan Parliament on 30 October 1954.*

*A similar agreement between Libya and France was signed on 10 August 1955 and ratified by the Libyan Parliament on 10 April 1956.*

## IN RETROSPECT

*Here I propose simply to ask myself a single question and try to answer it.*

*This relates to the petty deceptions which were used in order to ensure a Government victory in the elections, e.g. the slush fund, the fiddling with voting figures in some tribal areas, my own doctoring of returns to cover this up, etc. Could these be justified on moral grounds?*

*My view is that, if we had been living in a perfect, well ordered world, the answer would have to be a firm negative; morality should not give way to expediency. But in the very imperfect world in which we found ourselves in Libya in 1952, in an era of cold or near-cold war, I took the opposite view. Remember that the Opposition, the Congress Party, had their own slush fund and apparently used it effectively. Moreover, it became clear that, in some areas, they had engaged in intimidation. Pro-Government supporters could hardly be expected to allow such measures to go unchallenged.*

*Moreover it would have been a tragedy not only for Britain, but also for Libya, if Beshir Saadawi had won the elections in Tripoli at that time. Even supposing that, in Libya as a whole, the Government had obtained an overall majority in the new Parliament, but not a majority of the seats in the Province of Tripolitania, a break-up would still have occurred. The country would have been split down the middle and the whole flimsy structure might well have collapsed. The three Provinces would probably have gone their own separate ways and all the work so painstakingly undertaken in international conferences, in the United Nations and in Libya itself for a united country would have been wasted.*

*And even if by some miracle a break-up had been avoided, the Libyans were simply not ready for the kind of radical and xenophobic government which Saadawi and his henchmen would have provided. Libya's crying need at that time was [for] a period of calm and stability and this is exactly the opposite of what Saadawi would have given them.*

*My personal opinion is that, in Libya in 1952, HMG did no more and no less than any Government with imperial blood in its veins and some fire still in its belly would have done in similar circumstances. The measures which they either initiated or condoned were justified. My only real anxiety at the time was that, if things went seriously wrong, they might lose their nerve and use the men on the spot as scapegoats. Happily that situation never arose.*

*Some of these events had a bizarre, even an unsavoury flavour. But there were many redeeming features – a fascinating country at a crucial period in its history, good, enduring friendships, wonderful antiquities, endless contrasts. Libya was, by and large, a happy place for our small family. And the work, though demanding, was intensely stimulating. Moreover I did undoubtedly derive satisfaction from the feeling that I had played a part, if only a very small part, in the writing of a colourful chapter of North African history.*

# chapter 14

# EPILOGUE
## IDRIS, QADHAFI AND BEYOND

THE LAUNCH OF LIBYA as an independent nation on 24 December 1951 was claimed by the United Nations as one of its major early achievements. It was certainly an exit from colonialism that took place without any of the bitterness or major upheaval so often experienced elsewhere in the decades that followed. This was largely as a result of the close collaboration between the UN Commissioner Adrian Pelt and Britain (as the main occupying power) and of the continuation of Libya's relationship with Britain thereafter – to the extent that historians often describe Libya's status after 1951 as that of a 'client'. Helping to embody this subsequent connection was Sir Alec Kirkbride, the first British Ambassador, who revealingly noted some months after independence that 'it is still difficult to convince the French, Americans and Italians that we do not in some mysterious way still administer Libya.'[1]

A feature of the newly independent Libya was its federal structure, which was intended to ensure a degree of autonomy from Tripolitania for both Cyrenaica and the Fezzan. From the outset, the differences between the three regions were significant. 'Suspicions and rivalry persisted, as each province sought to serve and secure its own interests in the new power structures that had been drawn up under UN supervision,' writes historian Alison Pargeter.[2] For Britain, nevertheless, federalism had the special political advantage of helping to

---

[1] Note by A. Kirkbride, 17 May 1952, FO 371/97269, quoted in W. R. Louis, 'Libyan Independence, 1951: The Creation of a Client State', in *Decolonization and African Independence: The Transfers of Power, 1960–1980*, New Haven and London,1988, p182. Kirkbride had worked in Palestine and Transjordan since the 1920s, and had recently served as Ambassador in Jordan, only requesting a transfer following the assassination of King Abdullah in Jerusalem in July 1951.

[2] A. Pargeter, *Libya: The Rise and Fall of Qaddafi*, New Haven and London, 2012, p36.

minimise the potential Arab nationalist influence of Beshir Saadawi, leader of the National Congress Party, and the Egyptian government on any Tripoli-based government – the very theme that dominates Jeff Cassels's memoir.

Although Libya's achievement of independence happened to pre-date the new wave of decolonisation that was to sweep through Africa over the following two decades, many of its unresolved political issues were easily ignored, only to re-emerge in new forms under succeeding generations. However, it is nowadays often forgotten how poor Libya was in its first years, before the discovery of oil. Having no significant export products or sources of government revenue, the country was critically dependent on international financial and technical assistance. The USA and Britain provided the finance, while the UN provided a substantial technical programme. There were almost no Libyan doctors, teachers or other trained personnel, and there was no professional class.

## DEPENDING ON IDRIS ALONE

The constant factor in the British strategy towards Cyrenaica up to 1949 – and, after 1950, towards the whole of Libya – was its heavy concentration on boosting the authority of one man, Sayyid Mohammed Idris. The most senior British officials at the time were all too well aware of the risks of this exclusive focus, as Roger Allen of the African Department of the Foreign Office confessed in August 1951: 'He is not a commanding personality, he does not really want to be a King, he is an elderly man in poor health, and he has no obvious heir. But the plain fact is that there is no other person who can be head of the future State, and therefore we must deal with the Amir and make the best of him too. ... The future of Libya is in my view balanced on a knife edge.'[3]

Cassels's remarkably honest account of the transition during 1951 and 1952 provides vivid corroboration for the view of historian William Roger Louis that 'as the date of Libyan independence approached, the British went through what might fairly be described as a case of the political jitters.'[4] By the eve of independence itself, these jitters had at least calmed to the extent that the Permanent Under Secretary at the

---

[3] Minute by R. Allen, 11 August 1951, FO 371/90346, quoted in W. R. Louis, 'Libyan Independence, 1951: The Creation of a Client State', in *Decolonization and African Independence: The Transfers of Power, 1960–1980*, New Haven and London, p182.

[4] W. R. Louis, 'Libyan Independence, 1951: The Creation of a Client State', in *Decolonization and African Independence: The Transfers of Power, 1960–1980*, New Haven and London, p181.

Foreign Office, Sir William Strang, felt able to write: 'We are now reaching the culminating point in a three-years' political operation of great delicacy and complexity. ... We cannot even now say that nothing will go wrong, but we have good hopes. We have kept faith with the Amir, and he with us.'[5]

Under Idris, independent Libya was able to establish treaties, strategic alliances and airbases that were designed to protect British and US defence interests in the Mediterranean and North Africa. The first American Minister to Libya, Henry Villard, wrote: 'That was exactly what the Soviet Union feared and what Libya did. The strategic sector of African seacoast which had proved so important in the mechanised war of the desert was coming into its own as a place of equal importance in the air age.'[6] In Libya at least, if not always elsewhere, Britain's strategic aims were fully supported by the United States.[7] On an international level, Britain's success in staying on in the Mediterranean and the Middle East at this time was, as historian Saul Kelly has described it, 'undoubtedly a great triumph for Bevin, the Foreign Office and the Chiefs of Staff and their policy of defending Britain's global status.'[8] Nevertheless, when Anthony Eden reclaimed his post of Foreign Secretary after the Conservative Party's election victory in the autumn of 1951, it was clear that he and others in the British establishment would have preferred to have been dealing with a Cyrenaican rather than a Libyan state. 'Personally', Eden wrote, he would have felt 'safer' if the arrangement had been limited to Cyrenaica. 'However, we are now embarked on wider deserts. Let us hope that all will yet be well.'[9]

Throughout his rule, King Idris remained a firm ally of both Britain and the United States, allowing the RAF the right to continue using the el-Adem airbase near Tobruk, while the US took Wheelus Field, a much larger facility near Tripoli, for the use of which it paid $4 million a year after 1954. Britain sealed its friendship with a subsidy to the Libyan treasury of £3.75 million a year, which was paid regularly throughout

---

[5] Minute by W. Strang, 8 December 1951, FO 371/90350, quoted in W. R. Louis, 'Libyan Independence, 1951: The Creation of a Client State', in *Decolonization and African Independence: The Transfers of Power, 1960–1980*, New Haven and London, p159.
[6] H. S. Villard, *Libya: New Arab Kingdom of North Africa*, Ithaca, NY, 1956, p34.
[7] At this time 'Libya remained the key to the preservation of Anglo–American strategic interests in the eastern Mediterranean.' R. B. St. John, *Libya: From Colony to Independence*, Oxford, 2008, p94.
[8] S. Kelly, *War and Politics in the Desert: Britain and Libya during the Second World War*, London, 2010, p231.
[9] Minute by A. Eden, 9 December 1951, FO 371/90359, quoted in W. R. Louis, 'Libyan Independence, 1951: The Creation of a Client State', in *Decolonization and African Independence: The Transfers of Power, 1960–1980*, New Haven and London, p183.

the 1950s until the oil started to flow at the end of that decade. But with the Middle East remaining ever turbulent, there were inevitable setbacks in these relationships, not least during the Suez crisis of 1956 when Idris was painfully caught between friendship with Egypt and loyalty to Britain.

In July 1956, the then Prime Minister Mustafa Bin Halim was quick to express support for Gamal Abdel Nasser's nationalisation of the Suez Canal and made it clear that Libya would not allow the use of its ports and airbases for any British assault on Egypt. But as tension mounted and Britain mobilised its armed forces in readiness for an attack, Bin Halim demanded a guarantee that the facilities in Libya would not be used and that the British troops would be confined to base. With anti-British feeling starting to run high in Tripoli – much of it stirred by the Egyptian military attaché, who was encouraging Libyans to attack British installations and even distributing weapons – the British Ambassador, W. G. C. Graham, sent one of his staff, none other than Peter Synge's former colleague Cecil Greatorex, to talk to Idris in Tobruk, where the king now spent most of his time.

Greatorex persuaded Idris to travel to Tripoli in order to try to take charge and calm anti-British feeling. In this he succeeded, whereupon Bin Halim had to try to appease both Egypt and Britain by demanding the recall of both Greatorex and the Egyptian military attaché. Libyan historian Majid Khadduri speculated that Bin Halim was angry with Greatorex for going over his head in intervening with Idris.[10] After this incident, Idris turned a deaf ear to Bin Halim's subsequent efforts to renegotiate the treaty, but the king's loyalty to Britain eventually cost him the support of his people. 'It was a personal commitment that in the long run harmed his standing in his own kingdom, and Libya's in an increasingly nationalistic Arab world,' wrote historian John Wright.[11]

With little interest in maintaining the constitutional structures and institutions negotiated during the United Nations transition, Idris created a highly paternalistic system of government, with all power focused in the royal court, where tribal leaders from Cyrenaica held sway. With the cumbersome federal structure of the country remaining in place until 1963 (by which time oil had become established as the new source of wealth and patronage), the national parliament served little meaningful function. But eventually, in March 1964, it did summon up sufficient courage to make a stand and to insist on the closure

---

[10] M. Khadduri, *Modern Libya: A Study in Political Development*, Baltimore, 1963, pp269–274.
[11] J. Wright, *A History of Libya*, London, 2010, p179.

of the British and American bases, a demand to which the king finally acceded in a belated recognition of the overwhelming Arab nationalist feeling across the region.

Despite his declared reluctance to serve as a ruler, Idris held absolute power and there was little room for democracy, even if the tradition of holding elections every four years persisted into the 1960s. Political parties and meetings remained completely banned after 1952, and so candidates could only stand in an individual capacity. When the elections of October 1964 produced results that indicated support for opposition candidates, the king immediately dissolved parliament and ordered a new polling exercise, during which ballot boxes were blatantly tampered with by the police. That turned out to be the last time a nationally organised election was held until the much more recent electoral processes that were conducted in 2012 and 2014.

## SANUSSI RIVALRIES

One problem that kept recurring was the disharmony in the heart of Idris's extended Sanussi family. Some family members were highly favoured while others were disruptive. Three prominent figures thrived by being granted special privileges in the world of business. The politically powerful Abu al-Qasim al-Sanussi, who had served the British Military Administration from the beginning, was granted the financially advantageous right to collect and sell scrap metal from the tanks, vehicles, ships and other equipment that had littered the land since the war, which at the time was Cyrenaica's most profitable export. The eldest son of Idris's brother Mohamed al-Rida, Saddik Mohamed al-Rida, began to profit from the Cerasola farm that the British had handed to him. And another cousin, Abdullah al-Abid, was given assistance to set up a major contracting company, which, some years later, created political uproar when it was accused of having received overly generous government contracts.[12]

Idris sought to minimise these political intrigues by demanding that none of the Sanussiyya should hold office in the government, other than diplomatic positions, but there seemed little way that the king could insulate himself entirely from plotting within the family, as it was his own private office that instigated a good share of it. His personal secretary, Ibrahim Shelhi, made powerful enemies by promoting

---

[12] E. A. V. De Candole, *The Life and Times of King Idris of Libya*, published privately, 1990, p100. M. Khadduri, *Modern Libya: A Study in Political Development*, Baltimore, 1963, pp301–7.

the political and business career of Abdullah al-Abid, which at times ran counter to the interests of Abu al-Qasim.[13]

The inter-family rivalries of the Sanussis came to a head in the 1950s. The power of his long-standing personal adviser Ibrahim Shelhi was especially resented by descendants of Sayyid Ahmed al-Sharif, who still claimed the right of royal succession for their own branch of the family. On 5 October 1954, Shelhi was shot dead by a grandson of Ahmed al-Sharif, al-Sharif bin al-Sayyid Muhi al-Din, outside the Benghazi offices of Prime Minister Bin Halim (himself a favourite of Shelhi and credited with the rebuilding of Benghazi in an earlier role as Minister of Public Works). The incident shocked Idris to the core, to the extent that he vowed never again to visit Benghazi and withdrew to spend most of his time in a secluded residence near Tobruk.[14] The Manar Palace in Benghazi was assigned to become the home of the new National University.

Idris may have been king of Libya, but his primary allegiance was to his homeland of Cyrenaica, which differed from Tripolitania in its political culture and maintained its administrative independence under the country's federal arrangements into the 1960s. 'Tripoli and Benghazi appeared like the capitals of different lands,' noted Henry Villard, at the end of a two-year stay as American Minister to Libya in 1952–54, when he had to travel repeatedly between the two cities in order to have access to the king and his senior ministers.[15] Added to this were visits to al-Bayda in the summer months, where on at least one occasion Idris received Villard in the Rommel House. After Shelhi's assassination, when Idris became increasingly reclusive, diplomats had to factor in the need for accommodation in Tobruk if they were to have any chance of seeing him.

## LIBYA'S CENTRIFUGAL FORCES

As a ruling monarch invested with extensive powers, perhaps Idris's most obvious shortcoming was his preference for remaining almost invisible, and yet he did manage to play the role of symbolic figurehead in a fractious nation and occasionally turned his remoteness to good use. By standing above the divisive fray of politics, he could intervene when situations demanded it. In the early 1960s, Khadduri was still able

---

[13] M. Khadduri, *Modern Libya: A Study in Political Development*, Baltimore, 1963, pp76 and 233.

[14] M. Khadduri, *Modern Libya: A Study in Political Development*, Baltimore, 1963, pp249–51.

[15] H. S. Villard, *Libya: New Arab Kingdom of North Africa*, Ithaca, 1956, p88.

to write that 'Idris's greatest asset is perhaps his ability to hold a balance among disruptive centrifugal forces and competing personalities. In a country torn by tribal feuds and rival houses vying for leadership, the need for a man whose prestige and integrity are universally acknowledged is essential for the maintenance of internal order and stability.'[16]

Idris's ultimate failure to assert strong leadership in the turbulent 1960s and his government's ineffective handling of the country's new oil revenues so aggravated the challenges faced by Libya that by 1969, in the words of historian Lisa Anderson, 'the monarchy was almost universally considered an anachronism,'[17] Idris was out of the country for medical treatment in Greece and Turkey when the coup d'état of 1 September 1969 brought his faltering regime to an end; thereafter he lived in Egypt – his second spell in exile – until his death in May 1983, aged 94.

Soon after Muammar Qadhafi's regime took power, it systematically destroyed the Sanussiyya's power base in Cyrenaica by seizing their unused land and restricting agricultural subsidies that directly benefited the major tribes, sheikhs and families of the region.[18] This was part of a broader attack on those who had been favoured by the British, against whose continuing influence Qadhafi expressed a deep resentment.

As Libya's oil wealth rose exponentially and brought huge demographic changes in its wake, the old political order was easily swept away but, in its place, came a new disorder, often stirred deliberately by Qadhafi's quixotic and supposedly 'revolutionary' dismantling of state institutions, as well as by an even more personalised and unaccountable use of power than had prevailed before. The regime's reckless international adventurism – including arming the Irish Republican Army and other terror groups around the world – was matched by extreme and brutal measures against any domestic opposition. After one failed uprising in the mid-1990s, the alleged perpetrators, who mostly came from Cyrenaica, were incarcerated in Abu Salim jail in Tripoli, where in June 1998 around 1,270 inmates were massacred in cold blood.[19]

Following a controversial reconciliation between Qadhafi and the USA, Britain and other Western countries in the years after 2001, there was some show of remorse over such excesses but for most Libyans the sense of insecurity persisted, and no institutions stayed immune from

---

[16] M. Khadduri, *Modern Libya: A Study in Political Development*, Baltimore, 1963, p319.
[17] L. Anderson, *The State and Social Transformation in Tunisia and Libya, 1830–1980*, Chichester and Princeton, 1986, p 260.
[18] R. First, *Libya: The Elusive Revolution*, London, 1974, pp182–6.
[19] L. Hilsum, *Sandstorm: Libya in the Time of Revolution*, London, 2012, pp100–105.

the regime's interference. Democratic reforms that were repeatedly promised by Qadhafi's son, Saif el-Islam, never materialised.

In the absence of a functioning political system, Libyans have tended to fall back on their more constant family, clan and tribal loyalties. Following the uprisings and the final overthrow of Qadhafi in 2011, historian Dirk Vandewalle pointed out that the challenges faced by the monarchy in 1951 and by Qadhafi's regime in 1969 'were left unresolved and continue to persist today'.[20] The same kinds of competing visions of the future that in the 1940s divided the rural tribes from one other and pitted them against urban interests (and divided Cyrenaica from Tripolitania and the Fezzan) seem to have re-emerged – only in a much more complex, fragmented and dangerous form than ever before.[21]

Since the time of the 2011 uprisings, the number of armed militiamen is thought to have continued to rise, from an initial 30,000 to some 250,000 by 2014. Following the looting of the former regime's ammunition stores, it was calculated that at least 10 million handheld weapons – and it could quite possibly have been more than that – were in circulation among a total population of around 6 million. The uncontrolled flows of weaponry from the huge arsenals that Qadhafi secretly amassed over the years not only contributed to lawlessness across Libya, but also provided firepower for newly emboldened insurgent movements beyond its borders – as far afield as Syria, Iraq, Mali, Nigeria and the Central African Republic.

In 2014, Benghazi was once again a battleground, if not on the devastating scale of the RAF's bombing campaigns of 1941 certainly something of a much more unpredictable nature, with prominent individuals facing an increasingly high risk of assassination. By the middle of the year, rebel general Khalifa Haftar claimed to be leading a well-armed faction of the Libyan National Army in a series of targeted assaults on Islamist militants based in Benghazi and Derna. His campaign appeared to be winning support in some parts of the country, although his opponents continued to resist with suicide attacks, bombings and targeted assassinations. Around the same time, United States special forces raided Benghazi and captured Ahmed Abu Khattala, one of the alleged perpetrators of the attack on the US diplomatic compound in the city, in which, on 11 September 2012, US Ambassador Chris Stevens had been killed.

[20] D. Vandewalle, *A History of Modern Libya*, Cambridge, 2012, p208.
[21] See J. Pack, ed., *The 2011 Libyan Uprisings and the Struggle for the Post-Qadhafi Future*, New York, 2013. J. Pack, K. Mezran and M. ElJarh, *Libya's Faustian Bargains: Breaking the Appeasement Cycle*, Washington DC, 2014.

Although the international news about Libya tended to highlight the ongoing military confrontations and political feuding, in 2014 there were still positive indications that many citizens wanted peaceful solutions to the country's problems. Building on the aspirations that accompanied Qadhafi's overthrow, there remained a strong commitment to establishing a viable democratic process, based on elections to a Constitutional Assembly and a House of Representatives (with universal suffrage and a quota of seats guaranteed for women). And the United Nations, which brought Libya to independence in 1951, was once again trying to play a leading role in promoting reconciliation among competing factions. In sum, writes Alison Pargeter, the complete collapse of Qadhafi's regime left the country's new leaders with 'the heavy legacy of having to build the state almost entirely from scratch'[22] This includes no less than a functioning political system, a civil service, essential government ministries, a police force and a national army.

As efforts to re-establish viable governance continue, it seems more than likely that outside powers will find themselves drawn in, as was so often the case during Libya's long and troubled 20th century, but any prospects for stability will depend primarily on a fully representative cross-section of Libyans becoming, and remaining, engaged in determining the kind of future they want for themselves.

Since 2011, the biggest challenge has come from heavily armed tribal, regional and religious militias with uncertain and unpredictable loyalties, and as a result it seems likely that for the foreseeable future any central authority will face immense challenges to its legitimacy. By the end of 2014, stability seemed to have become increasingly elusive and out of reach, and the need to bring the militias under an acceptable form of central control was becoming even more urgent than ever. With so many false starts in the past, those attempting to establish a workable system of government will clearly have to be prepared for major upheavals and setbacks along the way.

---

[22] A. Pargeter, *Libya: The Rise and Fall of Qaddafi*, New Haven and London, 2012, p250.

# sources and bibliography

## PRIMARY SOURCES

**Peter Synge's diary:** quoted from extensively in Chapters 3–7, consisting of two consecutive, closely handwritten notebooks, in which he recorded events on a daily basis between January 1943 and February 1945.

**Peter Synge's memoir:** quoted from selectively in Chapters 3–10, consisting of a long first draft (handwritten in various notebooks), plus a shorter typewritten version, dated January 1978.

**Jeff Cassels's memoir:** 'The Libyan Federal Elections 1951/52: A personal account', by Gervase P. ('Jeff') Cassels, completed in typescript in March 1987, of which he left copies with his children and one in the library of St. Antony's College, Oxford.

The principal Foreign Office, War Office and Air Ministry documents consulted exist in several different series under file numbers FO 371, FO 1015, WO 230 and AIR 23.

## ABBREVIATIONS USED IN THE FOOTNOTES

AIR     Air Ministry

CAA     Civil Affairs Agency, Cairo (active after 1945)

CAB     Civil Affairs Branch, GHQ, Middle East Command

CAO     Civil Affairs Officer (post-1943)

CCAO     Chief Civil Affairs Officer (post-1943)

CinC     Commander in Chief

CPO     Chief Political Officer (pre-1943)

DCA     Director of Civil Affairs, War Office

DCCAO     Deputy Chief Civil Affairs Officer (post-1943)

DCPO     Deputy Chief Political Officer (pre-1943)

FO     Foreign Office

GHQ     General Headquarters

MEF     Middle East Forces

OETA     Occupied Enemy Territory Administration

PO     Political Officer (pre-1943)

WO     War Office

## SECONDARY SOURCES

Anderson, Lisa, *The State and Social Transformation in Tunisia and Libya, 1830–1980*, Chichester and Princeton, Princeton University Press, 1986.

Bagnold, Ralph A., *Libyan Sands: Travel in a Dead World*, London, 1935.

Baldinetti, Anna, T*he Origins of the Libyan Nation: Colonial legacy, exile and the emergence of a new nation-state*, Abingdon and New York, Routledge, 2010.

Bell, Sir Gawain, *An Imperial Twilight*, London, Lester Crook Academic Publishing, 1989.

Bills, Scott L., *The Libyan Arena: The United States, Britain and the Council of Foreign Ministers 1945–1948*, Ohio, Kent State University Press, 1995.

Bulugma, Hadi M., *Benghazi Through the Ages*, Tripoli, Dar Maktabat a Al-Fikr,1968.

Cannadine, David, *Ornamentalism: How the British Saw their Empire*, London, Penguin Books Ltd, 2001.

Casserly, Gordon, *Tripolitania*, London, T. Werner Laurie Ltd, 1943.

Cumming, D. C., 'British Stewardship of the Italian Colonies: An account rendered', *International Affairs*, Vol XXIX, pp11–21, London, Royal Institute of International Affairs, 1953.

Daly, M. W., *Imperial Sudan: The Anglo–Egyptian Condominium, 1934–56*, Cambridge, Cambridge University Press, 1991.

De Candole, E. A. V., *The Life and Times of King Idris of Libya*, Privately published, 1990.

Evans-Pritchard, Edward Evan, *Cyrenaica Handbooks Part VIII: The Tribes and Their Divisions*, 1943 (an internal War Office publication, available at the National Archives in FO 371/46112).

Evans-Pritchard, Edward Evan, *The Sanusi of Cyrenaica*, Oxford, Clarendon Press, 1949.

First, Ruth, *Libya: The Elusive Revolution*, London, Penguin Books, 1974.

Foot, Hugh, *A Start in Freedom*, London, Hodder & Stoughton, 1964.

Gunther, John, Inside Africa, London, Hamish Hamilton, 1955.

Haag, Michael, *Alexandria, City of Memory*, New Haven and London, Yale University Press, 2004.

Hassanein Bey, A. M., *The Lost Oases*, London, 1925.

Henderson, K. D. D., *The Making of the Modern Sudan*, London, Faber and Faber Ltd, 1953.

Hilsum, Lindsey, *Sandstorm: Libya in the Time of Revolution*, London, Penguin Press, 2012.

Kelly, Saul, *Cold War in the Desert: Britain, the United States and the Italian Colonies, 1945–52*, Basingstoke, Macmillan Press, 2000.

Kelly, Saul, *War and Politics in the Desert: Britain and Libya during the Second World War*, London, The Society for Libyan Studies, 2010.

Keyes, Elizabeth, *Geoffrey Keyes of the Rommel Raid*, George Newnes Ltd., London, 1956.

Khadduri, Majid, *Modern Libya: A Study in Political Development*, The John Hopkins University Press, Baltimore, 1963.

Louis, William Roger, *The British Empire in the Middle East, 1945–1951: Arab Nationalism, the United States, and Post-war Imperialism*, Oxford, Clarendon Press, 1984.

Louis, William Roger, 'Libyan Independence, 1951: The Creation of a Client State' in *Decolonization and African Independence: The Transfers of Power, 1960–1980*, Prosser Gifford and William Roger Louis, eds., New Haven and London, Yale University Press, 1988.

MacMichael, Harold, *Sudan Political Service, 1899–1956*, Oxford, *c.* 1958.

Monroe, Elizabeth, *Britain's Moment in the Middle East, 1914–1971*, London, Chatto & Windus, 1981.

Moorehead, Alan, *African Trilogy: The North African Campaign 1940–1943*, London, Hamish Hamilton, 1944.

Otte, T. G., *The Foreign Office Mind: The Making of British Foreign Policy, 1865–1914*, Cambridge, Cambridge University Press, 2011.

Pack, Jason, 'British State-Building in Cyrenaica during the War Years (1941–1945)', MSt dissertation, Oxford University, 2011.

Pack, Jason, ed., *The 2011 Libyan Uprisings and the Struggle for the Post-Qadhafi Future*, New York, Palgrave MacMillan, 2013.

Pack, Jason; Mezran, Karim; ElJarh Mohamed, *Libya's Faustian Bargains: Breaking the Appeasement Cycle*, Washington D. C., Atlantic Council Report, 2014.

Pargeter, Alison, *Libya: The Rise and Fall of Qaddafi*, New Haven, Yale University Press, 2012.

Pelt, Adrian, *Libyan Independence and the United Nations: A Case of Planned Decolonization*, New Haven and London, Yale University Press, 1970.

Peters, Emrys L., *The Bedouin of Cyrenaica: Studies in Personal and Corporate Power*, Cambridge, Cambridge University Press, 1990.

Rennell of Rodd, Lord, *British Military Administration of Occupied Territories in Africa during the years 1941–1947*, His Majesty's Stationery Office, London, 1948.

Robinson, Ronald; Gallagher, John; Denny, Alice, *Africa and the Victorians: The Official Mind of Imperialism*, London, Macmillan, 1961.

St. John, Ronald Bruce, *Libya: From Colony to Independence*, Oneworld Publications, Oxford, 2008.

Stark, Freya, *East is West*, London, John Murray Publishers Ltd, 1945.

Stark, Freya, *The Coast of Incense: Autobiography 1933–1939*, London, John Murray Publishers Ltd, 1953.

Stark, Freya, *Dust in the Lion's Paw: Autobiography 1939–1946*, London, John Murray Publishers Ltd, 1961.

Thwaite, Anthony, *The Deserts of Hesperides: An experience of Libya*, London, Secker & Warburg, 1969 (reproduced 2015 online version).

Vandewalle, Dirk, *A History of Modern Libya*, Cambridge, Cambridge University Press, 2012.

Villard, Henry Serrano, *Libya: the New Arab Kingdom of North Africa*, Ithaca, Cornell University Press, 1956.

Williams, Gwyn, *Green Mountain: An informal guide to Cyrenaica and its Jebel Akhdar*, London, Faber and Faber Ltd, 1963.

Wright, John, *A History of Libya*, London, C. Hurst & Co., 2010.

# list of figures

All the figures have been credited in the individual captions. I would like to note that Figures 12, 13 and 14, were reprinted from Keyes, Elizabeth, *Geoffrey Keyes of the Rommel Raid*, George Newnes Ltd, 1956, London. Permission was granted from the publisher, now Elsevier, and every effort was made to contact the author, unsuccessfully.

# index

## RICHARD SYNGE

Richard Synge has had a long and varied career as a writer, journalist and editor specialising in African political and economic matters. After first working for the monthly *Africa Research Bulletin* and the annual *Africa Contemporary Record*, he reported for over two decades on and from Nigeria for *International Herald Tribune*, *The Guardian* and several Africa-focused publications. In 2005 he became the founding Senior Editor of the Paris-based monthly *The Africa Report*, to which he continues to contribute. He is also Assistant Director of the Wolfson Press Fellowship Programme, Cambridge. His books include *Nigeria – The Way Forward* (Euromoney Books, 1993) and *Mozambique: UN Peacekeeping in Action* (USIP Press, 1997).

## JASON PACK (FOREWORD WRITER)

Jason Pack is President of Libya-Analysis.com and the editor of *The 2011 Libyan Uprisings and the Struggle for the Post-Qadhafi Future* (Palgrave Macmillan, 2013). His analysis and opinion articles have appeared in *The New York Times*, *The Wall Street Journal*, *The Spectator*, *The Guardian*, and *Foreign Affairs*. His Cambridge University PhD dissertation investigating the British Military Administration of Cyrenaica, its antecedents and implications will be published in book form as *Britain's Informal Empire in Libya? The Anglo-Sanussi Relationship, 1882–1969* (Hurst, Forthcoming, 2017).